# WEST YARD

### Integrity, Courage and Honour Inside the Chaos

## Dave Woodhouse

West Yard
Copyright © 2021 by Dave Woodhouse

West Yard Graphic: Josh Dueck
Technical Consultation Firearms: Chris VanDuyse
Editor: Mary A. Metcalfe, M.S.

Tellwell Talent
www.tellwell.ca

ISBN
978-1-7777220-1-2 (Hardcover)
978-1-7777220-0-5 (Paperback)
978-1-7713693-9-8 (eBook)

To Ron

" gARd up fr sure ´

W

Dave Wordham

# TABLE OF CONTENTS

# DEDICATION

This book is dedicated to the Officers.

# PREFACE

There were small Yard Shacks on the east and west sides of the prison yard that were the size of a garden shed. Inside them were a telephone, a lamp, a chair, and an electric baseboard heater. Between your winds (yard patrols), you would sit there and watch the inside of the prison for fire or attempted escapes.

I always enjoyed working in the Yard on a midnight shift. It was so peaceful sitting in your warm and cozy West Yard shack, especially in the winter months when the snow was falling. You could almost hear the snowflakes when they hit the windowpane.

It was a serene contrast to the noise, smells, and violence that assailed you constantly in the cell blocks throughout the day.

The West Yard shack was a sanctuary for me.

# INTRODUCTION

There have been a few books published recently by former employees of the Correctional Service of Canada (CSC). In the past, books such as these were almost nonexistent. There is a cost to committing yourself to writing about this kind of work environment. You have to be prepared to go back to that place in your mind where you have hidden all the violent and corrupt acts you have witnessed and been victim to. Most importantly though, you have to be mindful of what recalling those memories will do to you. I had to step back many times, regroup, and take stock of the risk of psychological damage that this act of recollection can do. Once you are out, it's not wise to return. This is why it has taken me over sixteen years to write this book.

But I feel the time has come to have the public see just what goes on Inside those walls that many have passed by while wondering what it's really like on the Inside.

My time on the Inside spanned two decades: the 1980s and 1990s. I like to think I was a Correctional Officer, level 1 (CX-1) rather than a guard. There is a vast difference between the two and I will examine those differences within this writing.

When I worked for the CSC, I was wrong a lot of the time. I suppose this entire book is about me being wrong. Finally, in the late '90s I got so very tired of being wrong that I left the CSC to become a police officer with the Toronto Police Service.

What I have written within are my firsthand experiences, boots on the ground, stab wounds and all. I was not one of the staff separated from the cons by armed guards, metal bars, and bulletproof glass. I did my time with them, where they lived, where they slept and worked. I swam with the sharks in the open ocean while many others viewed them through the safety of their aquarium of bulletproof glass and metal bars.

I was the one called upon as an Institutional Emergency Response Team (IERT) Leader when they rioted, in order to take back control of the prison.

What I write about within this book are not second-hand or events taken from other officers and staff. These are my experiences. I was there. I did it. I saw it. These are my wounds, my scars, my blood, and my many years of bad dreams.

I do not write so much about the inmates in this book. It's mostly about the fascinating and disturbing parallel subcultures that exist between the cons and the staff and the shocking and truly unbelievable corruption of the Correctional Service of Canada, that I experienced during my time on the Inside.

But I am only one of many people who worked for the Correctional Service of Canada who experienced one or more "Sensational Incidents". Mine are the memories of just one employee within this vast system.

The CSC fears a Sensational Incident. This an event within a prison such as a riot, murder, escape, or hostage taking. Anything that can bring serious outside scrutiny from Members of Parliament, the news media, law enforcement, lawsuits, or a coroner's inquest. Anything that shines a light upon what happens behind those walls and fences that the CSC, in my day with them, did all they could, sometimes illegally, to keep firmly contained within the walls and away from public scrutiny.

This book is a Sensational Incident.

*   *   *

Can even Hollywood with its limitless resource of creative minds, conceive of such lunacy? I have often thought that having worked in an environment where:

- corruption is the norm
- fear and evil are your day-to-day working companions

- you watch as your co-workers gradually lose their values under relentless pressure from their peers and supervisors to conform to a broken system
- the crimes that take place Inside the walls are sanctioned by the very people sworn to protect us from them
- Canada makes Federal Prison a nice place to be if you're a convicted criminal.

Welcome to a domain that consists of a nationwide collection of prison microcosms, each with their own unique environment, language, and subculture and yet they all share the same dysfunctionality. This is a field where every employee has at least one remarkable, unbelievable, or sensational story to tell about his or her employment within the beast that is the Canadian federal prison system.

Welcome to the Correctional Service of Canada.

Welcome Inside the chaos.

I began my work with the CSC in the early eighties. I was a volunteer Auxiliary Ontario Provincial Police Constable at that time and thought that working for the Correctional Service would be beneficial should I choose to enter full-time policing as my career, which I eventually did when I joined the Toronto Police Service years later. The CSC offered benefits and a pension and that was a great incentive seeing that the economy was in a recession at that time. I felt that the training offered and the exposure to working with inmates would give me a better perspective of the Canadian justice system from the Inside and the Outside. I also did this because I thought I would be able to contribute to the safety of our society.

After my training and assignment to Collins Bay Institution, I very soon discovered that what we were taught about how the Correctional Service of Canada was supposed to operate was not an accurate reflection of what really went on down Inside.

The reality, as an ordinary officer being witness to and victim of the concentrated impact of violence on the job that created physical wounds that have since healed but the scars are still there, you never really free yourself from that. Just as the West Yard graphic depicts by the dangling handcuff representing freedom, yet still tethered to the experiences of the past.

There are not many jobs that you go to each day where you are threatened with death and bodily harm by the inmates and the staff for doing your duty according to Canadian law and CSC policy.

Throughout my time with the CSC, I have documented my personal experiences and observations and I feel that I have a duty to write about them, so the events are not forgotten. These are my opinions and thoughts based upon what I experienced on the Inside.

Many former front-line employees of the CSC find recalling the events that they experienced in their careers triggering and difficult for them. For too long I have been discouraged from writing about these events for the same reasons. But after many years of being on the Outside and letting time soften the memories of corruption and violence, I was able to regroup, collect my chronicles, notes, and investigation reports in order to put them down on paper.

West Yard is now ready and invites you to take an unprecedented journey into the events that I experienced while working for the Correctional Service of Canada over thirty years ago.

# PART 1

## Recruitment and Induction Training - Fish

Mission: "The Correctional Service of Canada, as part of the criminal justice system and respecting the rule of law, contributes to the protection of society by actively encouraging and assisting offenders to become law-abiding citizens, while exercising reasonable, safe, secure and humane control."[1]

—*Basic Facts About Federal Corrections* (1999)

"The Canadian Penitentiary Service is desperate for persons to fill poorly paid and low-status positions in dangerous and unrewarding conditions working with undertrained associates in a hostile and low-morale environment."[2]

—*MacGuigan Report* (1977)

---

[1] Correctional Service Canada, *Basic Facts About Federal Corrections*, 1999, 12. Accessed October 7, 2020, www.publicsafety.gc.ca/lbrr/archives/hv%209308%20 b24%201999-eng.pdf.

[2] Canada, Parliament, House of Commons Standing Committee on Justice and Legal Affairs, Sub-Committee on the Penitentiary System in Canada, *Report of the Sub-committee*, 30th Parl, 2nd Sess, 1976–1977, para. 252 (Chair: Mark MacGuigan). Accessed October 3, 2020, https://johnhoward.ca/wp-content/ uploads/2016/12/1977-HV-9507-C33-1977-MacGuigan.pdf.

## In Service of the Mission

The Correctional Officer Training Program (CTP) was based upon what the Correctional managers envision the Service to be according to the corporate Mission. The idealistic crusade championed by a former Commissioner is a façade for the corruption and inhumanity that was the reality of the Canadian prison system in the time that I worked for them.

Those in positions of authority glorify the high-sounding words of The Mission that have no substance in this artificial environment and are not applied to everyone in the workplace on a consistent and equal basis.

Everyone in the CSC is issued a copy of "The Mission". In some cases, you had to sign for it. Often you can see a copy framed and displayed on the wall in the offices of senior staff members. It will usually be signed by everyone in the department as their commitment to the crusade. It's funny how trends go, the hypocritical are willing to embrace any policy or doctrine dished out to them provided a promotion or some other tangible benefit can be gleaned from it. My experience was that many would stand on their soapbox and extol the virtues of the Mission but not operate their department with honesty or uphold the moral content and the core values of the document itself.

The mission statement is a flag to be waved in front of the media, the public, and justice system partners. But when it comes to applying its values and principles consistently – where the rubber meets the road – some managers fall appallingly short of its minimum standards as I have witnessed.

## Correctional Officers Training Program

The CTP (Correctional Training Program) in my day began with the hiring of recruits who were given a training allowance and a uniform to attend the Regional Correctional Staff College: $280 a week is what you started at in the '80s. At one period in the 1990s, you got nothing, no uniform and no pay.

In the 1990s, you attended your classes dressed in blue track pants and a white T-shirt that you were to provide. This was your uniform. Something you can take pride in. You did not even know what a uniform looks like as none of the instructional or managerial staff wore one until the middle 1990s when two other officers and I began to teach there, and we wore our uniforms. It's all part of the theory that the offenders will be able to relate to you more closely if you do not appear too militaristic or authoritarian in your dress and demeanor.

A uniform served the additional purpose of drawing a line by separating the guards from the rest of the staff members.

Some recruits who arrived at corrections with a military or other disciplined background were shocked and appalled by this lack of professionalism. A uniform issued and tailored to new recruits was considered too much of an investment for the CSC if you happened to fail the course and leave the training program. Entering the Service as an officer back then you were already undervalued in the CSC by their own design.

If you were successful in completing the training program, you would be given a uniform to wear upon arriving at your respective institution but not to wear for your graduation. For a period in the 1990s, you were to graduate from the Correctional Staff College in a robe similar to what university grads wear. These robes were rented from a company in Toronto for the occasion.

I started in a year when the Service was structured like the Canadian military in the 1980s. In that period, you wore a uniform that reflected the rank structure of the frontline officers: dark green pants with a lighter green shirt, tie, and polished boots. Each officer was issued a dress uniform for formal occasions. Your rank insignia was fastened to the shoulder epaulets and on your shirt or tunic. Years of service badges and crossed pistols and rifles signifying a marksmanship achievement were sewn on the sleeve. You had a peaked cap with the CSC hat badge fixed to the front. This was your uniform of the day. This is what you were issued while on training to become a Correctional Officer at the Regional Correctional Staff College in Kingston in the 1980s. This what you were expected to wear on your day-to-day duties on the Inside of your institution and when on duty on the Outside.

Then, in the 1990s, the CSC uniform was changed in order to have a less threatening or authoritarian appearance toward the cons. It reminded me more of the clothes worn by workers at The Beer Store in Ontario or McDonald's at that time. It was a service industry uniform consisting of grey dress pants, light blue, or white and blue striped shirts. A dark blue blazer with the CSC crest embroidered on the breast, a blue tie, and to top it all off… a baseball cap.

This was the new image of the Correctional Service of Canada. There were no longer uniforms being issued to higher ranking managers such as Deputy Wardens, Wardens, Assistant Commissioners, and the Commissioner. That kind of look for them was now eliminated by design to distance them from those on the frontline working directly with the inmates on a day-to-day basis. We didn't know it at the time, but the Correctional Service members were being separated, distanced by the apparel they wore, to create a very broad and distinct line between the guard staff and all other members of the CSC.

The new uniform issued to the Keepers (Correctional Supervisors aka : zookeepers) was the same but had a white shirt rather than the blues to distinguish them from the frontline staff. Similar to the way higher ranking police officers have white shirts.

Some staff members wore their uniform shirts straight out of the package complete with wrinkles without washing them first, and a great many shirts never saw an iron. Seeing someone with their uniform shirt and pants pressed, with their tie on and boots polished was rare. In fact, as an officer, you were put upon if your dress and deportment were not consistent with those of the guard, that being shabby, dirty, and unkempt.

While on your training to be a Correctional Officer you had to parade before a senior officer at the morning roll call. The Officer in Charge would make sure you looked professional before you attended your classes for the day. The same kind of inspection is carried out at the Ontario Police College, RCMP Depot, and at police stations throughout Canada each day.

Afterward, when I got on the Inside, I wondered why they wasted all that time at the College marching you around the gym, preparing you to look and act in a professional manner, when it didn't really matter what you looked like or how you acted behind the walls. I found out that the reason this did not matter is that no one on the "Outside" sees what goes on "Inside" of the walls and fences of Canada's prisons, so the saying "anything goes" was, I found out, truly an understatement with respect to dress and deportment and many other aspects or working inside a prison.

## Induction Training

During your training to become a Correctional Officer in the 1980s you were required to perform military style drills and march in your uniform in formations to recorded music. There was training in how to use a wooden baton, handcuffs, body belts, and leg irons. You had first aid and CPR training as well as firefighting and being taught to use the MSA or Scott brands of Self-Contained Breathing Apparatus (SCBA). We spent a great deal of the training time on self-defence and arrest and control methods.

We attended the local firefighters' training facility and climbed through their smokehouse in our SCBA equipment while they burned a bale of hay using diesel fuel at the base of the tower to create the blinding, acrid smoke required to produce a realistic hazardous environment. Years later, it was determined that this practice of burning hay with diesel fuel was far too risky and dangerous for the students if their equipment should fail or they should panic and remove it. A smoke machine was used thereafter. Roughly the same kind that you can buy to create special fogging effects for your Halloween display.

The firearms training took place at the local army base in Kingston where the CSC maintained its own range. We learned safe handling and how to perform timed target shooting at stationary paper targets using different positions from measured distances.

The use and deployment of Chemical Agents (tear gas) was also taught with theory, live fire, and minimal exposure to the various gas used by the CSC.

There was a core of full-time instructors at the College some of whom may not have had extensive frontline foundational experience in some of the topics they taught but were excellent teachers just the same.

There were also a small number of officers, who did have foundational experience as frontline officers doing the work Inside a prison who were seconded to the College for a limited period of time to apply actual frontline practical knowledge to the lessons. Once their secondment was completed, another round of officers was brought in and on it went. The officers who were brought to the College to teach were acting in the position of a supervisor and were paid at the appropriate Master Contract Agreement negotiated level of pay.

The College provided in-house meals and accommodation to recruits from out of town.

Many of us had no knowledge or experience of the law as it pertained to the custody of convicted offenders in a prison environment, and this was something not taught at the time. As we gained experience on the Inside it was obvious that many senior managers of the CSC had no foundational knowledge of the law either, or if they did, much of law and policy was very often ignored.

## Graduation Day

I remember on our graduation day we were marched around the gym a couple of times and then we put on a display of self-defence for family members and friends attending the ceremony. Two officers were confronted by one of their class members role-playing as an inmate. The inmate confronted the officers with a rubber knife screaming at them, "You fucked with my TA ... now you're going to pay!"[3] And he attacked them full on with his knife.

The two officers subdued him using their newly acquired bare-handed self-defence skills, disarmed him, and applied handcuffs. They made the whole thing look easy. Some of the audience members were openly shocked and wondered aloud if this is what their family members would be facing in their new workplace. They had good reason to be shocked by this display.

No one who graduated that day or the many others who followed behind us had any accurate idea of just what was waiting for us behind those walls and fences.

[3] Temporary Absence Pass (TA).

**Collins Bay Penitentiary**

## "Disneyland"

> [Officers] "are under intolerable pressure not to break the
> rule of silence that the custodial staff, in their insecure and
> embattled insulation, have imposed on and tolerate among
> themselves. If they report such breaches of discipline, they
> are likely to find little support from their colleagues.

> —*MacQuigan Report* (1977), para 237

On the day that I and my fellow Correctional Officer Training Program
graduates arrived at Collins Bay Institution, also known as Disneyland due
to its imposing castle-like appearance, limestone walls, and turrets, we were
ushered up to the third-floor boardroom by the Staff Training Officer.
The STO was that in name only, they never conducted staff training as
they were more of a coordinator.

We were given a series of binders containing the *Commissioner's Directives* to read. We spent the day sitting there just reading over directives about finance, administrative services, health care, management services and other documents whose content was completely lost on us as new Correctional Officers.

## Fish

New officers and first-time inmates are both called "Fish". As in, we are only "a small fish in a big pond." This was our first introduction to the many cultural parallels between the Correctional Service staff members and the inmates. There were many, many more to follow.

The next day, we were handed our training schedules with the Posts that we were to attend in order to learn the routine of the Institution. We rotated through the Posts throughout a two-week period and were then placed into the roster and got to work.

There were no coach officers in place back then as there are in all police services in Canada. We learned from whoever was working on the post at that current time. Maybe you got lucky and the guard on that post actually spoke to you. Luckier still if you got one who taught you how to do the job. And luckiest if they themselves were doing the job according to:

- the Post Orders
- CSC Policy
- the law, and
- the way it was intended to be done.

\*   \*   \*

In the "Investigation Report into the Escape of Tyrone Conn from Kingston Penitentiary" dated May 1999, there was a reference to the poor induction training provided for new officers:

> *CSC failure to adequately provide training to recently hired correctional officers has left them concerned for their safety.*

*Newly hired correctional officers are supposed to receive formal documented orientation to the routines of all posts and to the operational expectations of Kingston Penitentiary.*

*The evidence, however, is that most correctional officers are handed a schedule of posts to visit during their first days at the institution. They are asked to request information from the officer on the post.*

*Staff interviewed by the Board advised that this process has mixed results in that some officers are not necessarily the best of teachers.*

*The Deputy Warden assures the Board that an improved process is in place. This, however, does not seem to be congruent with the testimony received.* [4]

Even in the years after I left at Collins Bay, this pitiful excuse for induction training was still ongoing within the institutions. The CSC invested very little for proper training of their entry level staff if they wore a uniform in that time.

Later, in the 1990s, I was designated to be coach officer to the new recruits. I arranged for the Warden to meet with the new staff, something that was never done when I started. I also arranged their training schedule around guards I didn't want the new staff being exposed to. I would show them how to do the job myself or ensure that a competent officer was training them to avoid them being exposed so early to the 'guard culture'.

There was such a large volume of new officers starting their careers with the CSC at that time that it was not uncommon to have a new recruit being trained on a post by an officer who only had two weeks on the job themselves.

In one instance, I had placed two new officers at the Main Gate control post with a good officer to show them the ropes. I went into the gate later to check on how things were going. I could feel the tension in

---

[4]   Report Number 1 410-2-395, p. 42.

the air as I entered. The new officers were sitting close together on a chair looking frightened and intimidated. Although I took steps to prevent this from happening, I could not control who came and went from the Main Gate control post. A guard had entered the post and immediately set upon the new officers with insults and the usual intimidating guard behaviour toward new staff. I removed the new officers from the post and explained to them that unfortunately they would be experiencing this kind of behavior from many of the guards. I wrote up a report on what took place at the gate between the guard and the new officers and submitted it to a supervisor.

At some point, the guard was spoken to by a supervisor about the incident because I received a call at my home from the guard threatening my life because I "ratted them out". Once the guard was through with their threats, I waited for a while and activated the telephone redial on the telephone number the guard placed the call from. The call was placed from the Institutional Hospital. The nurse on duty identified the caller and witnessed the threats. This guard was no stranger to this kind of criminal activity. There was an extensive history that included two assaults on other officers.

The next day, I submitted a full report to the supervisors in detail about the threats. The guard was spoken to about this criminal act but, as usual, the lid was on and that was as far as it went. But even with that behind them, the guard continued with this kind of threatening and abusive behaviour until they were given another job, transferred to yet another prison, and eventually awarded an Exemplary Service Medal.

"The Corrections Exemplary Service Medal, created on June 11, 1984, recognizes employees of the Canadian Correctional Service who have served in an exemplary manner, characterized by good conduct, industry and efficiency." A recent addition to the qualification statement for this award says, "that serves as a model for others".

All new officers to the prison at that time were immediately put upon, ridiculed, insulted, threatened, and harassed for sport. This was not a hazing; this was the way the place operated day to day when I started the job and continued still when I left it.

## Rewards for Violence and Abuse

The ratio of male to female officer recruits was close to 50/50 in my induction training class. Not many of the women who started in our training course lasted more than a few years in the service. There were very good reasons for this. I think that only two or three remained and made the CSC their career.

I noticed that one of the women in my training class would show up with a black eye. The result of walking into a door she said. But there were other signs of abuse as well: the telltale bruises in the shape of a thumbprint on each of the front of her biceps and the corresponding pattern of four fingermark bruises on the back of her biceps from being held forcibly by her arms. As it turned out, her husband worked at Collins Bay Institution, the prison I was going to be working at.

Once I got there, it wasn't hard to determine who her husband was, a tough guy who was only tough on woman. A "good guy to have around" when there was trouble, but always seemed to go the other way when there was trouble. A racist sexist loudmouth who never did his job in the units because he feared the cons. But over the years, he was promoted to a supervisor and eventually a senior supervisor, given an Exemplary Service Medal, and then pensioned off.

This was a pattern I observed throughout my entire time with the CSC: violent, corrupt and abusive guards being promoted, held out to us as leaders, and then honoured by the CSC with a medal for their "Exemplary Service".

## A Sexualized and Violent Culture

The Correctional Service of Canada was a totally sexualized culture when I began working for them, not unlike our military and police services at that time. In fact, much of the way the CSC was structured and organized was straight from military protocols even down to the office furniture, uniforms, and the manner in which the post orders were written.

At the time of this writing there is a massive lawsuit in place by victims of sexual harassment and sexual abuse against the *Canadian Armed

Forces. The Correctional Service of Canada was no different than the CAF with respect to the way it treated its own staff members.

And if you were not inclined to be assimilated into this kind of racist and sexist culture then you were labeled an outsider. You paid a very high price for being on the Outside while working on the Inside.

The female officers and some male officers were sexually assaulted and harassed all the time by the guards as well as the cons. Often, the male guards would bet money on who would bed the new female officers first.

When women first started as Correctional Officers in male federal institutions it was the early '80s and the guard dogs in the kennel were treated with more respect and dignity.

It was bad enough for the women facing this kind of disrespect from the people that they worked with, but they also had to put up with the inmates who would threaten to "slash and splash" them (stab you and then fuck your open wound) every time that they walked down a range.

- If you were gay, you were treated worse than that if it's possible.
- If you were of a colour other than white you suffered.
- If you were an officer rather than a guard you suffered.
- If you obeyed the law and policy, you suffered.

There was one well-known junior supervisor who you always had to be cautious with when he approached. You would never turn your back to him as he would grab you by the balls and twist. Nobody knew why he would do this other than for his own personal sadistic satisfaction in the act.

But he was one of those "good guys to have around", so many of his violent interactions with staff and inmates were ignored by the senior management staff.

---

\* In 2016 and 2017, seven former members of the Canadian Armed Forces (the "Representative Plaintiffs") initiated class action lawsuits ("Heyder and Beattie Class Actions") against the Government of Canada ("Canada") alleging sexual harassment, sexual assault or discrimination based on sex, gender, gender identity, or sexual orientation ("Sexual Misconduct") in connection with their military service and/or employment with the Department of National Defence (DND) and/or Staff of the Non-Public Funds, Canadian Forces (SNPF).

Another guard would sneak up behind you and pull your pants down around your ankles in front of all the cons as you were standing on the Strip (the Strip is a long hallway that runs three quarters of the length of the prison). These inflammatory acts would move to arouse the latent malevolence within some of the other guards as they thought it was entertainment and were not beyond doing the same themselves. They were emboldened and protected by the guard culture and so could get away with these abhorrent acts.

These are not one-off isolated acts of sexual assault and harassment ... these were reoccurring events as part of your workday.

Nothing was said and nothing was done by those who managed the prison when objectional behaviour like this took place. It was part of your day-to-day working environment in the Correctional Service of Canada, and you were just expected to "suck it up", thus establishing little or no incentive to break the cycle of these offensive and criminal acts.

The people on the second floor of the prison turned a blind eye to all of that. It's what they did best.

Even though there was a code of conduct for addressing the harassment, racism, and hate that was systemic in the Correctional Service of Canada at that time, it was just a collection of words on a piece of paper that were not enforced in any serious way by those in authority. *Commissioner's Directive 606 Code of Discipline* was detailed in its description of the standards set with respect to deportment and dress, interaction with staff, offenders, and the public, protection and sharing of information, and conflict of interest. Much of what is written today in these directives is the same that was written down in my time.

If you reported an incident to the Management Team, you risked being called out as a "rat" or a "whiner" or you were not "tough enough" to do the job. You didn't belong here.

On the very day that you made a complaint against a guard to the people who were responsible for and duty bound to manage the prison, you would find all four tires on your car slashed when you went outside to the parking lot at the end of your shift. There would be a dead mouse or rat stuffed into your mail slot or your locker would be spray painted or words carved into the paint with a knife.

This was the systemic culture of the Correctional Service of Canada nationwide at that time.

You had to be "one of the boys" or "the Old Guard" to be accepted into this kind of culture. That means you had to "go out drinking" often. You had to play hockey or golf or fish and hunt. You had to embarrass women with unwanted comments, lewd jokes and gestures, humiliation and gang harassment, sexually distasteful pictures, and leering looks. You had to be a racist and a con hater. If you amassed a lengthy record of criminal convictions, it demonstrated that you "didn't give a fuck", so you were now in with them. You had to stick together out of gender loyalty and prove yourself by demonstrating this kind of behavior in order to gain their trust, to belong, to become "one of them"…a guard.

You had to prove to them that you were a "tough guy" by exhibiting these behaviors. In my extensive experience in the justice system on the Inside and the Outside the only "tough guy" or woman were the ones who go to a job like this one every day that you didn't like to do. A job that you know is killing you and yet you do it for the love of your family.

The Old Guard set a terrible example for the rookies, who were compelled to believe their career and their survival Inside depended upon their affiliation with these guys and their sexist, racist, and corrupt way of conduct – and it did. If you did not bend to their influence, then you were ridiculed, threatened, put upon, and harassed every day.

Just like organized crime and gang culture, you were required to commit acts, some criminal, in order to be accepted into their guard culture.

**"If you did not bend to their influence, then you were ridiculed, threatened, put upon, and harassed every day."**

To report this kind of behaviour meant risking your career and your personal safety in the prison system. The constant repetition of these experiences day after day took its toll and was the main cause of overwhelming workplace fear and accumulated stress disease in the CSC at that time.

The image of a corrupt prison guard portrayed in Hollywood movies was not very far off the mark within the CSC in those days. In fact,

Hollywood could take some lessons from these very bad actors. The dismal image of sadistic Hollywood prison guards was brought to life every day in all its reputed brutality in the Correctional Service of Canada.

There were a great many prison staff involved in criminal behaviour both on the Inside and Outside. Our disgraceful reputation in the eyes of the public and the police was well-earned, and we had nobody to blame for it but ourselves and those who allowed it to perpetuate by their systemic neglect throughout the years.

# PART 2

## The Parallel Subculture

> The "guards' code" appears to be just as strong, and just
> as destructive, as the "inmates' code".

> —*MacGuigan Report* (1977), para 234

There is a very strong parallel between the prisoner subculture and that of the staff. In fact, there was a module taught to new Correctional Officer recruits on this very topic: How the behaviour and values of the offenders and the old guard is assimilated by some of the frontline staff. It usually begins with the manner of speech; it's mostly the swearing that staff will pick up first. Then it may progress to tattooing, drug and alcohol abuse, smuggling, theft, and so on, even to the point of joining a criminal organization. One guard I remember joined up with an outlaw motorcycle gang.

If you go Inside with a strong moral constitution and work ethic you will be challenged every time you step behind those walls and razor wire fences. And when you see inappropriate behavior being ignored and even endorsed and awarded by the managers you will begin to question the system and these Mission values that are run up the corporate flagpole.

Those who have manipulated the system to their advantage continue to do so with impunity, the golden rule in Corrections seemed to be "You can't touch me if I have the dirt on you." This is how the network of corruption was maintained in my time within the CSC. Leadership by hypocrisy is hard to contend with when you are a new recruit, and your head is filled with the Mission, and you are expecting these high-sounding words to be sincere and law and CSC policy to be respected. You are told that being a Peace Officer holds you to a higher standard than the general public but soon after entering your respective institution you find out just what a farce your training has turned out to be.

Your expectations of how the prison environment is envisioned to be, based on the training you received at the Regional Correctional Staff College will be soon shattered. Very soon after crossing the threshold of that prison, and you smell the stale pot smoke and urine, you will come to realize that the College version and the NHQ version of prison versus the reality of being down Inside are two very separate things that are worlds of reality apart.

## Life on the Inside

When you start at your assigned Institution, you're sized up by the guards in the same way the inmates size up the new fish. The guards have a pecking order just like the cons and were constantly on the lookout for weaknesses shown by new employees so they could exploit them. They wanted "something on you" to use against you in the future because this was the way the CSC was run in those days.

The guard hierarchy was the same as the cons', that being the most violent are often at the top of the order. They would try to threaten you and intimidate you to fall in line with their racist, sexist, and homophobic culture. This was not isolated to just one institution. It was a systemic problem within the Canadian federal prisons coast to coast at that time.

They wanted you to prove to them that you were one of them by conducting yourself as they did based upon their culture and what it took to be a "guard" in their eyes. This included a variety of expected behaviors such as heavy drinking, management bashing, con hating, racism, and womanizing.

Your first day on the Inside, the guards would check you out so they could label you. Usually, you'd be given a nickname, and not a pleasant one. This was done not in the spirit of camaraderie, it was done with the intention to embarrass, humiliate, and hurt. This was sport for the guards. Chances were that the name the guards labelled you with would remain with you throughout your career. I remember a former Deputy Commissioner who was called "paddle foot" behind his back throughout his career.

## Threats and Intimidation

Having had extensive experience working on the Outside in the field of law enforcement, I began to put together my experiences and evidence from working on the Inside and came to the conclusion that, at that time, the Correctional Service of Canada conducted its business using the exact same methods employed in the cultures of organized crime groups and street gangs.

One of the most frightening things I witnessed within the guard culture was just how much the guards talked like the cons. They had the same tone and inflection in their voices as well as using the same expressions the cons used. Sometimes, you didn't know if you were speaking to a con or a guard.

This was not the limit of how far the parallel subculture could go. Often, the guards used the same methods of intimidation that the cons used to try to get what they want. Guards used threats and physical intimidation and intentionally placed you in danger by not doing the minimum requirements of their jobs, including deliberately or negligently failing to lock the cell doors at the end of their evening shift thus leaving you alone in the cell block at night with some of the inmates having their cell doors left open. This was a risk to your personal safety, your very life, and placed the entire prison at the risk of takeover by the cons. This is what I witnessed and was victim to the entire time I worked for the CSC.

## The "Tradition" of Coercive Theft

When I first started working down Inside, there were two shift supervisors who had an ongoing scam involving the theft of money from new officers. The shift keeper would hire a brand-new officer for their first overtime shift. Then in the following month, when the overtime checks would arrive, the supervisor would advise the new officer that he was to sign over his check to him. The reason given was that it is "tradition" for the new officer's first overtime check to go to the supervisor who hired them for that shift. If the new officer objected, the supervisor would then remind them who does the hiring for overtime in the future and it's possible that the officer who does not comply with tradition would get overlooked for future shifts. There was no tradition. This was all just an act of coercive theft by these supervisors.

When you have a group of a dozen or more new officers starting at the same time it can be a lucrative payoff for the crooked supervisor in the following month. The new officers are too intimidated to complain so the scam continued. Who could they have complained to and done so safely? Being brand new to the job you have no idea who you can trust at that point. True to their word, I did not receive any more overtime shifts from these two supervisors. One of them was even honored by the CSC with an Exemplary Service Medal for his years of service to the Canadian public.

## Surveillance Camera Surprise

One night, a couple of guards on the midnight shift got the bright idea to steal the furniture from the third-floor lounge. They got the fire escape keys and unlocked the door on the west side of the building. They pulled their pickup truck under the fire escape and lowered the couches and chairs down with a rope. Good plan, except for the newly installed cameras recording their theft.

It was difficult to explain away their thefts when confronted by the videotaped evidence. These staff members were not fired or charged criminally for their illegal nocturnal shopping activity from the prison; they were simply asked to return the furniture. After all, they were both "good guys to have around" and they did learn their lesson from getting caught though and were much more careful when stealing from the Institution in the future.

## Creative Theft

Another method of getting stolen goods out of the prison was to bag it up and leave it at the bottom of the tower on the Inside of the wall. When you got up to the tower on the second half of your midnight shift you snagged the booty with the tower rope and hook, hauled it over the wall and into your car in the parking lot.

I remember one night, while working the West Yard post, I witnessed an employee, who had a knack for theft from the prison, use this time-tested system for stealing items from the prison Industrial Shops again and again.

A much easier way to steal from the prison with less effort was when you had an arrangement with the guard working the Main Gate post on that midnight shift and just walked out the front door of the prison with the stolen property.

Laptop computers were a hot commodity at the time and could be loaned out to staff members for their own use provided they signed a receipt.

Some years ago, in one of the Medium Security Institutions within the Ontario Region, a staff member returned a laptop with child pornography on the hard drive. This is what it took to get him fired.

Anything from toilet paper to audiovisual equipment was taken from federal prisons every day by staff.

When posted to the Yard, you were to walk around inside the perimeter every hour and check out the cell blocks, walls, and grounds for evidence of escape or fire. You were provided with a device called a Detex punch clock and obliged to make "punches" at several designated stations located within the walls. These Detex devices were a heavy round time clock placed inside a leather protective cover with a long leather strap to carry over your shoulder. At the bottom end there was a keyhole that corresponded to different metal keys that were strategically located within the walls and buildings of the prison. These keys made an imprint upon a small paper disk within the clock that recorded the times of your patrols. So, while on your four hours in the Yard you were obliged to make "punches" at these stations at least once every hour. It was the same routine if you were working in the cell blocks.

Some of the guards working in the Yard would make their first punches on that round and then they would detach the keys from the walls, pocket them, and retire to the Yard shack. There they could complete their punches without ever having to go outside again except to return the keys at the end of their shift. After your four hours on this post, you would then go up to one of the towers for the remainder of your shift.

## All in a Day's Work

Sometimes a staff member with a personal vehicle similar to the make and model of the prison's mobile patrol vehicle would exchange auto parts in the parking lot after dark. If your alternator was acting up, you could just exchange it for the one in the mobile patrol vehicle – as long as your vehicle parts were compatible with the CSC vehicle you plan to steal them from.

One guard who worked the Sally Port post (entrance to the prison where vehicles are searched prior to entering and leaving the Institution) would park his personal vehicle inside the wall and perform maintenance on it while he was supposed to be searching the cars. He never searched the vehicles passing in or out of the prison even once in his entire eight-hour shift all week long. He would just wave them on through. These are the kind of guards the cons watch for and make note of. They know that with someone like this on a post, the job was not going to be done. These are the guards that the cons plan their murders, contraband smuggling, and escapes around. There were many of these guards, so if the cons were clever, they got away with much because of them.

These are the kind of guards who permitted a van to leave the institution with two inmates hidden within. The van had been inside the prison auto body shop for months undergoing some renovations. These modifications apparently included having two inmates hiding inside the cabinets contained within the van. Once the van was driven out of the prison to the lower parking lot and left there, the two cons walked away.

# PART 3

## Prisoners of the System

"The evidence we heard on the position of the custodial staff convinced us they too are prisoners of the system."

—*MacGuigan Report* (1977), para 215

**"As staff members, we were just fodder to be consumed by this soul-killing factory."**

In the 1980s, there were no clear policies and procedures in place to deal with a complaint and no harassment awareness training or intervention strategy. There was no one to report these events to and do so safely. And if you did report, it often meant that victim blaming was the common outcome.

The widespread knowledge that this kind of behaviour among staff was permitted created a great mistrust of the senior managers who turned their back on it and even indulged in it.

The CSC allowed sexual harassment to go unchecked for years creating a lot of damaged people, destroying morale, destroying careers and motivation, and making the workplace even more of a living hell for their own staff. They often looked the other way when they had the responsibility and the power to make a difference. There needed to be tangible evidence of holding the perpetrators accountable. This was not the case in the CSC at that time as it was all hidden behind closed doors where deals were made to just make it go away. Often the victim did not even know the outcome of their complaint.

One former Commissioner's reaction to a publication on sexual harassment in the CSC was: "Well, boys will be boys." And this statement was from the CSC's first woman Commissioner.

If the CSC had any kind of employment equity back then to ensure a planned career path for everyone with a basis in merit rather than the buying of whisky, the staff vulnerable to those who abused their power and authority would have possibly gotten their chance at fair treatment just as the law and policy requires.

But many of the abused staff members quit if they could while others put up with it just so they could support their families. This was the only choice you had then.

Many suffered prolonged periods of stress not only from the daily abuse from the cons but from their coworkers and the indifferent neglect by our managers. There are many former CSC staff members who suffer to this day from the fallout of working in the most poisoned environment imaginable.

Even if an employee did have the courage to report a complaint of workplace harassment or worse, the chances of it receiving a thorough and professional investigation were, for the most part, non-existent. If you reported an incident to a manager you trusted, there was always someone above them, at some point in the complaint process, who owed their job to, drank with, played sports with, was related to, or owed a favour to the employee you were complaining about. There were no independent, trustworthy, professionally trained harassment complaint investigators in the CSC at that time, and the lower-ranking staff members paid for that dearly.

The victims of this systemic neglect deserved to know that the offending staff member would be held accountable for what they did and to have some security from being re-victimized. But that didn't happen because in those years the CSC authority made their decisions from well-appointed and comfortable offices over two hundred kilometres away having never experienced the reality of working inside the very prisons they managed.

The managers whose responsibility it was to enforce the rules and protect their staff just sat back in their padded chairs, closed their eyes and their office doors, and did nothing. They are now enjoying their retirement and pensions for being true cowards and compliant puppets ignoring the suffering and victimization of the people that they were duty bound to protect.

The Correctional Service of Canada Senior Managers built this kind of work environment through their neglect and maintained it as such over the two decades that I worked for them.

> In an ironic comparison, the 1998 CSC *Performance Report* spoke to the Management of Gangs and Organized Crime within the Prison, stating: "A safe environment free of fear, intimidation, coercion and negative influence is a fundamental condition for the successful reintegration of offenders into society as law-abiding citizens."[5] This policy was meant to apply to the inmates, not the staff members.

As I gained more experience on the Inside, I realized that what we were being taught at the Correctional Staff College was nothing like what really went on inside the prison. We were taught the law, CSC policy, and interpersonal skills but we were not taught the reality of being behind the walls. We were expected to buy a product from the CSC that just didn't exist and, as staff members, we were just fodder to be consumed by this soul-killing factory.

As an Auxiliary Ontario Provincial Police officer, I recall being assigned to go through the mug shot books at the local OPP detachment in order to create a photo lineup. Some of the photos I had to choose from were surprising to me in that I recognized many pictures of the guards who worked at my prison and some from other area Institutions. Some of them were even photographed while still wearing their CSC uniform. The guards would "go out drinking" after their shift without bothering to

---

[5]  Correctional Service of Canada, *Performance Report for the period ending March 31, 1998*, 35. Accessed September 30, 2020, www.csc-scc.gc.ca/text/pblct/perform/pdf/reporte.pdf.

change from their uniform before going to the local bars and getting into some trouble while there. This was not the type of dress and deportment the CSC expected of its employees, but nothing in the way of enforcment was done in those days.

This was at a time when the hiring of a Correctional Officer required little in the way of background checks, no vulnerability sector screening, criminal history check, no check to see if you are currently before the courts on charges or have an outstanding warrant, no fingerprint searches or RCMP and Interpol checks. No physical fitness requirement. No psychological testing.

## Playing the Game

If you happened to have had a few too many the night before while out drinking in your uniform, and just managed to drag yourself in for work late and still smelling of alcohol, that didn't matter, you were still good to go. You really didn't have much to worry about in any case because usually the Correctional Supervisor "Keeper" would put you on a post where you could sleep if off. A post like in a tower with a loaded high-power weapon or locked in a control centre with a toilet or bucket nearby to puke in. Or possibly at the wheel of the mobile patrol so you could drive around the back of the prison out of sight and sleep it off.

Or, in the case of the guard posted to the PIDS (Perimeter Intrusion Detection Centre) for the day, sleeping it off on the floor with a pillow, blanket, and his bucket in case he couldn't make it across the hall to the toilet to puke.

Within the Correctional Service of Canada at that time it was easy to be an open substance abuser because that kind of behaviour was, for the most part, ignored by senior managers from the day I started in Corrections to the day I left. In turn, some of the senior staff were themselves alcoholics and reported to work each day intoxicated or got that way on their lunch hours. Mostly, this kind of behaviour went ignored until something happens to bring the individual to the attention of the law enforcement part of the criminal justice system. This is more or less what it took for a staff member with a substance abuse issue to get treatment. Just like the inmates, substance abuse is a way of life for many and it's never a problem for them until a medical or criminal crisis draws attention to it.

I remember when I first started, one of the guards who had a chronic problem with drinking and driving had his licence suspended for the third time. Having his license suspended never deterred him from driving though. He required some time off from the shift so he could go into town and buy a case of beer. The shift supervisor not only gave him the time off but also loaned him a vehicle knowing full well that his driver's license was suspended. This same guard ploughed the mobile patrol vehicle into some parked cars in the lot after a night of drinking. It seems to be the shift supervisor's logic to have the piss tanks outside of the prison in the mobile or up in a tower, so they won't make a nuisance of themselves down Inside. It gave them the opportunity to go and park somewhere to sleep it off or to make one of those frequent trips to their car to get another bottle into them.

One night in the very early 1980s, while conducting an escape scenario exercise, one of the Emergency Response Team Leaders showed up falling down drunk. I had always wondered why the warden did not speak to him about his obvious condition of impairment as there was interaction between the two throughout the night. As it turned out, the warden was just as drunk. And, when the exercise is over, they both drove themselves home.

But many staff members did not have the tools required to cope with what they were exposed to day after day. Substance abuse was their antidote for the violence, stress, corruption, and the horror that went on Inside. In my time alcohol was the main go-to remedy, a lot of alcohol. Today, the substances used to cope with the unrelenting stressors of the job are limitless and many are even more dangerous and addictive than alcohol. Back then this was the answer for witnessing and being victim to the many horrors that go on Inside and it added yet another layer of torment to the already troubled lifestyle of many.

After a sensational incident, I have seen staff members whisked away to clinics to dry out, and upon their return being given an employee of the month award for completing the program for the second time, only to be back in the same situation within months. All the while, they were laughing at those who gave them the opportunity to clean up and maintain their substantive positions. They may have had "the cure", but they were put right back Inside and exposed to the cause again and again. No one is going to recover and heal if the cycle of abuse and stress keeps repeating itself.

The CSC did not know what to do with the victims of their own making. Stress-related illnesses were not recognized as an injury on duty in my time and those who suffered from it continued to do so their entire careers and lived miserable lives. In some cases, suicide was the final answer to end their suffering. A guard's personality was heavily affected by their time working in such a brutal environment. An environment that shapes and twists your disposition into a cynical and cold shell that is your only defensive shield for being exposed to the constant violence and corruption.

It is incumbent upon the CSC to offer these programs to their staff just as it is likewise to offer rehabilitation programs to the inmates. But, just like the cons, you must want to make that kind of significant change in your life for it to be effective. Otherwise, you are just "Playing the Game" like the inmates often do. I would hear the guards openly brag to each other about how many impaired driving charges or other criminal convictions they had accumulated in their day. About how the only difference between them and the cons was that all their criminal convictions have not drawn the attention of the prison management team yet and unless it was very severe – front page headline news – it was just overlooked.

Much in this book is about "Playing the Game"

## Prison Hygiene

Our prisons are dirty, filthy places to work and the further down Inside them you go, the dirtier they become. Many of the people who live there are not known for their personal or environmental hygiene, both guards and prisoners alike. Even though you have a large number of inmates who are unemployed and could be doing the cleaning, many simply do not want to work as there is an institutional welfare system in place to support them. Just like on the streets, you don't have to work if you don't want to work. The same with education, inmates were paid to go to school, but this was also a choice to be made. So, the cell blocks and many other areas of the prison had mice, rats, bats, insects, and lice. The smells of rotting garbage, human sweat, urine, stale cigarette and pot smoke were everywhere.

When I was giving tours of Kingston Penitentiary to the public after it closed, I noticed that high up on a window ledge there was a small plastic cup with a lid on it that was used to dispense medication to the inmates. This little cup brought back some repressed memories of the cons and how they would pick the lice off their body and save them up in these little cups.

Then, when you walked past their cells, they would throw them onto you behind your back. After a few days you would start to get itchy because you were now purposely infested with them. Another way to get the bugs was when you search an inmate's cell or clean out cell effects and their bedding. The sheets were ripe with the critters and now they are on you to take home with you.

Then, you would have them throwing things on you that made lice look like house pets. Mostly body excretions in the form of liquids and or solids, from a cup or bucket. The CSC did not know about or practice Universal Precautions in my time, and we had no bio-hazard protective equipment issued to us.

There was another item located in the Segregation unit at KP that brought back some bad memories that I would have chosen to keep buried. This piece of equipment was a plexi-glass shield on wheels. It was covered in scratches and stains from having things thrown and thrust at it over its years of use. The officer would push this shield before them while making a range walk to block and deflect the things thrown at them by the inmates from their cells. In three block, at Collins Bay there was another such shield that was used for the same thing. This was installed there as a result of an incident where, on the midnight shift, when you are patrolling alone in the dark cellblock something happened to an officer. The cons can easily hear you when you enter the range in the middle of the night to do a patrol. One inmate was standing on his chair at the window to his cell. When the officer slid the metal window covering open to check on him, the inmate had timed his masturbation in order to ejaculate in the officers' face when the window was opened.

This is what it's really like to work in a prison.

If you were the kind of officer that was aware of your environment, you never let a con walk directly toward you carrying a cup and a lighted cigarette or lighter. You simply cannot defend yourself after being doused in gasoline and set on fire.

One con saved his feces in a bucket for days. Kept it liquid by stirring it up and adding water to it when it threatened to dry out. He then shaved himself entirely and painted himself from head to toe in shit along with the walls, ceiling, and floor of his cell. He felt that no one would touch him if he were covered in it. He was right.

This same con would live off nothing but coffee for weeks. He would take a tray from the mess and fill it with Styrofoam cups of black coffee. It was his way of shedding weight for a power lifting competition he was entered in. I always liked this guy though because he wasn't full of shit, he was covered in it though. You knew exactly where you stood with him, usually upwind. Kidding aside, I truly did like him, and I enjoyed the many conversations that we had.

There were regularly scheduled movie nights where full feature films were shown on the big screen in the gym. There was a movie theatre quality projector in a small, designated room on the second floor above the front weight room in the gym that the inmates would operate. The floor was set up with chairs and there was even a large popcorn maker fired up and ready for the show. The entire prison population would attend. This was in the day before every inmate had a TV in their cell connected to cable. The officers would sit along the back wall closest to the gym exit doors. There were maybe four of five of us locked in the gym with the entire prison population and we were not separated by a control centre or a barred observation cage.

There was no "gun cage" overlooking the gym for our protection and no escape route. I will always remember the reaction from the captive audience of convicts when a cop or prison guard was killed or a woman raped. They would erupt in loud cheers and applause in reaction to these violent scenes that would go on for several seconds.

Along the back wall where the officers sat there were these marks on the wall above the backs of the chairs. They were perspiration and grease stains left behind by years and years of officers sitting there leaning back resting their heads against the wall.

When I started in prison, smoking was one of the things you had to do as part of being accepted into the guard culture. Even though there was a policy in place that offices, control centres, the hospital and the armory were designated no-smoking zones there was no enforcement in place at all.

Our institutional armourer smoked for years throughout his entire shift in the vault where the weapons, ammunition, and the gas were stored. If you complained, then victim blaming was always the result. If you spoke up about being locked in a control centre with a smoker you were immediately harassed, threatened, and had smoke blown in your face. The walls and ceilings of the control centres and the cell block offices were thick with years of accumulated nicotine residue. On humid days the moisture would run down the painted walls and exposed limestone of the jail collecting nicotine residue along the way and turning it into a river of black poison. Polite requests and written reports to have these areas of contamination cleaned were ignored. A formal complaint to Labour Canada was the only way that these areas of the prison were finally cleaned up.

The main currency inside all prisons among the inmates was tobacco. It's far more valuable today as there is a complete smoking ban in our federal prisons.

Most of the cons who smoked all the time like some of the guards, had yellow nicotine stains on their fingers and teeth. A lot of the cons' main diet was dedicated to their cigarettes and their coffee.

In the late 1990s, a smoking ban was instituted in the prison and only designated areas permitted it. Essentially, it was the same direction given in the 1980s but this time it was going to be enforced. You can well imagine how seriously this direction was taken and how well it was enforced given the culture of the prison at the time. Designated smoking rooms were identified and on the day shift when the supervisors were present the smoking was sometimes confined to these rooms. But on the back shifts it was all over the prison once again. There was even a designated smoking room for the staff in the Institutional Hospital.

## Unwritten Rules – Cons

There is an inmate code consisting of an unwritten set of rules that go back to the beginnings of incarceration.

The number one rule in prison has always been not to "rat out" a fellow con. The old "*omertà*" code of silence used to be the golden rule for all prisoners back in the day. I say, "used to be" because today the cons stand in line to rat someone out if there is something tangible in it for them.

Some cons have a direct telephone line to the prison's Security Intelligence Officer and are even rewarded for giving up information. It's a risky business to be a rat. If the cons you are ratting on suspect you, they can easily find you out by feeding you disinformation. If the disinformation is acted upon by Security, then they know where it came from and now your life is forfeit.

## Unwritten Rules – Staff

The guards use the similar technique for enforcing the same unwritten rule of not being a rat. One of the non-uniform staff members would come into the cellblock office every morning for their coffee and cigarette. They stayed for quite a while listening to the guard's conversation. Then they would go up to the Warden's office for another coffee and repeat what was heard. This staff member would be rewarded with training courses and other perks as long as the information was being supplied.

When the guards finally suspected, they would start to feed this person disinformation that would be acted upon by the prison management. The information started out to be plausible and then slowly progressed to the absurd after a period of time. A lot of resources and time were consumed to investigate the information supplied by the player who is now being played. Once found out, the morning coffee visits with the Warden stopped. They went from being a person known as a "comer" in the CSC into obscurity.

## Special Outings

Two guards were very much in demand by the cons to take them out on escorted passes within the community. The reason: they would take them to the local strip clubs and bars. Both of these guards presented as notorious con haters so it was a mystery to everyone as to why they would suddenly "get the Mission" and choose to assist the inmates in becoming law abiding citizens by escorting them out into the community.

This was only curtailed when one of them, practicing their special style of rehabilitation, was arrested when the offender he was escorting went out the bathroom window of the strip joint, across the street to the Royal Bank, robbed it, then returned to the club for another beer. A bank customer followed him and reported his location to police who arrested them both for robbery as they left the bar and were walking to their car in the parking lot.

Of all the other shit that these two did while employed by the CSC for years on end, it took a sensational incident, the indictable offence of robbery, to get them fired. And they were both "good guys to have around". One of them was even awarded the Exemplary Service Medal, because they "served as a model for others".

## Being Able to Relate to the Cons

Years ago, at the Camps (minimum-security), you often couldn't tell the staff from the offenders. The officers wore civvies with a magnetic nametag pinned to their chest to distinguish between convict and staff.

In some cases, I would challenge anyone to distinguish between the two without the ID badges. The Service was then all about how well you interacted with the cons. Interpersonal skills training is part of the educational process of becoming a guard. Dressing like a biker seemed to be part of that integration. The thinking behind the relaxed dress in the Camps was that the cons are more likely to relate to a staff member dressed casually than if they were in a military style uniform. It was all about being able to relate to your Correctional Clients in order to bring about that "law-abiding citizen" goal of the Mission. The cons saw through these attempts; you were still a "screw" to them regardless how of you dressed.

I have to mention now that I call the cons, cons. I have yet to meet a con who didn't want to be called a con. Being on the Inside is all about image. You cannot present as being weak in the world of crime and the word con is more forceful than the word inmate. At one time in the 90s a commissioner insisted that we not use the word con, but that advice fell short when he was observed using the word while on a tour of one of the institutions. The CSC tried using the term "correctional clients" for a short time but that wasn't long lived either. You must understand the social dynamic of being on the Inside before you attempt to make changes to the culture of the prison environment, be it inmates or guards. Learn the nature of your correctional clients before trying to apply remedies that may be effective with those on the Outside but end up being embarrassing when applied to the people on the Inside.

I remember being involved in an arrest in Toronto of a man who was a federal inmate on a release program. He had with him his identification card that was issued by the CSC, and it acknowledged him as being an inmate from Millhaven Institution. Of all that had happened to him on that night the greatest concern to him was that he got his prison identification card back. This card represented great worth in the value system of the criminal in that it gave him street cred. This card gives him high standing in his circle of peers because it signified that he came from a maximum security prison. Had he been released from Kingston Penitentiary rather than Millhaven he would have never admitted to that because it would have classified him as a protective custody inmate and in the circles of the criminal lifestyle, this is a label that you definitely need to avoid at all costs.

## Dressing for Court

I recall one day I was posted to the cell blocks rather than to the external escort post that I was scheduled to be on. There was an outside escort of an inmate going to Appeals Court that day. I was dressed as I usually was, with polished boots, pressed shirt, and tie. The individual chosen over me for the external posting was obese and unshaven, reeking of alcohol from the night before. He was on the sixth day of his eight-day shirt, dirty running shoes on his feet, uniform shirt undone down to his naval with a T-shirt on underneath printed with a sports team logo. He had a big old brass belt buckle with the word "Bullshit" embossed on it. This guard was going out in public escorting an offender to Appeals Court. Even Hollywood couldn't have created him! He just reinforced the public's poor opinion of guards as did the supervisor by letting him appear outside of the walls of the prison looking like that.

Another time, I remember attending Criminal Court as a witness to something that took place on the Inside and the con was facing "Outside charges" as the result of his actions. Several officers and guards were subpoenaed as witnesses as well, along with one manager. A couple of officers were dressed in court attire, that being properly turned out in uniform or suit and tie. The guards who attended were dressed in short pants, tank top, paint-splattered clothing, sports team shirts, dirty running shoes, flip-flops and unshaved.

Everyone sat in the courtroom together awaiting the start of the trial. Just as the proceedings were about to begin, one of the police officers in charge of the case asked these guards to step to the front of the courtroom with him. As they stood up at the front of the courtroom, the judge asked the police officer what this was all about. The officer replied that these were "Correctional Officers" who were appearing as witnesses in his next trial.

The judge looked at each of them in turn and then told the officer to remove them from his court and instruct them on the proper attire for witnesses appearing in the Courtroom. The police officer then marched them from the room and the trial had to be delayed because of their lack of respect and decorum. The CSC manager who was sitting in the courtroom never said a word to the guards; he just stared straight ahead and pretended nothing was wrong.

## The Making of Prison Brew

> "The inmate population, in general, when they get into CSC, upon admission,… about 80 per cent have a history of substance abuse."
>
> —Dr. Ivan Zinger, Correctional Investigator of Canada

Prison "brew" is homemade alcohol. It is quite the industry and moneymaker for some of the inmates known as "brew-masters". You don't have to be a brew-master though to make your own alcohol inside a federal prison. The basic ingredients are provided to you during meal parades.

Yeast, fruit, and sugar are all you need to get started. If you can't arrange to have a small packet of yeast smuggled out of the kitchen, you can do nicely with just a loaf of bread. The residual yeast in a loaf of bread is enough to get your brew started. It takes a little longer to cook because of the secondhand yeast, but the results are the same. Fruit is also served at most meals. You just have some other cons on your range bring back their apples and some sugar packets from the mess.

A garbage bag is all you need to cook it in, so now mix your ingredients with some water and get started. It's best if you can place it near a source of heat as it speeds up the breakdown of the fruit and sugar. Hiding it from the officers can be an exercise in creative thought but it's not that often that the "Coppers" search your cell or the ranges so you should have all the time you need to cook up your brew.

Some place the bag inside the leg of their jeans or the sleeve of their coat hanging in their cell. Some hide it on the range at the bottom of garbage pails. They can always tell when it's a good time for them to do this sort of thing by looking to see what staff members are working the ranges that particular week of shifts.

If they are known to the cons as slackers then it's all right to go ahead and cook up a brew right on the range because these guards are not likely to perform regular searches or even walk down the range for the entire week that they are posted to the cell block.

I often wondered why some of us fought the battles we did with the cons to get them out of their beds for work and school every day, perform searches and window bar checks, get the inmate cleaners out of bed to clean the cellblock.

Once the administration lets the discipline lapse, it's an uphill fight to get it back. However, those who allowed it to slide are not the ones on the frontlines fighting to regain that lost ground.

## Look for Fruit Flies

There was even a full-on distillery discovered behind the drywall in the upper vestibule of Cell Block 2. An old office had been walled up years gone by but the cons got inside and began a large-scale brewery. They were cooking it up by the gallons inside large garbage pails before it was discovered.

One of the most important steps to making a brew is to vent it. If not, it will explode. But the ventilation allows the odour of the brew to escape, and the officers can sniff it out. One of the methods to disguise the smell is to vent it through a bottle of shampoo. As the gas from the brew mash bubbles through the shampoo it masks the smell of the brew.

But you now have a cell smelling of fragrant soap rather than the usual body odour of the con. That alone may be enough to tip off the officer that something out of the ordinary is going on within that cell. The smell of a brew in the making very often attracts fruit flies, lots of fruit flies because it's so sweet. It's not that hard to find it within the cell block with a great cloud of flies hovering around.

Once the mixture has cooked for a few days you strain it through a pillowcase and discard the leftover mash down your toilet. It's best to dispose of the mash because if the "Coppers" find it they know that there is a brew cooking on the range.

Once filtered, it's ready to drink.

When I worked at the Staff College teaching the new recruits, I decided to cook up a brew in my office to show the recruits how it's done and what it looks and smells like. One Friday afternoon, I gathered all the components and constructed my still. I put the ingredients together and sealed them inside the container. The following Monday morning I thought that I had my brew all cooked up ready to go. But I failed to vent the container and it exploded all over my office – wall to wall prison brew. Truly a rookie brew master mistake.

I remember some cons in segregation making a brew out of ketchup.

All the ingredients were delivered to right their cell three times a day on their meal tray. They hoarded their ketchup, sugar, fruit, and bread for their brew. Ketchup is a great ingredient in a pinch because it is made from fruit and has loads of sugar in it.

Once cooked up, they drank it all in one sitting. They gorged themselves on it and ended up puking it all up. It was quite a sight with their cell floors covered in bright red regurgitated ketchup brew.

The Institutional Emergency Response Team (IERT) was called in to secure these two and have a medical examination due to their high degree of intoxication. They were removed from their cell, placed on the floor and handcuffed while getting them washed up and relocated to a clean cell.

## Extraction from Segregation

Once on the day shift, the Response Team was deployed to remove a con from his cell in Segregation as he was drunk on brew. He had gotten possession of a floor mop, which he had broken and was using the pointed end to jab at the officers as they walked past his cell. This con considered himself a jail-house lawyer and would advise other cons on the law and CSC policy all the time. He was quite outspoken to say the least. In the jail vernacular, he was a "mouthpiece".

Eventually, he had to be removed from the general population once it became known what his actual crime was. It was the type of offence that the other cons look down upon, to say the least. He knew that the Response Team had been called so he prepared for them. He stood his bed up against the door and wired it in place against the cell bars with a coat hanger and then reinforced the barricade with his mattress and his desk. He also took apart his radio and used the electric cord to wire the cell bars up to live electric power. He ran one wire into the socket and then into a pool of water on the floor outside his cell. He then wired the cell door bars with the other one.

The staff in Segregation saw what he did and reported it to the Team Leader. The Team Leader had the prison electrical maintenance staff shut off the power to the cell in the service ducts before the team deployed to remove him.

The team entered the cell block to begin the extraction. When the first team member touched the cell door there was a pop and a shower of sparks. The con shouted out, "Live wires, baby… get 'em into you!" Every time after that fiasco, when the power or the water needed to be shut off, the Team Leader ordered that a Response Team Member accompanied the maintenance staff into the ducts to make sure that it was indeed completely turned off.

The con was removed from his cell, strip searched and put into what was called the "China Cell" (a cell with nothing in it except a bucket to shit in) for the remainder of the day while he sobered up. Later that night, the Response Team had to go in after him again. During the day, he had one of the inmate range cleaners give him another mop to break and use as a weapon where he would attempt to stab at everyone who passed his cell.

The tactics were a bit different this time. The Team Leader made sure that the power to his cell was really turned off this time around. He had barricaded his cell once again with items given to him by other cons. He stripped himself down naked and was trying to poke staff with the sharp end of his stick through the bars.

He was ordered to surrender up his weapon but declined the invitation to do so. He was warned that he would be gassed. But he felt that he was up to the challenge of a fight. This time, a munition called an SGA-110 Ferret was fired from a shotgun into the back wall of his cell. This is a small plastic munition about the size of your thumb and looks like a little rocket with stabilizing fins on it. It is designed to shatter upon impact with a hard surface and dispenses the CN gas as an aerosol mist. When you fire gas into a cell you always give a little time for it to get working on the con before you enter the cell.

Because he had removed all his clothes, the gas mist covered all of his body to great effect. He was soon a very compliant con. He was removed from the cell and taken up to the showers to be decontaminated.

The CSC soon issued a policy stating that an SGA-110 was not to be fired into a cell while the con was inside because they feared the con being accidentally struck by the projectile. Probably a wise move, as I can see a great potential for this happening accidentally or with intent.

In the future, the Team was issued with a gas dispenser called a Mark 9 or a Mark 10. This is an aerosol can about the size of a small fire extinguisher that contains either Mace or Pepper Spray. It was ideal for cell extractions because it could contaminate the whole cell without any projectile danger and without cross-contaminating the whole range.

## Chemical Agent Use Requires Extensive Decontamination Procedures

The decontamination procedure for exposure to CN gas, Mace and Pepper Spray in the CSC is extensive. You have to remove the inmates from the contaminated area and shower them with Sunlight dish detergent. The surfactants in this brand of soap cut through the chemical agent more thoroughly than ordinary soap or shampoo. Then you have to give them clean clothes and have them examined by a nurse right away, and by a doctor within 24 hours. You also have to remove all their bedding and clothing from their cells and have it washed, along with the walls and floor of the contaminated cell.

The entire range also has to be scrubbed with water mixed with baking soda. For severe contamination, the area has to be sealed and heated up to a certain degree for a measured period of time, vented out, and repeated. This procedure breaks down the components of the chemical agent.

Any food stuffs in their cells have to be replaced and any electronics that may have been damaged also have to be replaced by the Canadian taxpayer. So, the cons have nothing to fear about being gassed or pepper sprayed other than the immediate discomfort. Decontamination measures for exposure to pepper spray from the Police are very different than those used in the CSC. There are no showers, no Sunlight dish detergent, no health care examination, no fresh clothing and no doctor examination within 24 hours. Canada makes prison a nice place to be.

\*   \*   \*

...Years ago in the 80's and 90s' at the Correctional Staff College induction training, you had to learn some thing called the LCT Factor for applying Chemical Agents (gas) to a given area. Lethal Concentration Time Factor was the length of time a person could survive in a contained CN gas contaminated area before death. You were tested given the square footage of the area you were intending to gas along with the CN content of the munition in grams. You were then to compute the time factor at which the occupants of that room would be in danger. I had often thought that this was a moot exercise as the volume of air and CN gas in the room would never be constant given that the first thing to be destroyed in a riot is every window in the entire place. The cons always enjoyed smashing their windows. It finally came to light in the late 1990's that yes, this was the case. The LCT computations were finally thrown out of the testing criterion for chemical agents and not used at all in the future.

Large-scale use of Chemical agents was restricted in certain areas of the Prison. They were not to be used in the Institutional Kitchen, as the replacement of the gas contaminated foodstuffs would be costly and it was not to be used in the Institutional Hospital.

## Moonshine and Aqua Velva

Another option in the manufacturing of alcohol is that you can go a step further in your brew making by cooking up some prison moonshine. You need to have something to cook it in like an empty gallon Javex bottle, large soap container or similar vessel, preferably with a screw-on cap. You put in your strained brew along with a device called a "dunker". This little homemade gadget has been around since the cons had access to electricity.

A simple one is made from coiled wire or two razor blades tied together with string or thread separated by a small piece of rubber or wood between the blades. Attached to both the blades is a piece of electrical wire and a wall plug. You immerse the blades in a cup of water and plug it in. In no time at all the water will boil. This was commonly used in the time before the cons had electric kettles and microwave ovens to heat the water for their coffee, tea, and Mr. Noodles.

Prison Dunker

In order to vent this compact little still you will require a length of tubing for the boiled off vapour to be cool down by flowing through it. You can steal this from the industrial shops or find it in other areas of the prison.

One con stole a stethoscope from the hospital and used the rubber tubing off that in his still. Affix the tubing into the container cap after lowering your dunker down into the bottle. Make sure the cap is well sealed so none of the odour escapes.

Often, the cons will get some ice from their ice machine on the range and pack it around the tubing so the liquid will cool down rapidly. Now plug in your dunker and begin the process of making moonshine. If you do a good job, the shine will come out clear and potent.

Brew is powerful enough, but it does not compare to prison made shine for alcohol content. You get a con high on shine and then mix with it some pills smuggled into the prison and you have a man totally out of control.

Some cons even go as far as drinking the windshield washer fluid or antifreeze from the institutional vehicles in the garage where they work.

One Christmas, an inexperienced Social Development Officer (SDO) allowed the cons to have a pound of raisins each along with a bottle of Aqua Velva aftershave lotion. Aqua Velva straight up is quite a cocktail to celebrate the holidays with and the raisins were the perfect fruit for the many brews cooking up over New Years. So, we had a lot of drunk cons on our hands over the holidays. But at least they had nice smelling breath after drinking their aftershave. This was a suspicious occurrence to have the SDO purchase these items because he did the same for the inmates in a former prison he worked at.

## A Lesson Learned

The punch clock records vanished after a midnight shift where a con committed suicide. This was very embarrassing for the supervisor giving his testimony at the Coroner's Inquest, as he simply could not explain how these records were no longer in existence. But no repercussions were forthcoming for him or the guard on duty in the cell block that night who was supposed to be doing his patrols. No big deal for Regional or National Headquarters either way because there was no complaint from the dead man's relatives as to why and how this evidence went missing or how his body was not found until the day shift. There were no relatives or friends attending the Coroner's Inquest for the dead man.

After his lifeless body was discovered, I witnessed the supervisor on duty that shift permitting two other Indigenous cons to enter his cell and perform a smudge ceremony over the body without supervision. This was done before the Joint Penitentiary Squad (police) got on scene to begin their investigation into the death. So much for the preservation of evidence at a death scene.

### "GO AHEAD AND JUMP!"

A former supervisor was showing a group of brand-new officers around the prison as part of their orientation as he now held the position of Staff Training Officer.

I remember him leading them around back of the Institution to the exercise yard for the segregation unit. It just happened at that time one of the offenders from segregation had climbed up onto the roof of the

Institution and was threatening to jump. There were officers in the Unit trying to talk him down. I was one of them.

Then this buffoon comes around the corner and tries to induce him to commit suicide by encouraging him to jump. The warden, who was on the phone with the officers in segregation, had heard the supervisor yelling at the con to "GO AHEAD AND JUMP!" She had him up to her office for a little talk afterward, but that was all, a little talk. Encouraging a person to commit suicide is an indictable offence under the Criminal Code of Canada. A great example of interpersonal skills demonstrated during a crisis by a supervisor for the new recruits to see their very first day on the job. This was the same supervisor who was running the "tradition" of handing your overtime checks over to him. He managed to do a great deal more damage in the years that he remained on the Inside before his retirement, with a full pension and an Exemplary Service Medal.

# PART 4

## Shivs and Other Prison Weapons

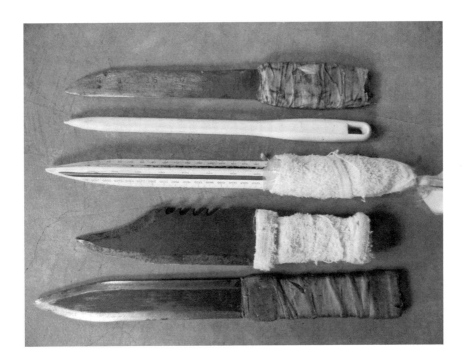

Knives, or 'shivs' or 'shanks', as they are known in the institutions are the most easily obtainable and most common tools used as lethal weapons in our prisons. The public often wonders where the cons get them. In the 1980s, they were given to the cons to eat with. The same type of dinner knives and forks that you and I use every day were freely handed out to the offenders three times a day and not accounted for at all at the end of the meal parade.

The cons picked them up in the mess hall before their meals and were supposed to leave them behind at the end of it. They were on the honour system back then because none of the cons leaving the dining hall were ever searched, and the knives were never counted. They would sharpen them up using power tools in the shops, sandpaper, or just rub them against the concrete floor or the wall of their cell to put a fine edge on them. One con had a combination electric can opener/knife sharpener in his possession and would run off the honed shivs like an assembly line.

In the 1990s, the offenders were given "camp sets". These are a thin metal knife, fork and spoon combination that fit together for easy storage. The metal is too thin and flexible for stabbing but, in a pinch, is good enough to slash a throat.

The cons used to complain that the flimsy metal knife camp sets were useless for cutting their steak.

## Designed for Maximum Lethality

The cons in my time were issued old-style safety razors. Boxes of razor blades were always available on the ranges and the cons could take many as they wanted. Constructing a simple throat slasher using these blades and melting them into a toothbrush was easy. The plastic toothbrush and the very thin metal of a razor blade melted into it would not activate the metal detectors so the cons could carry them anywhere they went. Another use that some of the inmates would put the razor blades to was to swallow them as a means of self-harm. I had often wondered how they were able to do that, swallow a razor blade. I found out one day while working in segregation. Being brittle, the razor blades would be folded upon themselves and break cleanly in two. They would be folded again and again until they were in small pieces. The inmates would wrap these little bits of blade in toilet paper and swallow them with water.

Other times the cons would fasten razor blades to the handle of their cell door so when the officer grasped the handle to close the door they would get cut.

There is a very lethal looking crossbow constructed from melted toothbrushes, dental floss, and razor blades on display at the Correctional Museum in Kingston. The bolts have a very destructive broadhead made from razor blades meant to inflict a major wound channel. Then they were coated in feces to infect the open wound and render it more lethal. This was a method that was used often to ensure that additional damage was done to your victim. Even the average shiv would be coated with a thin layer of shit in order to infect the wounds inflicted by it.

Have you ever noticed the fire escape orders printed and posted up on the walls of every government building you have ever gone into? Often, they are covered with Plexiglas to protect them. The cons remove the Plexiglas and make knives from this plastic-like material. The plastic will not set off the metal detectors when they pass through the security checkpoints, so they are transported all over the prison and to outside escorts in the community without being detected.

Plexiglas Shiv

Most weapons could be made quickly and easily in the metal shop, automotive garage, carpentry, or electrical shops to a custom design if you wished.

You could design your shiv to accommodate your needs and give that drawing to a con who works in the metal shop for construction. I remember searching the metal shop once and seeing several knife designs drawn on a large piece of sheet steel waiting to be cut out and sharpened.

A once popular design is a hollow metal tube with a threaded nut welded to one end. Then take a metal rod and grind it down to a spike with the dull end threaded to match the nut in the end of the tube.

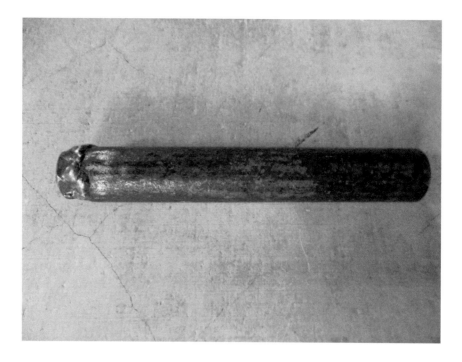

When concealed, the pointed end of the spike is encased in the hollow part of the tube, screwed in place and then inserted until needed. When you decide to deploy it, you simply unscrew the spike and remove it, turn the spike around and thread it onto the other end of the tube.

When I say the hollow tube is inserted, I am suggesting that because of its smooth round shape and compact size, the offenders commonly insert it into their rectum. This type of weapon can be carried within the prison all the time or when the offender is escorted to hospital, on a transfer or court appearance within the community. A strip search will not turn the weapon up so the con can carry it outside the jail concealed until he is ready to use it in an escape attempt or as a murder weapon.

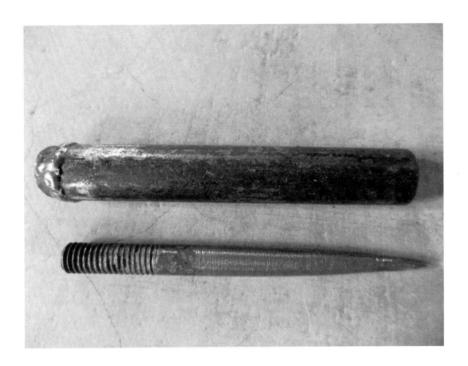

If you are really serious about your stabbing weapon of choice you have to wrap the handle in cloth. It's preferable to have a material like a cotton towel on the handle rather than tape, bare wood, or steel. With the towel fixed to the grip, your hand does not slide down the shaft of the blade when you strike bone, thus cutting your own hand. It also won't slip when your hands are covered in blood. This will prevent evidential cuts to your own hands that may show up in court and convict you should it go to trial. The serious gladiators will grip the shiv in their hand and wrap duct tape around their entire closed fists to prevent the knife from being accidentally dislodged during the attack and possibly used against them.

I have seen the attacker suffer serious wounds themselves during the offensive because in their lust to strike again and again they will often inflict wounds on their own body as they swing down, miss, and plunge the knife into their own leg or arm. A serious knife fight is dynamic and unpredictable.

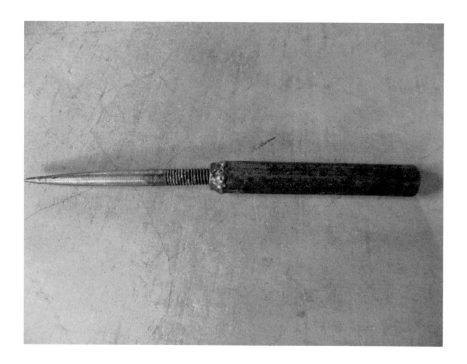

The cons never attack head on. They prefer an ambush from behind, a blitz attack in numbers, or when the intended victim is sleeping, in the shower, or somehow otherwise disadvantaged. The goal is to kill the person. You are not going to give your victim a fighting chance to run away or defend themselves. You also have to do it out of sight of the cameras or the staff if you don't want to get recorded doing it or get shot at.

One guy got it while he was bench pressing during his workout, when both of his hands were being used to keep the weight bar up. He was in no position to defend himself. The attackers brought down a weight bar across his legs, breaking both of them. It was not until after these attacks that cameras were installed in these areas of the prison. But a camera is only useful if someone is monitoring it.

I find it interesting to watch some of the Hollywood movies where a victim gets stabbed once and falls dead instantly. That's just not the case with most of the knife fights I've witnessed and even been victim to. I have seen only one offender get stabbed once and die from that lucky, or unlucky wound, depending upon the perspective. I remember an offender in 3 Block got hit once in the heart and bled to death on his bed in his cell.

I can still see him lying dead, face up on his bed, with his blanket covering him up to his chin. The blood dripped out from under the bedsheets, congealed, and formed a perfect cone on the floor like a stalagmite. But that is not usually the way it goes down. Most cons I have seen suffer numerous stab wounds.

I have seen offenders eviscerated and still come back for more. It's not uncommon for an offender to survive twenty to forty stab wounds.

Of course, there is no limit to the type and number of weapons available in prison and even the supply of sporting goods available to the cons can be used for anything but sports. Aluminum and wooden baseball bats and 45 lb. Olympic weight bars always come out of the gym and are used with great effect when there is a prison riot.

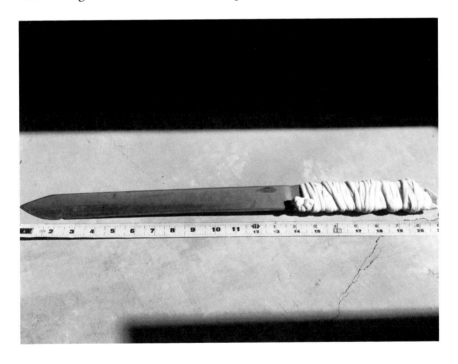

File Cabinet Support Arm

Other ingenious fabrications such as the bar spreader were constructed inside the metal shop of a maximum-security prison. This device is of solid heavy metal construction with counter rotating threaded wheels on each end. It is placed between the window bars and a metal lever is inserted into a hole in body of the centrepiece. This lever then turns the body of the bar spreader, providing torque to the outer wheels and spreads the bars enough for the inmate to get between them and outside to freedom.

Bar Spreader

There was a business that an inmate in the carpenter shop was running successfully for a while. He would make these very fancy hash pipes out of wood. They would be carved with designs, sanded, and varnished and a little metal grill was fixed into the bowl end of the pipe. They truly were masterpieces of drug paraphernalia. His creativity was not limited to just the creation of these pipes. Somehow you have to smuggle them into the main prison. The inmates are given those little variety boxes of cereal with their breakfast and they would bring them to their work to snack on. Sometimes they would not eat the cereals and so would bring them back into the prison after work. Within the cereal boxes was concealed a contraband pipe. The cons would hide the pipes inside these boxes and then seal the box back up with carpenter's glue. When the guard inspected the box and found that it was properly sealed it would not look suspicious and would simply leave it with the inmate.

Prison made hash pipe

# PART 5

## The Untouchables

### "The Island of Misfit Toys"

It is rare that the Correctional Service of Canada fired their problem staff members in my time on the Inside. Usually, they hide them for a period of time until the heat is off, sometimes within the offices of other Justice Canada partners. Then they are reintegrated into the mainstream and sometimes even promoted.

Just as the cons are reintegrated back into society, so the problem staff are sent back to the prison after their time-out. Another staff inmate parallel– reintegration.

The most common place to hide the problem staff members used to be at Regional Headquarters. It was most often referred to as "The Island of Misfit Toys". You may remember the classic Christmas movie *Rudolph the Red-Nosed Reindeer,* where his travels take him to such an island. The new island of misfit toys was the now-defunct Prison for Women until it eventually closed and was sold to Queen's University. It was then referred to as the "Prison for Managers". The old limestone building and the site is now in the planning stages for condos, offices and shopping.

It was closed to the offenders many years ago but was still operational within the Service as a location where the ass grabbers and corporate criminals languish for a few years until people forgot about their misconduct and they were integrated back into a prison again, transferred, or promoted.

It has been my experience that the best indication of future performance is past performance, but this is a lesson that the CSC has never learned. After all, "We believe offenders have the potential to become law-abiding citizens." It has been apparent that they believe some of their corrupt and violent staff have that same potential. It has been long evident that some staff in the CSC are not held to a higher moral standard than the very criminals it incarcerates. Once again, a very strong parallel can be drawn between this kind of problem personnel management and that of offenders being transferred to higher security prisons for the crimes they have committed while at lower security institutions, only to be brought back should they display the potential to abide by the rules.

You would be surprised at who the CSC holds out to the public as leaders. Some staff members have longer criminal records than the cons. It always comes back to bite them without exception when they cover up and forgive the criminal offences their staff commit. They get into a jackpot by retaining staff who have committed serious criminal acts only to have them re-offend again and again. In the CSC, the harassment and abuse often escalates for individuals whose behaviour goes unchecked. It's a lifestyle very much like that of the cons. Once they become entrenched within a system that protects them, they become bolder in their transgressions knowing that they are untouchable and unaccountable.

This in turn sets up the system to enable other staff members to use the same line of defence and skewed logic when they too are involved in disciplinary or criminal acts in order not to be held accountable or to keep their jobs. How can you proceed against me when officer so-and-so did the same thing without repercussion? Knowing where the bodies are buried seemed to be the key to your success within the Correctional Service of Canada in that period. As an OPP Auxiliary Constable I also knew where the bodies were buried…in fact I knew where entire cemeteries were.

There just didn't seem to be any modelling in the CSC in those days, and frankly, there wasn't much to look up to.

## Tracking Disciplinary Issues

There was a time that the Correctional Supervisors would try to keep track of officers arriving late for work, improper dress, and other disciplinary issues by recording these events in a memo book they kept on the desk or in an unlocked drawer.

After a time, the offending guards would get ahold of this book and write their own comments in it about other staff members and their opinion about them. Or they simply ripped out the many pages that pertained to them.

This went on for quite a while. It filled up with racist and sexist comments and insults until I removed it, placed it into a sealed envelope with the appropriate security classification upon it, addressed to the Warden and hand delivered it up to his office. I included all the violations of the *Privacy Act* that insecure record keeping of this type encompassed. The book was never seen again. No action was taken against any of the people who accessed the book, made comments in it, or made it available to other staff to read.

An employee has committed an infraction, if they:

> "Fail to properly safeguard all documents, reports, directives, manuals or other information of the Service.

> —*Commissioner's Directive No. 060*
> *Code of Discipline*
> *Protection and Sharing of Information*

## Season's Greetings!

One December night in the 1980s, I was posted to 3 Block on the midnight shift. This was the perfect opportunity to do some searching of the common rooms and cell block ranges. The cons are either sleeping or watching TV all night, so things are quiet.

Most of the guards are doing the same thing as the cons… sleeping.

Not being one of the officers who preferred to sleep on duty I always searched.

The Inmate Committee Room was located in the 3 Block vestibule, and I decided to have a look around for hidden contraband. Usually, the cons don't hide prohibited items in areas such as this because it can lead to having their privileges suspended and them being locked out of their room.

They had three plants in the room. Two were healthy and green. The third was dried out and shrivelled up. One of these things is not like the other.

I used a pencil to probe the soil in the pot and came up with a couple of folded plastic wrapped pieces of paper. When unfolded, they were found to be a list of names, addresses, and home phone numbers of all the staff at Collins Bay. This particular copy was more up to date than the one in the supervisor's office.

I guess this would explain why some staff members were getting Christmas cards from inmates mailed directly to their homes. This was not done in the spirit of the season; it was done to intimidate.

In an attempt to control this information in the future, any copies of Protected Information of this nature were numbered. That had nothing to do with the physical security of the information, it was just a means to identify what department of the prison the missing copy was from.

In the late 1990s, the same thing occurred at Joyceville Institution. The cons got a copy of the staff's personal information: names, addresses, and phone numbers. There was a class action suit against the CSC and its failure to protect this information. As a result of the suit, each staff member affected by that loss of information received a cash settlement. Looks like we at Collins Bay Institution were ten years too early for our cash settlement.

# PART 6

## Visits and Correspondence

**"Some will even pack drugs or cash on their children, thinking that staff won't suspect that anyone would endanger a child by committing such a grossly negligent act."**

Within those fences and walls of the Canadian prison system the Criminal Code of Canada as those outside of the system know it, does not seem to exist.

As a small example, I was working in the visits and correspondence department one afternoon. In this capacity, the officers are to monitor visits between the offenders and their family members and friends.

Many people on the Outside would be surprised to discover that visits in Canadian prisons are not so much conducted between glass barriers as most movies depict. This only takes place if there has been a history of passing contraband, assault, or inappropriate sexual behaviour between the parties. The majority of visits take place in an open common area. Offenders and their visitors sit at a table and are able to openly express their affection for or their dissatisfaction with each other, up to a point.[6]

In one case, dissatisfaction was expressed in the form of a domestic assault. The offender had walked around the table, took his common-law

---

[6] This was pre-Covid-19.

wife by the throat, and throttled her. He then slammed his fist down on the hand of the woman's three-year-old daughter who had touched some coins on the table. All of this was recorded on videotape by the many cameras located throughout the visiting room. I ended the visit and completed a report on the assault. I noted that very same inmate was scheduled for a trailer (conjugal) visit the following weekend with this same woman and her child.

I was astonished to discover that no criminal charges or institutional charges of assault were even considered by the management team. The weekend trailer visit with the victim of the assault and her child went ahead. The Unit Manager interviewed the offender and decided it was all right to proceed with the trailer visit. She counselled the offender, and he agreed not to beat up his wife and child anymore. My written reports and the videotaped recordings of the assaults disappeared.

I had no idea that the authority of a Unit Manager with the Correctional Service of Canada superseded that of the Solicitor General of the Province in matters of domestic violence. But violence in federal prisons is hidden from public view and public scrutiny. When it's out of sight in this manner, it just doesn't exist.

In Ontario at that time, the Solicitor General directed that domestic violence would not be tolerated. Police officers were instructed to arrest in *all* cases of domestic assault. But historically, within the Correctional Service of Canada, the *Criminal Code* does not have any bearing.

## How Many "Wives" and Girlfriends"?

When conjugal visits first began in the federal prison system in the mid-1980s, the offender was permitted privileged visits with their immediate family members only. These visits were called "trailer visits" because the CSC bought full-sized trailer park trailers. There were initial difficulties in getting these trailers inside some prisons, as they were too large to fit through the doors of the sally ports. In some cases, the CSC had to hire a crane to lift them over the prison walls and fences to get them set up on the Inside. Later, small townhome-style buildings were constructed within the walls and fences.

General food orders and special food orders were supplied to the inmate and their guests throughout their trailer visit. Televisions and VCR/DVD players were provided as well, and the inmate could choose from a number of movies from the collections held in the V&C Office. There was also an outdoor BBQ to grill your steaks on. Outdoor play equipment was available for the children and there was a stock of toys and board games in each trailer for them as well. If the con wanted some photos of his trailer visit, then the inmate photographer went over and took them for him.

When I worked for CSC, it seemed that 'anything goes' with respect to whom the cons could have Inside for their trailer visit. There were some offenders who had a different woman in the trailer every few months and nothing was ever said of this. The way to arrange this was to have your current girlfriend sign a document stating that you co-habitated with the offender prior to their incarceration thus establishing a common-law relationship.

So, this month you could have your current wife in the trailer with you. The next month you could have one of your three common-law wives. The month after that you could have one of your three or four baby mothers in. You could even bring your family pet in for a trailer visit. Or if you were just too stressed out from day-to-day prison life you could have the trailer all to yourself to get some peace and quiet if you knew how to play the game. This was called a "solo trailer visit." Life is good when you are on the Inside of a Canadian prison and you know how to play the game (as the notorious prison escape artist Tyrone Conn did).

I remember one woman who would arrive at the prison for a trailer visit with her incarcerated son. Upon searching her luggage, we found it to contain a variety of sex toys among the lingerie outfits she had packed for her stay. When asked why she thought she needed these items when she was visiting her son, she replied that she "didn't want him turning queer" while he was on the Inside.

One incident I reported was the ongoing correspondence between an offender who was incarcerated for living off the avails of prostitution, among other criminal offences. His "wife" was keeping up his business on the street by reviewing applications for potential escorts that she was actively recruiting, and then sending the prospects to him through the mail.

He would receive a photograph of a woman who may have the potential to work for him, along with a short bio written by his wife. The photo was usually of a nude woman posing for the camera. He then would get word back to his wife whether or not the applicant had what it took to be one of his prostitutes.

The report I submitted to the managers was ignored, and I was instructed to return the photos of the naked women to the offender who continued to run his business from the jail with impunity. The photos would be stuck up on the walls of the Con's cell using toothpaste as glue or passed on to other Cons for their entertainment and personal use.

## "Special" Deliveries

Trailer visits and staff members are just a couple of the vehicles by which most of the drugs and other contraband enter Canadian institutions. Drones are being used more and more lately because it's less risky for those involved in the conspiracy to smuggle in the contraband. Drones, depending upon their size can pack a sizeable cargo of drugs, cell phones, and even firearms onto their payload, fly them over the walls and fences and into the hands of the cons. Today in the Kingston region there is an epidemic of drones delivering contraband over the fences and walls of the areas prisons.

Some visitors will insert items into their body cavities, a process commonly known as 'suitcasing' or 'hooping'. Some will even pack drugs or cash on their children, thinking that staff won't suspect that anyone would endanger a child by committing such a grossly negligent act. But it's done more often than people on the Outside would think. If you are ever on a tour of the old Kingston Penitentiary, look for the painted outlines of feet near the entrance to the visiting area. This is where the visitors used to line up for the drug dog to inspect them. At the end of the line of painted feet are much smaller prints to represent the location at which the children would stand.

People entering the prison for visits are not usually strip-searched. It is rare for that to take place. The institution has to have reasonable grounds for performing a strip search on a civilian and at that point the police are involved.

In many cases, where the grounds do exist, the visitor may be given the option to be strip-searched, or they can leave the institution. Often, the visitor will go down to their vehicle in the parking lot and remove the contraband from their body and return without it, consent to the search so they can continue with their trailer visit. Usually, you will see them with a black eye the next day because they did not deliver the goods. More people than just the cons involved in the smuggling plot must pay for the goods not being delivered on time.

That is why the CSC had family violence patrols. After several notorious assaults and even murder within the trailers, the Visits and Correspondence Staff were required to have Family Violence Training and be able to identify the signs and characteristics of domestic discontent while the cons and their family members are within the walls and fences on their trailer visit.

The officer is supposed to walk out to the trailer three times a day and the inmate and their visitors are to present themselves at the front door… that was it.

Upon observing the occupants of the trailer, you have been so highly trained by the system that you are able to tell if there has been any family violence with just a glance over a distance of several metres between the fences that surround the trailer. Often, if the weather was bad the guard doing the trailer check would not even get close to the trailers. They would simply walk a short distance outside of the main building and wave at the con and his visitors without getting a clear view of them. As long as a live body waved back, they were good to go. This is of course a Band-Aid solution to the problem that CSC has put in place to address any of the recommendations that may have been suggested by a coroner's jury or any other external investigative body.

It was a rare that any of the staff working in the Visits and Correspondence office even had that Family Violence Training in the first place as it was not a requirement to work in that department. This is one of many tick box solutions that the CSC developed in response to a sensational incident.

**"Cigars in your own personal humidor."**

Then there were the two brothers from Southwestern Ontario who were incarcerated within our fine system who fancied themselves organized crime bosses. They were in for conspiracy to commit murder. Each weekend when their family members came to Kingston to visit the boys, they brought in high-end cigars for them. On one occasion, they brought down a whole box of expensive cigars so the boys would not have to wait a full week in between stogies. For their convenience, the cigars were kept in a humidor located in the Visits and Correspondence office.

The manager of the department told staff to hand out the cigars on demand when the boys required them. So, the boys would walk up to the office and bang on the window glass while they made a "V" with their index and middle fingers. That was the sign that you were to get up and get them a cigar from their own personal humidor.

This is completely against all CSC policy and law. You can't bring any tobacco products into the prison for the inmates as it is contraband and to allow it to happen is trafficking. This activity was reported to the senior manager in charge. Yet, the senior manager continued to allow it to go on. And so, it did for a while, but after the word got around down Inside the institution, the humidor and its contents disappeared one midnight shift.

So now when the boys wanted a cigar, they had to wait until their relatives came for their Sunday visit. The department managers continued to permit this.

My question is which or how many CSC managers were being paid off to allow this practice to even exist let alone continue for the length of time that it did? Just what other reason could there be for such blatant disregard of CSC policy and the law?

I liked both these inmates, and we used to have long conversations and a few laughs when they were in the V&C area. After they were released from prison, the younger brother was shot and killed in his driveway outside his home in 2017. In 2019, the older brother was shot a number of times when leaving his lawyer's office. He survived that attempt on his life but a year later he was gunned down again in a Burlington plaza parking lot. This time he didn't survive.

## To Stamp or Not to Stamp

Postage stamps as currency were always a hot item in the prisons. You can buy them in the prison canteen for the same price as stamps on the street. However, some of the cons would have their friends and family members mail in books and books of stamps so the con could "write home more often". This is, of course, considered a contraband item if it was not purchased in the prison canteen. The cons would use these contraband postage stamps as cash on the Inside.

Meanwhile, the Visits and Correspondence officer would pass on the letter to the con but return the stamps to the sender along with a list of the contraband items that are not to be mailed into the prison, the area listing Postage Stamps as contraband would be highlighted on the letter. The officer used one of the contraband stamps as postage to return their letter to the sender along with the remainder of the books of stamps. So, what naturally happens? The con submits a grievance that the officer used one of "his stamps" to return the letter. The manager dealing with the complaint of course sided with the con and reprimanded the officer. The same manager who permitted the cigars to enter the prison.

The cons would also peel the used stamps off their incoming mail and use them again if they were not completely cancelled by the Post Office sorting machine during processing. So, when the V&C officer received the mail, he would take an indelible marker and run it over the stamps that were not cancelled. Again, the cons would grieve that action and as a result the Cigar Unit Manager told the officer not to do it any longer. Canada Post will continue to be cheated out of postal revenue because a CSC manager decided to bend the law and side with the cons. After all, to them, what are a few stamps in the greater scheme of things provided that the lid is kept on?

You can't expect offenders to strive toward that "law-abiding citizen" goal of the Mission when a CSC manager neglects their duty by actively encouraging this sort of behaviour.

## Tax Time!

Another scam the cons would run would be at income tax time. There was always at least one savvy con in the joint who would complete income tax returns for the cons at a price. He would claim GST rebates for items purchased through the prison canteen so a federal government cheque would appear in the mail for some cons in payment for that legitimate tax claim.

But some outlandish tax returns were filed on the cons' behalf as well as the legit ones. There were some very creative claims submitted in order to receive deductions on properties, rent, heating costs, hydro bills, property maintenance, and other deductions for cons who had been inside for several years and had never maintained property on the outside or paid these costs in the first place. Just because you're on the Inside doesn't mean you still can't continue to commit crimes for profit beyond the walls and fences.

When questioning the Cigar Unit Manager about these cheques, he would instruct us to "Just deposit them in the inmate's bank account" and "Don't ask these kinds of questions." Again, what was being deposited into the cigar manager's bank account in order for him to ignore this? What other possible reason could there be for this kind of indifference and neglect of duty, law, and policy?

The Visits and Correspondence position was the last one I was in before joining the Toronto Police Service. Two of the heavies (inmates who ran the prison) came to see me and say their goodbyes on one of my last days working for the CSC. They both gave me a hug and told me, "Sorry to see you go, Boss. You were one of the good ones."

Years later as a police officer, I remember working on the streets of Toronto and getting a radio call that one of our officers had just stopped a full patch biker at Lawrence Avenue and Markham Road. I was in the area and so stopped by and parked across Markham Road from the officer and the biker. I just got out of my scout car when the biker yelled from across the street to me, *"Boss! Hey, Boss!"* as he ran across the street arms wide open to give me a big hug. The other officers reached for their weapons as they thought the biker was going for my gun. We had a long talk about our days spent together in prison and exchanged business cards, laughs, and well wishes.

# PART 7

## A Night in "The Ghetto"

**"The Correctional Supervisor on duty that night 'lost'
my six-page report."**

Within my first year inside a federal prison, I met with the experience that everyone who has ever thought of working behind those walls, fears.

One Block is the notorious subdivision of the institution where the new inmates are housed. It was called "Gladiator School" or "The Ghetto" and for good reason. It was built as part of the original structure of Collins Bay, consisting of two cell blocks divided by a central hallway called the Strip. During the early '80s, the rate of federal incarceration offenders was increasing but the cell accommodations were not.

The institutions began to double bunk offenders. It began with the installation of a small number of bunk beds into cells designed for a single offender. The cons became upset by these new living arrangements and demonstrated their displeasure in the common way most offenders do, by acting out. "Acting Out" is the politically correct term used within the CSC for displaying violent behaviour.

Within the institution, the common and effective way to exert control over offenders is to limit their movement. Most Canadians are under the assumption that the cons are locked up 24/7. It's just not the case. The only time the offenders are completely locked in their cells is between the hours of 23:00 and 07:00. The officers lock the cells only periodically through the day. Every hour they are unlocked for about ten minutes to allow the cons to go to work, school, or recreation.

The officers have to go down the range to unlock these cells manually. Few prisons in Canada had automated door-locking devices on the cells at that period in time. There you are, often by yourself down a long range surrounded by convicted criminals with only one way out should things go wrong. You do not carry a firearm; you do not carry a baton, Mace, or any other form of weapon to defend yourself in case of attack. You do not have body armour. If the cons decide they want you, there is nothing you can do about it because it's a long way from the back of a cell block range to the front where the only exit door is, and you are greatly outnumbered.

You are supposed to be watched by a fellow officer if they are doing their job. Often, they are not. If a hockey game is on TV, if they have a good book, card game, or even if they're engaged in conversation with other guards these diversions will trump your safety down the range every time. Even if they are watching you, the only action they can take on your behalf is to summon help and then lock you down the range with the cons so that the violence can be contained.

Today, most officers are issued with a "PPA" a Personal Portable Alarm. This device is a little larger than a pager and is slides onto your belt. Once activated, it notifies the Control Room that there is a problem, and an officer will summon help on your behalf. This is provided the officer staffing that post is awake, sober, or even within the control room itself to hear the alarm being activated. There was also no established procedure for an organized response to a PPA or a Riot Alarm within the prison. I have seen chaos abound when an alarm is activated. While on a control post that monitors the length of the Strip, I have seen the response to an alarm activated in the kitchen with the guards running like the wind down the corridor not thinking to stop at the Control Centre to pick up a pair of handcuffs, mace, or even the very keys that give them access to the kitchen. They'll run down the Strip and stand in front of the kitchen barrier staring inside and ringing the bell for access. If the staff member holding the keys is the one activating the PPA and is being stabbed or beaten there will be no help forthcoming. This information comes from my direct experience in being the one on the kitchen floor fighting with the con and awaiting help that doesn't come because no one thought to get the kitchen keys from the control centre.

Even when an adjacent door is available for staff to enter through, they are so single-minded that they do not think of an alternate access route. I have witnessed this take place several times in a week with the same staff members responding to the alarm and standing outside looking in and pressing that damn bell.

Much of the problem with the CSC is that they do not learn from past mistakes and its own corporate history as a whole. When the suggestion of organized responses to alarms was brought to the attention of the Institution's management team in the form of an Officer's Statement Observation Report dated January 4th, 1990, it was ignored because they did not see a need for it. They would never be in a position to respond to an alarm down Inside themselves and there was no risk to their personal safety, so they had no concerns.

In the early 1980s, there was no technology to aid the officer if a situation got out of hand. You relied upon each other.

So, on one particular night, an officer monitoring the meal parade overheard a couple of offenders from the ghetto, discussing how they felt the matter of double bunking was going to be resolved this night. In the report written by an officer who overheard that conversation he quoted an inmate by name saying, *"We will have to get someone in one block to do him in"*.

This report was not acted upon.

Two other officers and I were working in 1 Block that night. Under normal conditions there are only two officers per cell block. But, because of the double bunking, the tension being high along with the rumour that there would be some form of protest over it, an additional officer was posted to the cellblock. The cons were riled up and began throwing fruit and one-pound bricks of margarine at our office door and windows. Then they set some garbage pails on fire and tossed them into the cell block lobby and even bounced one off the roof of our office. We put the fires out using the extinguishers at hand.

On one of the hourly walks, I could not help but notice that they had smashed their twenty-six-inch colour televisions all over the range. When I returned to the office, I started to write up a report on the destroyed TVs.

It's rare that they would do something like this because the TVs belong to the entire range and so to destroy them usually means they are serious.

I remember one of the other officers asking me what I was writing. I told him that they smashed their TVs. How could he miss it as I could hear his feet crushing the glass from the broken TV screens as he walked over the debris. He still didn't believe me until he went and looked down the range for himself.

Then he laughed and said, "I guess they're upset at something." With all this violent activity going on in the cell block, I assumed it would be locked down for the night especially when they started to smash and set fires.

I was wrong.

An hour later, we went down for another range walk. As I entered the range some of the cons were looking at me in a peculiar way. As I reached the bottom of the range and turned around, I could see that most of the cons had now gone into their cells, which is out of character. There were only four of them out on the range. Being new to the range, I did not recognize any of them.

I looked at the entrance to the range and did not see the supervisor who was supposed to be watching my back as I did my walk. I started to walk back up when a con quietly said, "Hey, Boss." I turned to look at him and he nodded toward a shiv sitting on the bars of the vacant cell next to him. I picked it up and began to walk farther toward the cell block entrance.

The four cons formed a line across the range blocking my exit. I could see that one of them was holding a metal bar (the broken leg of a chair) along the back of his leg trying to keep it out of sight. The others were concealing items in their pockets, but I could not see what they were at that distance. As I got closer, I kept looking for the supervisor to appear at the top of the range. He never did.

One of the cons asked me "What's that for?" indicating the knife I had. I told him, "I know what's going to happen here tonight, and if I have to go down, I'm not going alone." I turned the shiv over in my hand so that the point was along the ulna bone of my right arm. In this position, it can be used to slash as well as to stab.

Many knife fighters will hold the knifepoint outward toward their objective. This is only good for poking at the target and the cons know that this method of knife fighting is the sign of an amateur.

As I approached the group, I was trying to decide how to make a run for it. Should I shout a warning hoping someone would hear? Should I turn around and run back down the range? Should I try to run for the open door to the lobby?

I chose to run for the lobby. I started to run, and the group closed in on me. I swung the knife up and around in front of their faces, and they parted and fell back enough for me to break through their line. They weren't expecting such an aggressive unexpected move or for me to put up a fight. Just as I made it to the entranceway, another con came out of the shower located next to the exit door. He had been standing "six" (meaning lookout) since I came on the range. He was not as easily intimidated like the others by someone else armed with a knife.

When I slammed into him, I lost the shiv the con gave me and had to grab onto the con's knife hand with both of mine to prevent myself from being stabbed. I pushed him back into the shower and got out of the cell block.

My major concern then was what was happening to the other officers I was working with. I checked down the other ranges and both were just leaving without incident.

The supervisor who was supposed to be watching us while we were downrange was outside the cell block on the strip trying to make time with a female officer from 2 Block across the hall. He was not even in the cell block watching us do our range patrol.

What happened to the cons? Nothing. Some were transferred to a higher security institution but no criminal charges of assault or attempted murder or assault causing bodily harm were ever brought against them. The entire incident was not even reported to the Joint Forces Penitentiary Squad. The Correctional Supervisor on duty that night "lost" my six-page report. He should have locked down the cell block after being informed of the pre-indicating factors that led up to the assault. But he did not; he was trying to cover up for himself by telling me that he had everything in hand and that he was dealing with the matter. Several knives and a metal bar were found outside the cell block windows by the officer patrolling the yard on the midnight shift. The cons were getting rid of the weapons that they were going to use on me.

Being new, I believed and trusted my supervisors. I never made that mistake again. This was also one of the Keepers who was running the "tradition" of handing over your overtime cheques to him.

The supervisor of the cell block that night who was supposed to be watching us while we were downrange was found across the hall in 2 Block. He disappeared after that night, and I never saw his face again to this day. Was he paid off to be absent from his area of responsibility in our cell block at that particular time or was he just saving his own ass?

I'll never know.

I experienced my first lesson in how the Service really works that night, and I almost paid for it with my life. There were many more like this to come.

> "Gladiator School" is a popular nickname given to Collins Bay Penitentiary, a medium security federal institution in Kingston, Ontario, as well as generally to other prisons where it is perceived that prison life serves to reinforce criminality and foster the very behaviour they purport to control.
>
> —*Michael C. Chettleburgh*

# PART 8

## Stay Out of the Kitchen

> Post Traumatic Stress Disorder (PTSD) is a disorder that can develop after an individual has experienced, witnessed or been repeatedly exposed to a major trauma.[7]
>
> —Anxiety Canada

The institutional dining hall is exactly what you would expect: a large open area with the tables and stools bolted to the floor. A central island contains loaves of bread and condiments, salt, pepper, and bricks of margarine. I have seen the cons take an entire loaf of bread and dump it in the garbage can just because they wanted the plastic bag that the bread was in.

Some cons controlled the seating arrangements in the mess. They would have designated seating that the weaker cons would have to pay for if they wanted to sit down to eat. The enforcer would always sit at a table just inside the doorway so he could see everyone who entered. He would make note of the ones who sat in 'his area' and would visit them afterward to encourage them to take part in his pre-paid seating arrangements. Your option was to pay, refuse and get beat up, or starve.

---

[7] Anxiety Canada, "Post Traumatic Stress Disorder," accessed January 4, 2021, www.anxietycanada.com/disorders/post-traumatic-stress-disorder/.

Along one wall was an area where the cons would queue up and receive their tray through a hole in the wall that separated the dining hall from the main kitchen.

The cons who were vegetarians would tell the kitchen steward at the window so and would receive a veggie meal. Those who did not eat meat for religious reasons would state the same. They had to present a meal card to the kitchen steward to prove that they adhered to this kind of diet. Very often though, they would see what was on the regular meal line and if they thought that was better, they would go for it regardless of what their religion or their veg diet card stated. Ever the con artists.

Two officers stood inside the dining hall at the very back near a locked door to the main kitchen. They had no weapons, no radio, no keys. They only had a fixed-point alarm and a telephone on the wall while standing there surrounded by the entire prison population.

In order to get out of the dining hall during an emergency you had to make it across the entire length of the mess through all the cons if you could. And, if something went down, you and your partner were locked inside the dining hall with all the cons.

## Hit the Riot Alarm!

One con had just returned from having his tonsils removed at the local hospital on June 13, 1987, and he received two bars of strawberry ice cream and some fruit juice for his meal as he could not eat solids for a couple of days post-op. He took exception to this meal, as he did not like the flavour of ice cream and demanded something else. He approached the door to the kitchen to complain about it to the kitchen steward. As the door was being opened to let a kitchen worker in, this inmate pushed his way through into the main kitchen.

This is something that is never done, letting unauthorized inmates into the kitchen. Because if the cons took the kitchen, they could hold out for months with the food stores contained inside or they could destroy the food stocks and that would cost thousands to replace. If they damaged the equipment in the kitchen the prison would have to send out for their meals thus costing even more money. So, letting unauthorized cons inside the main kitchen was something that wasn't supposed to be done at all.

Also, there are a lot of very big and very sharp knives readily accessible in the main kitchen.

The con rushed in and wound up to punch the kitchen steward in the face. I came in right behind him and blocked the punch. So now I'm the target of his assault. The other officer in the dining hall came in with me and the kitchen steward locked the door behind us. Then things exploded as we were on the floor fighting this con while half of the inmate population on the other side of the wall were screaming for our blood. Some of them slid their dinner knives under the door for the con to use on us. He got hold of a pair of salad tongs and stabbed me in the back with them several times. While trying to restrain him I could feel his fingers in my eye sockets trying to gouge my eyes out. My partner, who was over sixty years old, slipped on the ice cream, fell, and struck his head on the floor, receiving a concussion. He was out of the fight.

My head was full of all the self-defence twist locks and wrist locks we were trained to do at the Correctional Staff College. It was impossible to use any of these CSC "Approved" self-defence moves while being covered in slippery ice cream and trying to apply them to someone who was more intent on stabbing you to death than listening to your "verbal non-violent crisis intervention strategy/resolution methods."

I'm trying to deal with this guy without having to punch him out and thus provoking the ire of the other cons that work in the kitchen, locked inside with us and they all have access to very large, sharp kitchen knives. The thoughts of the last two officers who were killed at Collins Bay Institution were on my mind because they were murdered in this very location, one of them almost decapitated by a con using a kitchen knife and then joking afterward that the officers would not be home that night for their dinner.

The struggle went on for quite some time as the officer who was supposed to be watching us on our post in the dining hall was off doing some socializing. She did not see the play go down in the dining hall and so did not summon any help. She did not see the cons clambering over themselves to see the action through the small windows to the main kitchen. She did not hear them screaming encouragements for the con to kill us.

She was not on her post.

It was the kitchen steward who hit the riot alarm and got to a phone to alert the Control Centre that there was an assault taking place inside the kitchen. There was a great response to the call for help but, as usual, no one responding to the alarm thought to stop at the Cell Block Control Centre and get the emergency access keys to the kitchen. I could hear the kitchen doorbell ringing and the responding officers yelling "Key up!" Did they expect me to ask the con for a time-out while I opened the door for them?

So, the struggle continued.

## Bring Some Handcuffs!

Eventually, a guard came strolling in through an alternate kitchen entrance with his hands in his pockets, not assisting in any way. He stood over me and the con fighting on the floor and said, "Okay, I'm here. You can let him up now."

I told this guy to come back another time, and when he does, to bring a pair of handcuffs with him. He just continued to stand there, hands in pockets.

Finally, a group of officers arrived with the Mace and handcuffs. The con was taken to segregation and my partner, and I reported to the Institutional Hospital. I remember passing the Inmate Committee Chairman on the Strip and him asking me, "How you doing Boss?"

I replied, "Oh... not so bad" – for someone just having to fight for their life and being covered in blood and strawberry ice cream.

The next day, I got a phone call from a supervisor at the prison wondering when I was coming back to work as they had to pay overtime to cover off my post. The managers could not even wait until I had my stitches out. The only person in the entire prison to ask me how I was the Chairman of the Inmate Committee, a con. Not a single supervisor from the Warden on down made any effort to inquire how I and my partner were after the assault.

I even had a hard time trying to get my torn and and blood-stained uniform replaced afterward.

> **"I had to get the guy who just tried to kill me out of his cell each day and give him a shower, let him out to the yard and bring him his meals. Effective protection from being re-victimized just didn't exist."**

When I did return to work, I was posted to the Segregation Unit where the accused was being held. So, I had to get the guy who just tried to kill me out of his cell each day and give him a shower, let him out to the yard and bring him his meals.

Effective protection from being re-victimized just didn't exist. Proven once more by forcing me to have day-to-day contact with the very person who just tried to kill me and in fact, wait upon him. This was not the only time I experienced this insane practice… this was just the beginning. There was a future incident, similar to this one, that almost cost me my life.

I spoke to the Institutional Preventive Security Officer about this arrangement, that of putting the criminally accused and his victim together. All he did was to call me out for being a coward for not having the guts to be working around this guy.

It was clear that officers did not deserve to be protected in those days. There was great systemic and profound indifference and abuse toward staff that was common in the CSC then. There was little recognition of the harm caused to the victim by the accused and there was no reparation from harm and no restoration of the victim's self-worth, in fact it was the opposite of this in the CSC at the time.

## Charged and Convicted

The con was street charged with Assault Cause Bodily Harm and Assault Peace Officer, times two. The accused pleaded not guilty to these charges but was convicted at trial and an additional four months was added to his sentence. Events like these never made the papers at that time. The CSC made sure of that.

Prior to my insisting that outside charges be pursued (criminal charges), I was strongly encouraged by the CBI management not to proceed with that and deal with the assaults within the institution under the *Corrections and Conditional Release Act*. This way, the con does not have additional time added to his sentence and yet another criminal conviction added onto his lengthy record. The "encouragement" by the manager was a direct threat to torpedo any career aspirations I may have had with the CSC. The other officer and I did proceed with outside charges though, and the con was convicted at trial. And, making good on the threat, I never achieved a higher rank than CX-1 while employed with the CSC. I was Terminal Ranked. The second officer posted to the kitchen with me that night never returned to work after that assault.

You had only two choices when you wore a uniform to work in that period of time. You sold out and let yourself be manipulated by those invested with power and authority who are skilled in developing ways of intimidating you. Or you did your duty according to the law and CSC Policy and you paid the price for it.

# PART 9

## Did you get an Ambulance?

> "The Service shall take all reasonable steps to ensure that penitentiaries, the penitentiary environment, the living and working conditions of inmates and the working conditions of staff members are safe, healthful and free of practices that undermine a person's sense of personal dignity."
>
> —Section 70, *Corrections and Conditional Release Act* (1992)

The Cell Block Control Centre was a bulletproof glass, steel-reinforced bunker located at the junction of the main corridor (the Strip) and the entrance to the gym. It is staffed by an officer on rotational shifts for sixteen hours a day and controls the movement of cons and staff through these strategic areas. It also contains a series of CCTV monitors, which enable the officer to see what is going on in the gym. These CCTV monitors were not video recorded in my time.

On one evening shift, an offender was lured into the back weight pit and brutally butchered. Dying from his wounds, he was still able to crawl out of the weight room into the gym looking for help while leaving a trail of blood and viscera.

The guard in the Control Centre was unable to see all of this on the monitors because the newspaper he was reading at the time of the murder was in the way. It's also hard to be looking up at the monitors when the cable television is located under the desk out of direct sight, and you have to have your head and eyes looking down all the time to see your hockey game.

I liked this inmate. He saved my ass one day on the Strip as I was standing as a barrier in between two cons intent on killing each other. He walked over and physically picked up one of the combating cons and carried him away while I dealt with the other one. While all this was going on, the other guards just walked around the battle pretending they didn't see what was going on. Or they stood there and nervously watched, too intimidated by the violence to act as was their duty.

While at the Main Gate Control Centre one night, I was listening to a guard who had recently transferred in from Prison for Women as this correctional facility was being shut down after the scathing Justice Arbour Report. The guard was complaining that nothing exciting ever happened around here and that she was bored. No sooner had the words left her mouth when I looked down the Strip and saw two cons coming through the barrier at the Cell Block Control Centre. One was leaning on the other for support and appeared to be injured.

I picked up a radio and went down Inside to see what was going on.

The two cons were brothers. Both were well known troublemakers to staff and to the other cons in the institution. One of them had been stabbed while they were in the gym. They had used the lid from a garbage pail to defend themselves just as a gladiator would use a shield; it was covered in puncture marks, scratches and blood. A few of the stabs got through or around their metal lid/shield though. Another officer and I opened the gate to the institutional hospital and got them inside.

**"Did you get an ambulance?"**

**"No," was the reply.**

**"You get on that phone and call an ambulance *right now!*"**

The CSC had removed the nurses from the institution on the back shifts to save money (although the back shifts are when most of the violence, suicides, and overdoses normally take place), so there was no nurse on duty. It was up to me to treat the offender's wounds using the contents from the trauma bag located on top of the stretcher.

I got the con onto the stretcher and removed some dressings from the trauma bag and applied them to his stab wounds. I called the Main Gate Officer via my radio and told her to call for an ambulance – an inmate had been stabbed. The guard at the Gate acknowledged the transmission. Half an hour later I called her again: "Did you get an ambulance?"

"No," was the reply.

"You get on that phone and call an ambulance *right now!*" I ordered her. Eventually, an ambulance arrived, and the con was escorted to the hospital.

## You're Not a Supervisor

I walked across the hallway and asked the Correctional Supervisor on duty if she had heard me tell the Main Gate guard to get an ambulance the first time I asked for one. She told me that she did hear that. I asked her if she heard my second radio broadcast one half hour later telling her to call for an ambulance once again? She told me that she did.

I went down to the Main Control Centre and asked the officer in charge of that post if he heard the radio transmissions from me calling for an ambulance? He said that he did. So, there was no mistake that these transmissions were made, acknowledged, and recorded.

The next day, I approached the Correctional Supervisor on duty that pervious night and asked her if she discovered why the guard at the Main Gate did not call an ambulance as instructed. She told me that the guard did not think that I, not being a supervisor and only a low-ranking officer of terminal rank, had the authority to tell her to call for an ambulance.

Now as I remember from my First Aid training, a first responder personally designates someone to call for an ambulance. This prevents incidents where a person shouts, "Someone call an ambulance!" and no one does because they think that "someone" has made the call.

This very act took place many years ago when a con in one block was stabbed and an officer shouted, "Someone call an ambulance!" and no one did because they all assumed that "someone" was calling for an ambulance.

What happened to the guard at the Main Gate who did not initially call an ambulance as ordered? Nothing. But. she was soon promoted to a supervisor and then to a senior manager.

# PART 10

## Dispute Mechanism – Guard Style

### "I'll see you in the lower parking lot after shift!"

The lower parking lot at Collins Bay Institution.

The designated place to settle disputes between guards.

"I'll see you in the lower parking lot after shift!"

Okay, if that's the way things are done around here, so be it.

I remember spending a lot of time in the lower parking lot, all by myself, watching all the off-duty guards driving by on their way home. The next day, when you asked them why they were not there to meet you in "the lower parking lot" you usually got no response. If you get any response at all it will be how you are their best buddy now.

"I was only kidding, bud," they would say.

"I'm not your fucking 'bud', asshole."

### The First Guys Out the Door

In my extensive experience, some of the guards labeled "a good guy to have around when trouble starts," have always been the first guys out the door when the trouble starts. Or they are the ones to start the trouble in the first place, then they walk or run away leaving you to deal with it.

These are the guys who talk tough all the time. The guys who want to "See you in the lower parking lot." The guys who constantly trash talk management and other staff. The sexist, racist, homophobes that sit with their feet up on the desk and read the newspaper all day because they won't go down range near the cons because they are afraid of them.

The guys who won't lock up a con's cell because they are afraid to say "no" to them.

"Oh, I was running to get the Mace."

"Oh, I was running to get a radio."

No, you were running to save your ass.

## Predators Talk Big Yet Rarely Show Up

These are the tough guys who are only tough against women and children.

These are the tough guys who take the specially arranged trips to developing countries to have sex with children. If that's not bad enough, they sit around the cell block office bragging about it and having the other deviant guards hanging off their every perverted word – justifying their exploitation of children by explaining how they are helping them and their families by paying for sex with their children so the family will have money to buy food.

Not wanting to hear about their sickening pedophile perversions I'd go out and stand on the strip with the cons. The inmates have a very strict social order and those who exploit children are at the very bottom of it. This was not the case with the guards it seemed. Then I get the taunts from them about how you must be a queer or something because you don't enjoy their degenerate stories. So, I'm waiting in the lower parking lot again, waiting to meet the predator pedophile who doesn't show up.

I spent a lot of time in "the lower parking lot" waiting for the "good guys to have around" to show up. But they never did.

## A Gun with Hollow Point Bullets – Pointed in My Face

I came in for work one morning and there was a redneck guard at the Main Gate entrance who always worked the midnight shift. He pulled out a revolver loaded with hollow point bullets and pointed it at my face and threatened to "blow my head off."

He was standing behind bulletproof glass at the time, but I didn't want that "bulletproof" claim tested on me. He was upset that a friend of his was arrested for impaired driving during the night and blamed me for it because I was an OPP Auxiliary Constable even though I was not involved in that occurrence.

I made sure not to linger too long in front of the open gun ports as I passed by and went down Inside to report this Indictable Criminal Offence to the supervisor in charge off the prison.

What happened to this guy? Absolutely nothing.

But at least he was never promoted to supervisor before he retired with a full pension and given his Exemplary Service Medal.

I experienced this form of harassment all the time from many of the guards who ended up before the courts on criminal charges or for even having just received a ticket or warning from the police. It was always the cop's fault that they were arrested and/or charged, never their own.

Some of the guards would try to pick a fight with me because they got caught doing something criminal just because I represented what they perceived to be the cause of all of their troubles just as the inmates do.

Yet another parallel behaviour between the guards and the cons.

## Selling Out to Move Up

It's been my experience that the most militant and anti-management tough guy, pro-union and staunch "never rat out another officer" guard, after a while, when they could no longer cover up their cowardice, their thefts, and when they ran out of supporters and had no place to turn, they suddenly got "the Mission" and turned pro-management and sell out to protect themselves. Once they were supervisors, they could really make the lives of other staff hell. And they did.

It's that Guard/Con parallel once again where, like the guard, the con gets in over his head in debt or 'beaks off' at the wrong person or group and has to run for protective custody.

The CSC has a long and continuing history of placing and maintaining these staff members in positions of authority over others and even awarding them with medals. Much to the detriment of the officers who have integrity and a solid work ethic.

## Multiple Alarms… and Responses

During my stint, there was a post within the institution called Administration Security that required you to log in, search, and keep track of inmates who had access to the Administration part of the prison when they reported to their Institutional Parole Officers (formally called Classification Officers) and when they went for their visits. The offices were located two electronic gates away from the front door, i.e., freedom. Often, at least one of these gates would be left open because the guard in charge of the Main Gate forgot to close it or couldn't be bothered to keep it closed. So, their freedom could be easily gained by rushing the gate when it was opened and having a car waiting outside the front door. Or grab a staff member and use them as a bargaining tool to force the door to be opened for them.

As the officer on this post, I always made frequent patrols of the hallway containing the offices of the Parole Officers. If a con got some bad news about his parole or temporary absence **"You cannot ignore a Fixed-Point Alarm."** application, he might act out. Each office had a Fixed-Point Alarm (panic button) on the wall. If things went wrong for the parole officer, they could push it and summon help.

One of the parole officers arranged her office so the button was directly behind her chair. The chair, being on wheels, would be pushed back when she got up and bump directly into the alarm button. The alarm would be activated in the Control Centre and the officer there would dispatch a response to her office. The first officer to respond would be the one on the Administration Security Post as they were the closest. So, every time she got out of her chair the alarm would go off, and we would have to respond.

This happened several times a day, day after day, week after week. She was advised of this ongoing issue and was politely asked to rearrange her office. She ignored this request mostly because it came from someone who wore a uniform; thus, the person and the request were beneath her notice. But responding to alarms is part of your duties; you cannot ignore a Fixed-Point Alarm.

Seeing that lesser measures to resolve the problem were ignored with attitude, I was compelled to write a report about this ongoing issue. So, instead of having her change her office furniture around, the Management Team called in an electrician to move the alarm button to a new location for her.

## Convict Fodder

It was a simple fact at that time in Corrections that if you wore a uniform you had no worthwhile contribution to make to the Service in the eyes of Senior Management at all levels. And the further down you were in the rank structure, the less value you had. You were convict fodder and very much disposable. And some the supervisors had no difficulty in informing you of that at every opportunity.

"You're just a guard, what do you know?"

"He's a guard. You'll have to speak slowly to him."

"If I want your opinion, I'll rattle my zipper."

"Go back to turning keys and pushing buttons."

"You don't have a university degree; you'll go nowhere here."

"You wear a uniform; this is no place for you here."

"You're not one of us."

"I'll see you in the lower parking lot."

The Correctional service of Canada has a long and thriving history of throwing guards under the bus. Many managers were well aware that "shit rolls downhill" regardless of the evidence to prove otherwise in most cases. It is true that many guards dug their own graves through their actions and deservedly so. But in those days, you did not have much to look up to in the form of leadership by example.

Honesty, integrity, ethics, leadership, workplace encouragement, education and staff development were, for the most part non-existent on the Inside if you wore a uniform. This was all accurately documented in the *MacGuigan Report* a decade before I began working in the CSC.

Indeed, in the '80s and '90s, the higher-ranking officers were encouraged not to wear a uniform to further distance themselves from those who worked down Inside. There were a few who held on to their good qualities amid the pure toxic, oppressive, sexist, racist, and corrupt work environment that the CSC created and perpetuated over decades. But even those few could survive only so long in this soul-killing factory without being severely damaged by it in some way.

Even the good ones, somewhere along the line, had a puppet master pulling their strings for them. Everything you believed to be moral, right, just, and honest was hammered at you every single working day in some way from someone behind those walls.

Fear and threats of violence are what you faced every time you put on your uniform and reported for work and not just from the cons.

### "You look into their eyes and there is just nothing there."

It's not your average fear that those Outside the wall may experience a few times in their lives. It's not the fear that you can't walk or run away from. In prison, there is no place to run or hide. You have to come back the very next day and do it all over again.

It's walking down a range alone. A range that is filled with killers, many of whom have access to weapons. People who you know have committed truly vile acts without any remorse shown whatsoever toward their victims.

People without a soul.

You look into their eyes and there is just nothing there.

People who have caused and continue to cause so much pain and suffering in the lives of others without remorse that you question if they are even human.

You have this to cope with every working day you go down Inside. It's the kind of thing that you can never leave behind at the end of the day.

The fight or flight reaction that you experience eight hours a day cannot simply be turned off at the end of your shift.

It follows you home and invades your dreams. It poisons all your relationships eventually. It steals away your quality of life.

As humans, we are hard-wired to respond to a threatening environment instinctively. The constant threat of brutal physical violence, intimidating actions, and direct threats by inmates and staff keep that wiring taut all the time. The human body and mind are not capable of withstanding this kind of ongoing punishment without breaking down. In those days, it wasn't that the CSC senior managers neglected to provide psychological services to its staff, they simply never even considered that because they themselves were not exposed to it. This environmental punishment did not affect them directly, so they had no idea of the cause and effect that working down Inside had on their people. And, in my time on the Inside, they didn't even care.

# PART 11

## Internal Discipline

"The absence of the rule of law is most noticeable at the management level, both within the prison and at Regional and National Headquarters levels."

— Madam Justice Louise Arbour (1992)

### Keeping A Lid on the True Statistics

Offenders threaten officers and their families with assault, death, and bodily harm day after day. Offenders assault officers and often nothing becomes of it. To seek any kind of justice, the officer victims would often be forced to take their case outside of the institution to a court of law. You were taking a big chance in doing this as the Collins Bay management team preferred that you deal with it through charges under the CCRA. There was a high price to be paid if you brought these criminal acts to the attention of the police.

Within the walls, you may charge an offender under section 40 of the *Correctional and Conditional Release Act.*[8] Disciplinary offences include:

---

[8] *Corrections and Conditional Release Act,* SC 1992, c. 20, s 40.

(a) disobeys a justifiable order of a staff member;

(b) is, without authorization, in an area prohibited to inmates;

(c) willfully or recklessly damages or destroys property that is not the inmate's;

(d) commits theft;

(e) is in possession of stolen property;

(f) is disrespectful toward a person in a manner that is likely to provoke them to be violent or toward a staff member in a manner that could undermine their authority or the authority of staff members in general;

(g) is abusive toward a person or intimidates them by threats that violence or other injury will be done to, or punishment inflicted on, them;

(h) fights with, assaults, or threatens to assault another person;

(i) is in possession of, or deals in, contraband;

(j) without prior authorization, is in possession of, or deals in, an item that is not authorized by a Commissioner's Directive or by a written order of the institutional head;

(k) takes an intoxicant into the inmate's body;

(l) fails or refuses to provide a urine sample when demanded pursuant to section 54 or 55;

(m) creates or participates in

(i) a disturbance, or

(ii) any other activity that is likely to jeopardize the security of the penitentiary;

(n) does anything for the purpose of escaping or assisting another inmate to escape;

(o) offers, gives, or accepts a bribe or reward;

(p) without reasonable excuse, refuses to work or leaves work;

(q) engages in gambling;

(r) willfully disobeys a written rule governing the conduct of inmates;

(r.1) knowingly makes a false claim for compensation from the Crown;

(r.2) throws a bodily substance towards another person; or

(s) attempts to do, or assists another person to do, anything referred to in paragraphs (a) to (r).

## The Starry-eyed View of Prison Reform

Many of these offences are criminal, yet behind the walls they were often not considered that and were dealt with internally. This gave the impression that the Mission of the Correctional Service was well and truly on track and the inmates on the road to redemption.

Charges classified as minor are heard by a Correctional Manager. Major charges are heard by the Independent Chairperson who is someone appointed by the Minister of Public Safety for no more than five years but may be extended. They come into the Institution once a week or as needed.

He or she acts as a judge who hears and decides on the disposition of the charges. One of the essential qualifications is that they have recent experience in the legal or criminal justice process.

The cons can represent themselves or if they choose, may be represented by a taxpayer-funded lawyer on internal charges that are not even considered criminal.

Punishment ranges from a stern warning to fines or time in Segregation upon being found guilty. Sometimes, offenders enter into a "behaviour contract" between themselves and a manager. A written agreement is drawn up and both parties sign it. The offender agrees not to repeat the behaviour stipulated in the agreement. Just have the accused sign an agreement not to sell drugs or assault his wife in the visitor's room again and release him…justice satisfied.

The majority of these offenders are hardened criminals and treat this like the joke it is. Those expecting justice out of this sort of absurd settlement are not fooled by it. This is just another way of "keeping the lid on" and keeping the statistics low to make it appear to the public and the Parole Board that the cons are indeed on that road to becoming law-abiding citizens.

## No Intent to Protect

This is why some supervisors sometimes destroyed minor institutional charge forms that were brought before them, it keeps the numbers down. It's been my experience that some Correctional Managers would try to induce the victimized officer to lay an internal charge under the CCRA rather than go with a *Criminal Code* charge of assault on a Peace Officer. This inducement was often in the form of a direct threat to derail any career, acting appointments, or training aspirations you may have. This keeps the numbers down and it appears the system is working. It is just another insult to the officers on the frontlines who are assaulted and then victimized further by a lack of support from their managers.

I remember being told by a manager that if I attempted to have a con charged criminally for assaulting me that I would be the one to suffer for it. He told me that the con was being released soon and therefore could not be criminally charged. This lie was just another means to fast track the offender to freedom and make it look like our methods of rehabilitation are working.

It's tough to cope with that kind of injustice and ignorance from your employer. The people who are responsible for protecting you by law have no intention at all of protecting you, your rights, or seeing that the law is respected as long as the crime is taking place behind those four walls, out of sight, so the law can be averted and the crime covered up to make it appear that our system of rehabilitation is working.

## A Con Named "Tex"

There was a con called Tex (not his real name) who was a very tall and skinny fellow. He was always a source of entertainment for the staff as he did some very bizarre things.

**"The entertainment value overshadowed the prison rules on this one."**

Tex would scrounge the ranges and the yard for cigarette butts so he could remove the leftover tobacco to roll his own. He didn't work so he got his tailor-made cigarettes by providing a service to the other cons in exchange for his smokes.

Tex would sit himself down on the strip and display items the other cons wanted him to sell for them: Hobby crafts, radios, lamps, DVDs, CD's, and items of clothing. He would take a percentage of the cigarettes paid for these things. It was against the rules, but we looked the other way because of the entertainment value. Now, Tex was well-known for the size of his cock. Any officer who had to strip search him knew that. So, he put what God gave him to good use while selling the goods on the Strip.

One day, Tex was set up on the Strip between 2 and 3 Block with his wares for sale gathered around him. On this occasion, Tex had a new twist to his sales campaign. He got hold of an officer's black leather winter glove somehow, placed it over his erect penis and was waving it around at everyone who passed. Again, the entertainment value overshadowed the prison rules on this one.

How are you going to write up the charge on something this bizarre anyway?

One thing was for sure, the officer did not want his glove back after that.

# PART 12

## A Culture of Distrust

> If employees perceive that their employers do not take their concerns about harassment, discrimination, and violence seriously, they are less likely to report their concerns. Issues that are not reported cannot be resolved and may affect employees' health.
>
> —Auditor General of Canada (2019)[9]

During my time with the CSC, there was a well-earned and profound lack of trust between line staff and management. Many victims of the corruption, abuse, and criminal offences perpetrated by their peers and supervisors did not even report the abuse. This, in turn, gave the perpetrators more power over their victims and the abuse just continued and, in many cases, escalated in the form of death by a thousand cuts.

There was absolutely no victim support strategy or network in place in the CSC in those days for staff who were victimized by the cons or by other staff members.

---

9   Auditor General of Canada, *2019 Fall Report of the Auditor General of Canada, Report 1: Respect in the Workplace* (Ottawa, 2019), www.oag-bvg.gc.ca/internet/English/parl_oag_201911_01_e_43530.html.

There were just so many layers of nepotism and cliques within the CSC that you could not trust anyone to be completely unbiased with respect to an investigation into any accusation made against another service member.

The Correctional Service of Canada was not accountable to anyone outside the walls and fences and that was the way they wanted it. As a result, the corruption simply grew unabated to the point where managers and staff just did whatever they wanted knowing that there was no reliable reprisal system in place that could be trusted.

Most staff gave up on seeking fairness and justice and just sucked it up or gave in to it and became part of it as a means to survive. The latter was the most prevalent…a means to survive in the jungle.

Truth and reconciliation just didn't exist in the CSC in those days.

## Managers with Little Integrity or Ethics

If you made it out of uniform and you now to came to work in a suit and tie with a higher pay level, little to no inmate contact, and no more shift work, the last thing you wanted to do was go back down Inside, so you placed your soul on the market to keep that arrangement static.

Some would do anything that was asked of them if they wanted to keep themselves from going back down Inside. This included committing criminal offences against your own subordinates, covering up for your supervisors, performing all manner of underhanded acts, lying, cheating, disposing of evidence and manipulating competitions to place a preferred candidate in the position. I witnessed it all and was a victim of much of it.

I liken this arrangement to the story of the Sword of Damocles. An allusion to the imminent and ever-present peril faced by those in positions of power. The sword is hanging above your head by the single hair of a horse's tail, point downward. You always have to watch in fear and anxiety against the danger that the hair may part and the sword fall at any time should you choose to go against the wishes of your masters. Those in power would assuage any guilty conseience you my have toward performing unethical acts by assuring you that you will be protected. That they will have your back, that this is the way we do things here and you'll comply if you know what's good for you. This insidious abuse and gaslighting is intended to coerce and manipulate you.

I had made my mind up a long time ago that I would not be sucked into the guard culture and be a part of the corruption and sell out my integrity for the sake of a promotion. Having made that decision, the corrupt managers had no hold over me, no carrot, and no stick to use against me.

They did not have to shred my training requests or pretend that they were lost anymore. In the final few years that I was with the CSC, my supervisors did not even waste their time completing a mandatory annual assessment on my work as is required for all employees. Their implemented PDP form (Personal Development Plan) was nothing but paper waiting to be recycled if you wore a uniform to work because the CSC did not invest in their frontline staff.

The *MacGuigan Report* observed:

> *The lack of continuing training for persons who have made a long-term commitment to the Penitentiary Service. Such training is necessary to enable career officers to upgrade skills in order to qualify for advancement. In the absence of adequate educational programs, we find a widespread conviction among correctional staff that promotion standards are unfair, arbitrary and sometimes based on favouritism and nepotism rather than established abilities.*

And after twenty years, this report was still accurate and reflective of the unrelenting way that the CSC treated their own dedicated staff members.

## Lack of Professional Development

Professional development for the custodial staff simply did not exist in my time with the CSC and the line staff did not even receive the *Commissioner's Directive*-mandated annual refresher training like firearms/use of force and first aid/CPR.

Yet I was the one they would call upon to save their prison for them when the riots broke out. I was the one they used to train their new officers and to give refresher training to their experienced staff. I was the one to coordinate the Annual Peace Officers Memorial March in Ottawa and to organize the funerals. They put me on public display when they needed an officer who presented in a professional manner.

I tried to keep an open mind throughout all of the backstabbing and corruption, but I was a fool to think that any of it would change. I had enough Goodyear tire tracks on my body from being thrown under the bus as a low-level employee in the service, I needed to get out.

> People management in CSC wasn't done through engaging and inspiring, it was by threats and intimidation in my time. This was kept alive through a successive legacy of prison managers who perpetuated this style over decades from institutional to regional and national levels. They are the ones who were directly responsible for the systemic harassment, corruption, and appalling working conditions their staff were forced to endure just as Mark MacGuigan reported back in the 1970s.

## Maintaining Your Distance

Most cons will not engage in a casual conversation with a guard. It doesn't look good to the other inmates, and it could get you killed if you are suspected of being an information pipeline to 'the man'. In areas removed from the sight of the general population, you can have meaningful conversations with some of the cons, but it is still, in many ways, a risk to both parties.

The CSC constantly uses the phrase "meaningful interaction" between staff and offenders. It's part of their Mission document. But those who do not work closely with the inmates cannot accept the age-old fact that the cons are always on the lookout for other inmates who get too chummy with the guards. Unless it's for the purpose of lugging contraband into the prison for them, or some other tangible interest for the con, like a sexual relationship with a guard, your life is on the line as a suspected rat.

It's no secret that many cons hate the police/guards and blame them as the cause of all the suffering in their lives.

For this reason, day-to-day interaction with offenders remained static throughout my entire time in the CSC.

# PART 13

## Perpetual Survival Mode

"When something traumatic happens at an institution, there's quite often the sense of 'I need to be strong. I can't tell anybody what I'm feeling at nighttime or when I'm home with my family.' And I think there's still that stigma."

—Jeff Wilkins, President, Atlantic,
Union of Canadian Correctional Officers

After just a few years spent on the Inside experiencing direct daily contact with the inmates, you will begin to notice changes in your personality. The way you conduct yourself at home and while in public undergoes a dramatic change, and not for the good.

You are going to be much more aware of your surroundings while out in public places. The observations you make of your environment are going to be sharper and analytical. Even though you could be looking at the same surroundings and the same people that others are, you will see them in a very different light. You are now constantly looking and listening for signs of threat. You are living fight or flight 24/7.

You don't like strangers walking behind you.

You sit in public places facing the door while all the time looking for the exit locations and where the fire extinguishers are located. You watch every person who enters the establishment to determine if they have the potential to be a threat. You use the glass in windows and doors on the streets to see the reflections of the people around you.

As you walk down the streets, you are able to tell if the person coming toward you has done time by the way they walk. You look to see if they are "packing" (carrying weapons). If you notice something about them that sets off the alarm bells, then you cross the street for your own safety.

When I went to work for the Toronto Police, I already had a great advantage over my peers from the knowledge and experience I gained working on the Inside. Being able to "read the streets" and the people around me accurately would sometimes baffle my partners. Even the experienced street-smart officers I worked with were confounded by the accuracy of my seemingly casual observations.

I would point out to one of my rookie officers a certain car in a parking lot and announce that it was stolen. They would ask how I know this, and I would tell them I can tell by the way that it's parked. I would be able to tell them that a certain person hanging out on the street corner is packing a gun.

Those on the streets who are holding weapons, especially firearms, want others around them to know they are packing because it gives them street-cred (status). These observation skills, or curses, apply aptly on the Inside as well as on the Outside.[10]

All these observations can be performed in a matter of a few seconds of casual observation because it's now become instinctual. These observations can mean your survival on the Inside and on the Outside as well. You can't turn it off because it's part of who you are now.

## A Life Sentence of a Different Kind

Survival mode is perpetual for someone who works with and is exposed to dangerous people and corrupt supervisors as part of your daily working environment. Your mind and body are damaged by this kind working environment. Physical injuries sustained in the line of duty are with you for the remainder of your life. It's not like in the movies where you take a

---

[10] "Characteristics of an Armed Person" is a well-known course offered by the Toronto Police Service for their officers that has been challenged and accepted as being reasonable in court.

beating or stabbing and in the following scene you are whole again. The physical and psychological injuries you suffer on the job continue to cause you pain and suffering for the remainder of your life.

Then to compound your injuries, you have the people who are supposed to be looking out for you, watching your back, making it a safe workplace, supporting, and educating you. And, over your years of frontline experience, you come to find that they are not Public Servants at all. A great many of them are serving no one but themselves and often at your expense, risk, and the cost of your physical and mental health and even your life.

It's never the decision-makers who suffer from their own inexperienced input imposed upon the frontline staff. Those who make the policy decisions are so far removed physically from the prisons they manage that they are never in any danger of being harmed by their own blunders. They often don't see the end results of their machinations and never have to deal with, or take responsibility in the aftermath of their misguided policies and agendas.

### "If it was so bad, why did you stay?"

I spent many years being victim to this meat grinder. People often ask me, *"If it was so bad, why did you stay?"* My answer is the same as many others I know of who stayed inside so long: *"I thought it would get better."*

I thought, *"how long can something this broken continue in its present form?"*.

I trusted my leaders to make it better.

I thought that with every new Commissioner, new Warden, Supervisor, and Principal that things would improve.

I was wrong.

They made their speeches, they wrote their Missions, they laid down the law with respect to racism, sexism, obeying the law, and CSC policy, but it was all just betrayal and cheap talk to their employees and the Canadian public.

They had their Management Teams sign a copy of the Mission document as their commitment to the values within it. The document was framed and placed up on the wall as a symbol of their devotion to its content. This was a new era in Corrections that would erase all the harm caused in the past and usher in a bright future for the staff and the cons.

They were wrong.

At the end of the day, the Correctional Service of Canada exceeded the very definition of a poisoned work environment in every aspect of the term.

## The Effects of Incarceration

A prime example of just how deep being "Institutionalized" can go is the unconscious actions that can carry over even years after being on the Outside.[11]

Cons do not open doors in a prison. An officer opens all doors for them, either with a key or electronically for the duration of their incarceration. The cons become so used to this that even when released they will forget themselves and stand in front of a door waiting for it to be opened for them.

I found out that this subconscious reaction is not just limited to the inmates.

In 2013, Kingston Penitentiary was closing and in the process of being decommissioned. During the fall months of that year, the prison was opened up to guided tours to raise money for the United Way and Habitat for Humanity.

This was a very successful venture as it raised thousands of dollars for each of these organizations. The tickets were so popular that the sanctioned sites for electronic sales crashed repeatedly due to the overwhelming number of people trying to purchase them. People were coming from all over Canada to walk behind those walls and get a look at what was on the other side of this iconic and infamous piece of Canadian History.

These prison tours have continued through the St. Lawrence Parks Commission and are just as popular and even more profitable than they were in 2013.

There were so many volunteers that signed up to either be guides or to help out taking tickets, cleaning, and organizing that many people simply never got the chance to get Inside and help out.

I volunteered as a guide and reported for my shifts at the North Gate. I went down to Keepers Hall and had my coffee and walked back up to

---

[11] Angela MacIvor, "Number of prison workers suffering from PTSD much higher than official stats, union says," *CBC Investigates,* May 11, 2017, www.cbc.ca/news/canada/nova-scotia/canada-prisons-corrections-ptsd-first-responders-coverage-1.2735583.

collect my tour group. As I approached the North gate from the Visits and Correspondence area, I came to a closed electronic door. I yelled, "key up" the standard prison request to open the door. No response. I pushed the door buzzer so the person in the control centre would know I was there. No response. So, I turned around and walked away.

I never even tried the door.

It was open the whole time.

I was still institutionalized after well over a decade of being on the Outside.

# PART 14

## Counting Up the Bodies

How often in CSC history has the body of a murdered con been left in his cell for days as staff members on three shifts over several days failed to discover him? How many times have they counted his dead body? Was it the smell that eventually gave it away? Was it another con tipping them off that maybe they should look more closely at him? Was it because his vocational work or school called for him because he hasn't shown up for a few days and someone was forced to check up on him? Or the many times that a dummy was counted as a live body over several shifts after the inmate had already escaped from the prison.

I remember having to search for an inmate whom we were unable to locate when the school called reporting him absent from class. We searched his cellblock and looked into his cell. The bed was neatly made up, which was unusual because nearly all the cons never made their beds, so this was truly a rare occurrence and thus cause for suspicion. We opened his cell and discovered that he had neatly draped his blanket over the bed so that you could not see under it. Here he had a second mattress, pillows, and blankets on the floor under the bed and was found sleeping there. At that point in time in our search, we were suspecting an escape and just about to call an institutional count to check the numbers.

## Dummies for Dummies

The making of dummies has been a longstanding ruse for diversion and escape from prison since the beginnings of incarceration. Some of the designs and materials used to create these doppelgängers are truly creative.

The prison barbershop was the only approved place to have your hair cut. The hair would be collected and placed in the garbage so it could not be reused for other means.

It used to be an internal charge for a con if they were caught cutting hair on the cell block ranges because they would collect it and use it for making dummies as a means to make them appear more genuine. If the officers noticed a con with all his hair cut off, it usually meant writing up a report on it.

The cons would sometimes make *papier maché* impressions of their face and paint them flesh colour, then glue the hair and eyebrows on after outlining the facial features with paint or markers. It didn't have to be perfect since escapes were often attempted at nighttime when you couldn't see into the cells as well as you could during daylight.[12]

The making of the body involved use of their own clothing and stuffing it to resemble their body mass. Some cons would steal the hockey elbow pads from the gym and use them for the accurate articulation of the elbow and knee joints on their creation. Often, they would make a waist-up only dummy and use their blankets to cover the lower portion because it was faster to assemble and not as much raw material to have to keep hidden before its intended use.

The cons knew which Guard Towers were occupied on the night shift by the glow of the television screen reflecting off the windows. Televisions were not permitted on any of the guard posts in prison at that time yet there they were. They were called "tower survival kits" by the guards. Many were even spliced into the inmate cable TV system. This knowledge was all part of the intelligence gathering an inmate had to do prior to going over the wall.

---

[12] Some of these creations can be seen at the Correctional Service Museum in Kingston along with homemade ropes, grappling hooks, and all manner of equipment used in actual prison escapes.

# Board of Investigation into the Escape of Tyrone Conn

File# 1410-2-395, 06 Oct 1999[13]

While at KP, Tyrone Conn in his final prison escape, went a step further by using a speaker in his dummy and a microphone leading to the cell next to him. So, if a passing officer spoke to his replica, another con could reply for him using this microphone and speaker arrangement. He also had his accomplices change the position of the dummy on the bed as well as turn on or off the cell lighting, TV, and computer to give the indication that there was someone alive in there. He got some of the other cons to give the officers a hard time while they were doing their walks down the range as an incentive for them not to spend too much time nosing around.

---

[13] *Board of Investigation into the Escape of Tyrone Conn.* File# 1410-2-395, 06 Oct. 1999.

# PART 15

## The "Demerit" System

> Irregular enforcement procedures by the staff may even be
> seen as useful to the system to keep things "looking good
> on paper". The smaller the number of formal disciplinary
> actions required to be taken against staff, the more
> effective the management of an institution seems to be.

> —*MacGuigan Report*, para 298

Leadership at all levels is the bottom line in the Correctional Service of
Canada. Strong leadership with integrity and by example is what the
Service needed in my time to pull itself out of the dismal morass it was in
since before the publication of the McGuigan Report published in 1977.

For example, you can't expect staff members who have managed
for years by corrupting and bullying their subordinates to change just
because you hand them a memo stating that they now are required to
have integrity, morals, and a value system. You should be in possession
of those traits prior to becoming a supervisor or a Peace Officer for that
matter. How many times have I seen a Keeper shred an officer's overtime
check just because they didn't like them? Countless times I've seen the
shift supervisor arrive at work still drunk from the night before wearing
a shabby uniform and still smelling of booze. None of this behaviour

changed because the commissioner introduced his Mission document with the naive expectation that this would fix everything.

Those staff who have integrity and perform the job to the best of their ability are most often left back in favour of the squeaky wheels, liquor buyers, and ass grabbers that have to be shuffled around from jail to jail because of the damage they do and the danger they pose to other staff members.

## Degrees for Everyone

In the 90s National Headquarters imposed a university degree requirement across the board for most career advancements. They made it very clear that if you did not have a degree, you were going nowhere in this organization. Some staff would simply lie on their competition application about having that required degree. Some were found out, some were not. When this deceit was discovered, future candidates would have to provide university transcripts and other proofs that they indeed held a degree.

The CSC made it possible for those who wished to get their degree to do so via distance learning. But in that period of time distance learning was not what it is today. The service arranged for certain selected individuals to have access to a series of instructional video tapes for the purpose of furthering their education. These tapes were supposed to be shared by the staff members participating in the program. That didn't happen because there was no accountability and competent management of this program. After about year or so, it was determined that there were not enough university degree-holding staff to fill the vacant positions regardless of the system they provided to achieve higher education, so the university requirement was dropped. But the damage to the morale of many staff members was already done by imposing this unrealistic condition for advancement and promotion within the Service.

## Scamming the System

There are endless ways and opportunities to take advantage of the system if you put a little thought into it. The chances of being caught are slim and even if you are caught you will rarely be held accountable for what you do. The better your ability to run a scam, fake an injury on duty or work a connection of nepotism the more advantage you have over the staff member who works with integrity. Amazingly the successful scammers, who openly bragged about working a connection or scam were admired by the other guards.

Some say you can't blame the frontline staff for attempting to cheat the system given the miserable working conditions they have to tolerate every day.

The staff who scam the system like this are in no way concerned about the negative effect this has on others who may for example have a legitimate injury and are struggling to get compensated for actual on-the-job injuries. Oddly, the scammers is proud about their deceit and seem to take pleasure and satisfaction of putting one over on the system.

Just like the cons who brag to each other about the lengthy history of crimes that they have committed.

As Union President, I witnessed staff members fake an injury on duty in order to get time off with pay. I saw them forge the signature of a physician in order to a "certify" a medical form to get even more time off work. I do not accuse them or even blame them for trying to escape the frightening and corrupt environment of Corrections by having a few extra days off. You have to experience this kind of poisoned work environment for yourself to see just how far a person will go to survive it or escape it.

One officer who was an expert at this kind of deception would be on constant lookout for opportunities to make it appear that he got hurt on the job. One such incident occurred in the Segregation unit when we were trying to restrain a con that attacked an officer. After we got him handcuffed and he was on the floor, the obese, chain-smoking officer walked up and kneeled down on the con's back. Then he got up and proceeded to the health care centre to report his being injured on duty. He was "injured while attempting to restrain a combative inmate," the report said. He took the summer off and played golf.

Another of his favourite scams was to look for a wet floor, pretend to slip on it, and report an injury due to a fall. Of course, there was an investigation and that prompted the purchase and use of the yellow "Caution Wet Floor" signs to prevent it from happening in the future.

## Intentional Self-Injury

The cons used to have a prison-wide network for broadcasting to their TVs in the cells over the cable network installed in every cell. The CSC would rent VHS tapes from a local video store and play them to the prison population. The cons would place their movie requests by filling out a form pasted to the wall.

One of the junior supervisors on the midnight shift used to think it was cool to bring in his VHS porn tapes and play them on this network for the cons. This was the same guy who used to steal the weightlifting equipment from the staff gym and from the con's gym. He would walk right out the front door with it on the midnight shift.

This clever guy was also a Response Team Member. I recall one night having to do a cell extraction in Segregation. The team piled into a cube van with the back door open and were being driven into the prison. We went over a slight bump in the road, and everyone was tossed into the air slightly. I see the look on this guy's face, and I read him seeing himself intentionally flying off the back of the truck on the next bump.

Sure enough, he purposely flipped himself off of the truck on its next bounce and landed on his head. Another intentional injury on duty.

The electronic control panel at the Main Gate Control Post operated all of the barred sliding doors around the entrance to the prison. If the guard

> **"They, or any offender that they may have passed that information to could easily walk out the front door of the Prison."**

at "The Gate" was lazy, he would simply leave all the doors open. They wouldn't be bothered with opening and closing them one at a time like it is supposed to be done according to Post Orders. So, the inmates who worked in the Administration building were able to identify these guards and know that when they were working on that post, it was an open-door policy for the prison. They, or any offender that they may have passed that information to, could easily walk out the front door of the prison.

This negligent and lazy practice only ended when the electronic control panel had an interlocking system installed in it. Then doors could only be opened one at a time with this device activated. There was also an interlock cancel switch incorporated. This switch turned off the interlock system and all of the doors could be opened at the same time in the event that you were trying to get paramedics with a stretcher into the prison for example. This switch was locked in place with a key and that key had a plastic seal on it. The only time you could remove the seal and turn off the interlock system was when the correctional supervisor gave you permission to do so.

These are the kind of extremes that you had to go through because the guards would not follow the rules.

How lazy was the senior guard in charge of the Main Gate Control Centre who had duct-taped a wooden ruler to his ankle so he could use his foot to activate the buttons on the electric gates while reclining back in his chair? This was the same guard who, when called into the prison for an emergency, being drunk, drove his car off the main highway and onto the front lawn of the prison. It remained there in a snowbank for all to see for a week before it was finally towed out. This guard was eventually promoted to a supervisor.

> **"One of the hardest experiences in the CSC is seeing the corrupt staff promoted and then having to work under them."**

I remember when the maximum and medium prisons were having a beefed-up electronic perimeter security installed and how the guards and the union were up in arms because they were going to take the officers out of some of the armed tower posts. This was a battle that was lost before the fight even got started.

How can you justify keeping these posts staffed when the inmates went over the wall right under the tower guard's nose? A glaring example of this was when the cons piled up the picnic tables right under a manned tower and climbed over the wall to escape. As a result of this act of neglected duty, all the picnic tables in every medium and max prison are now chained to the ground. I can see management's position on this issue: why pay to staff these positions when the guards posted to them can't do the bare minimum of their job?

# PART 16

## Short-term Gain for Long-term Pain

[Parole] Board members assess each case individually in terms of risk and public safety. The Board's assessment of the risk presented by an offender on parole is based on three major factors:

1. Criminal history.
2. *Institutional behaviour*[14] and benefit from programs.
3. Release plan.

—Parole Board of Canada (2001–2021)[15]

> **"Many of the guards who took advantage of this arrangement are now supervisors due to the casework that someone else did for them ..."**

### Ghost-writing Casework Reports

During my time with CSC, in order to be considered for a promotion you had to demonstrate that you produced casework records and other

---

[14] David Woodhouse: italics added.

[15] Parole Board of Canada, "Parole Decision-Making: Myths and Realities," modified March 16, 2021, www.canada.ca/en/parole-board/corporate/publications-and-forms/parole-decision-making-myths-and-realities.html.

reports related to the offenders assigned to your caseload. These reports were recorded on the Offender Management System (OMS). They were accessed through your password-protected computer account. When computers were installed in the offices in the 1990s there was no training provided to the officers, so they had to learn to use them on their own and the first thing they learned to do was how to install computer games on them. The use of the computer was essential to completing casework records and other reports directly related to your job, but the CSC did not give the officers any formal instruction in their use ... it would have cost money for their training.

Some of the guards who were competent in the use of the computer system in the 1990s, would write casework records on cons that were assigned to other guard's caseloads – for a fee.

They would charge them cash or have that officer work a shift for them as payment called a "mutual". Many of the guards who took advantage of this arrangement are now supervisors due to the casework that someone else did for them in receipt of payment.

For me, this practice raised some serious questions:

- Did the guards writing the reports actually communicate with the offender they were writing about?
- Did they have firsthand knowledge about their day-to-day behaviour within the institution?
- Did they even work in the same cell block where the con lived?
- Did they even know what the con looked like?
- Were the reports an accurate reflection of the behaviour of the con?
- Did these reports eventually go before the Parole Board of Canada as part of their decision-making process?
- Was the information recorded in these reports used to decide the release or detention of the inmate?

It seems like such a small bit of corruption for the sake of a day off, a small payment or a promotion. The Correctional Managers were aware of all of this, but the fact that the reports were being completed seemed to override the scamming that went on. It seems that they didn't even notice that the date on which some of the reports were locked into the OMS system were on days that the guard who was supposed to be the author of the report was not even working.

Many staff members in the CSC back then were primarily motivated by money and an opportunity for advancement rather than by the guiding principles of the mission or a sense of Integrity, Courage and Honour Inside the Chaos.

## What Charge?

Then there were some Correctional Supervisors who were required to hear and decide upon minor institutional charges. They would throw the completed charge forms in the garbage in front of the con because they feared the con might flip out should they decide against them.

So, does that make them the con's "buddy" now?

Were they being paid off for neglecting their sworn duty?

How does destroying a charge under the *Corrections and Conditional Release Act* help the decision-making process of Institutional Parole Officers and Parole Board of Canada members?

How can an appropriate decision concerning a con's release or detention be made when no accurate record or profile of their institutional behaviour has been documented correctly?

All this because you think that if something happens down Inside that "your buddy" the con will bail you out or somehow save your ass.

That's not the way the cons do business with a guard.

This act of neglect of duty actually plays into the role of making it appear to the Canadian public that the road to being a "law-abiding citizen" and fulfilling the Mission document is well and truly working out as planned.

## Can You Trust the Casework Records?

Information about a con's behaviour is supposed to be supported and documented by casework records and other reports completed by the guards as partners in their Case Management Team. Given the report-writing scams, whether those guards completed the assigned records or paid to have someone else do it for them is unknown.

Add to this, the con will tell his parole officer whatever they want to hear and do whatever it takes to get back on the Outside. Any inmate worthy of his jail house tattoos is also a con man (confidence man). I have heard many cons coaching each other on what to say and how to appear when they are in front of a Parole Board hearing. The very first piece of advice is to accept responsibility for what you did and how sorry you are for your actions.

Express remorse and look like you are trying to hold back some tears when they question you about the suffering you inflicted upon your victims and their family. But don't overdo the theatrics. Tell them how you have applied yourself while on the Inside and took the offered programs and educational opportunities the CSC has provided for you.

I remember standing in a Parole Board hearing listening to the Academy Award-winning performance one con was giving to the Board. When it was finished, I escorted him back to segregation, listening as he boasted about the "acting job" he did on the Board; the other cons giving him high fives and joking about the whole scam.

I have often wondered if the weight of all of this deceit was heavier on the cons' side or the CSC... most likely equal from my experience.

# PART 17

## Zero Drug Tolerance – CSC Style

> *Drugs are available in prison. Studies examining rates of substance use indicate that the per capita use of drugs in Canada's prisons is substantially higher than on the street. In addition, drug trade is also much more violent in prison than it is on the street.*

—Canadian Centre on Substance Abuse[16]

There is a device at the front entrance to most medium and maximum institutions called the Barringer Instruments Ionscan. This very expensive machine is designed to detect drugs or explosives, depending on which substance it is calibrated for.

When someone enters the institution, a piece of identification like a laminated driver's licence, car keys, or wallet is wiped with a cloth swab. This swab is then placed into the machine and a sample is taken by rapidly heating the swab to produce a vapour. The vapour is passed through the scanner and any narcotics present in that sample can be detected. The

---

[16] Canadian Centre on Substance Abuse, "Substance Abuse in Corrections FAQs," (Ottawa: CCSA, 2004). www.ccsa.ca/sites/default/files/2019-04/ccsa-011058-2004.pdf.

results are then displayed on a computer screen and those results may be saved or printed out.

Often, you would see the visitor using their own alcohol swab to wipe down their ID before presenting it to the staff member for inspection. They would hold it by the edges to try to prevent their fingers from contaminating it. Or wear gloves when handing it over. What does this kind of behaviour tell you?

A high reading on the machine used to mean that their visit would be cancelled. But often this was not the case because too many visitors complained.

## An "Allowable" Threshold Limit

In managing the complaints, the CSC created a threshold limit for the amount of heroin, cocaine, meth, hash, and PCP they permit you to have in your system and still be allowed to have your visit. Apparently, you can have these drugs in your body as long as they are below the established threshold limit. So, a little drug use is acceptable according to the CSC so long as you don't go over their allowable limit. This is the CSC example of zero tolerance when it comes to drugs in Canadian prisons in my time. This is the corporate spin they put on it so the Canadian public is fooled into thinking that there really is serious drug enforcement going on behind the walls at that time.

Another way around the scanner is to have a bogus prescription in your hand that states you are on some kind of opiate medication that would account for your high reading on the scanner.

More often than not, if you go over the top on the scanner, the Correctional Supervisor will let you enter the prison once they determine your degree of impairment. How they are able to judge this was a mystery to me in my day. Possibly they judge it against their own degree of impairment at that time.

## And If the Scanner Doesn't Scan?

CSC also has advanced colour X-ray scanners they can use to check packages entering the institution. I remember being trained on this device and passing a briefcase through the scanner that belonged to the instructor sent from the company. I hid several rounds of .9mm ammunition in his case. The certified instructor was unable to detect the ammunition inside his own briefcase using his own hi-tech scanner.

In the past, most of the staff members who run these machines were not even trained by qualified personnel and were not certified to operate the machine by the company that makes them. Most were "given the onceover" by the person they relieved from the post. Hence, you have a very expensive piece of equipment that tax money has paid for and that is, for the most part, useless unless there is a trained and experienced operator at the controls.

Most often, when you suspected a visitor of bringing drugs into the institution in those days, the end result was that the drugs were seized and their visits suspended for a couple of weeks. Then, they went before the visitors screening board where they promise not to do it again and most often their visits are reinstated, or they are permitted a visit behind the glass. Again, the law that applies to everyone else outside the walls with respect to possession of drugs being a criminal offence in Canada is suspended within the criminally sanctified walls of our prisons in my time.

# PART 18

## Prison Searches and Contraband

There are many places for inmates to hide their contraband within their cell or on the range. If they know a search is coming they have time to prepare. It's advisable not to get caught with items like your drugs, your cash, cell phones and weapons so the smaller valuable items are often hooped. When they hoop it, regardless how well it's wrapped, it still comes out smelling like shit after a while in the cooker. I remember retrieving a package of cash that had been hooped by an inmate in segregation. Even being wrapped in plastic the currency still smelled bad.

There was an isolation cell installed in the segregation unit at KP that had a glove box style toilet in it. The inmate suspected of hiding contraband items in his rectum was placed here until he passed the items. Some cons would excrete the items and then swallow them again immediately to prevent their loss. Once the inmate made a deposit into the toilet, it was then the guards' job to sift through it using the glove box. Being a guard is not a glamorous occupation.

During major institutional searches the inmate will be removed from his cell and taken up to the showers and strip-searched. He then waits there until his cell had been gone through. In some cases where the search may go on for a few days in order to do the whole Institution the cons will have a great build-up of garbage in their cells consisting of old food, pop cans, candy wrappers and the like. Often the cons will hide their contraband items inside their garbage because the gaurds will not search through their smelly trash. I got around that by taking out their garbage for them. You always knew when they had something hidden in there because when they go back to their cell the first thing they do is look to see if you found their stash. Then you hear …."The fucking coppers took out my garbage!"

Another good place to hide your valuable drugs and money if your ass is too full or sore, is to wrap it up in plastic and stick it in your toilet bowel below the water line just under the lower rim in the bowl. Of course, you have been filling the toilet for days without flushing so as to have a nice build-up of smelly slimy shit in there. The officers are not going to reach into the full toilet to search for anything so it's a pretty safe place and the smell ensures that they are not going to linger in your cell any longer than necessary. I always flushed their toilets for them. Again, you always knew they had hidden contraband in there by the reaction you got when they were returned to their cell. "The fucking coppers flushed my toilet!" We don't have it, but you don't have it either.

## The Cost of Prison Debt

There is still a price to be paid if you were the one holding the cash and or drugs for someone else. Regardless of how you lost it you still are liable for it. Hard core drug dealers are not very forgiving, so your options are to repay it somehow or go into protective custody because now your health and safety are on the line.

Some dealers are flexible in their repayment plans. You can have someone on the Outside, like your friends or family send in a nice computer or maybe some PS games, or the latest in sports clothing such as team sweaters or high-end running shoes in the same size as whom you owe the debt to.

Commonly you are instructed to have someone deposit the debt into a bank account for them. During a search it's common to find a debt lists and often they are written in code and within the code is a bank names, account, and branch numbers. The amount expected to be deposited is included on the list along with the name of the person owing.

If you are known to be having an upcoming trailer visit, then your visitor may get a package delivered to their front door containing the money or drugs that they are expected to bring into the prison on their next visit.

Or maybe, at an Institutional Social, your debtor has taken a liking to your wife, girl friend or maybe even your daughter. A few moments alone with your loved one out of sight in the bathroom and you may be eligible for a lower interest rate on the money you owe to him.

Being in debt to someone in prison is very much like having a death sentence hanging over your head. If you can't pay you will be press ganged into performing criminal acts for your lender, carrying his cash, drugs or weapons for him. Smuggling contraband into the prison for them, making or holding their weapons, enforcing payment and even murder to settle your accounts is all part of the interest you are required to pay on the Inside.

Another way out of your immediate debit situation is to get transferred to another Institution. There are several ways of doing this but the quickest is to assault a staff member. You pick a victim who presents as the weakest and less likely to be able to defend themselves and you punch them in the face. You get a bus ride to higher security that very day. I have seen this happen more than once.

But the debit still follows you. Just because you're in another institution doesn't mean that the debit has been cancelled. The person you owe very likely has connections in the prison you have been transferred to, so debit enforcement is inevitable. Even if you are released to the street, whom you owe will find you.

## Tattooing and a Disturbing Photo

I remember searching a con's cell who was a jail house tattoo artist, and it was a good bet you could get a homemade tattoo gun out of his drum (cell). These machines were constructed using the electric motor out of an old cassette player, a CD player or, the ideal electric appliance was an electric shaver as the rpm in the motor was just right for a tattoo gun. The motor would be connected to the bowl portion of a tablespoon via tape or wire.

The spoon would then be bent at a right-angle providing a down shaft to which was fixed the barrel of a pen. The cleaned-out ink storage tube from the pen would then be inserted through that hollow shaft and a sewing needle melted into the old ink tube using a lighter.

You could pick your tattoo from the many choices of patterns that he kept in his photo album or you could design your own. These component patterns were all labeled "hobby craft" and the inmate had a permit for them to be in his possession.

There was plenty of ink available from ordinary pens or you could use the different colour inks you ordered from the hobby craft department as part of your "artistic drawings course".

In early prison times you would have to resort to burning pages from the Bible and mixing the ash with small amounts of water to make use of the residual ink from the printing process. Poke the holes in your skin using a sewing needle and rub the ink and water mixture onto the skin. It was crude but effective.

While searching through this con's photo album I came across a disturbing photograph. It depicted a bar in an outlaw bikers club. Their colours were prominently displayed on the wall behind the bar. In the photo was an inmate I knew from some years ago. While inside, he kicked in some other con's head with his steel toe boots. Since that assault, all the cons that are required to wear steel toe boots in the prison shops now have to leave them behind when their workday is over. With him was another upstanding member of the gang. Both were standing with big smiles on their faces and a bottle of beer in their hands held aloft in salute. They had their pants down around their ankles and in their other hand they held their dicks in the face of a young woman kneeling on the floor at their feet. Her clothes were torn and hanging off of her. In the picture she was trying to cover herself up. Her makeup was running and smeared down her face. You could see the streaks in it on her face made from her tears. She was sobbing. She was beaten and bloody. I removed the picture and wrote a report on what I had found and submitted it.

I was thinking that there had to be an investigation as to the identity of this woman and what became of her after this assault. Seeing that one of the suspects in the photo was known to us, it would not be a hard task to locate him and question him about the photo. I was wrong. There was nothing done.

The con I took the picture from was questioned and he must have had a good explanation because I was told to give the photo back to him. I often wonder what happened to that woman after that picture was taken. Did they let her go when they were through with her or did they kill her to prevent her from going to the Police? I'll never know.

# PART 19

## Segregation aka: Structured Intervention Units

Purpose:

To ensure administrative segregation is only used for the shortest period of time necessary when there are no reasonable and safe alternatives.

> To ensure that the administrative segregation of an inmate occurs only when specific legal requirements are met and that restrictions are based on the least restrictive requirements to meet the objectives of the *Corrections and Conditional Release Act*.
>
> —CSC Administrative Segregation Guidelines (2018)[17]

Recently, there has been a great public and media outcry about the use of Segregation[18] in our federal prisons. Inmates are not forced into segregation

---

[17] Correctional Service Canada, "Administrative Segregation Guidelines," modified December 21, 2018, www.csc-scc.gc.ca/politiques-et-lois/709-1-gl-eng.shtml#s2.

[18] In November 2019, new federal legislation came into effect renaming Segregation Units as Structured Intervention Units (SIUs). In February 2020, the Supreme Court announced it would consider two challenges – one brought forward by the Canadian Civil Liberties Association and another by the British Columbia Civil Liberties Association on the use of solitary confinement in federal prisons.

units; they are there for the same reasons that they are on the Inside of a prison in the first place.

Segregation is a prison within a prison. It's the jail within the jail for the prison population. Even while in prison, inmates still commit crimes that are as bad or worse than the ones that they have committed while out on the streets.

So, what do you do with them? You can't leave them in the general prison population to continue with these actions. The Service can charge them under the *Corrections and Conditional Release Act (CCRA)* and have a trial, at which time they are represented by legal duty counsel for offences that are not even criminal.

An Independent Chairperson will render a verdict based upon the evidence presented by witnesses and pass sentence upon the offender under the guidelines of the CCRA. If found guilty, the con can receive anything from a warning, a fine, or time in Disciplinary Segregation, or time served just like on the Outside.

Once placed in Segregation, the unit staff have to padlock his cell because when the other cons find out that he's in "the Hole" they will steal everything he has. The unit staff also have to pack up the items in his cell that he wants to take to Seg with him, like clothing and personal entertainment equipment.

Once admitted to Segregation, the con gets his TV and Nintendo, Game Boy, PlayStation, books and magazines, movies, exercise, phone calls, and showers, visits from family, medical or dental and psychology appointments, his school lessons are delivered to the cell door, the nurse comes every day and the doctor every week. Condoms, lubrication, and even bleach kits to sterilize the tattoo needles and hypodermic needles that you are not supposed to have are also available upon request. The Correctional Manager is in every day to see that his needs are met by the unit staff. His meals are delivered to his door.

**"Most inmates who "run for the Hole" do so because their life has been threatened."**

Disciplinary Segregation is time-limited. There is a minimum and a maximum amount of time that the inmate has to serve depending upon his sentence and he is then released back into the general population or, if the offence is serious enough, a transfer to a higher level security prison may be in order.

Administrative Segregation, in many cases is ordered because the con wants to be segregated from the prison population. He or she is in there for their own protection, and many don't want to leave because if they do, they would be killed for sport in the general prison population. Some of those seeking voluntary segregation are often notorious sex offenders, killers of children and women and known rats. Prison debt is a big reason for "checking yourself in."

Most inmates who "run for the hole" do so because their life has been threatened or they may even have been assaulted in the general prison population and managed to survive, so they don't want to press their luck by remaining in "Pop". Sometimes they have been told outright by the other inmates to "check yourself in" or you may not live to see another day. They may run into a situation where they have to "pay protection" to another inmate to ensure that their lives are spared. Often, many have debts that they can't pay back and now their life is forfeit.

In one local maximum-security prison, the protected information concerning some inmate crimes was breached by the CSC when it permitted the cons to use older computers that were no longer required by their staff. The machine was never vetted properly, and information fell into the wrong hands that was used as leverage over some of the cons to extort money.

In other cases, an inmate from a different prison is transferred in and our con has "a beef" with them. There will be violence and there will be blood, so they have to be separated until something can be worked out.

Many options are looked at to get a con out of voluntary segregation. Cooperation with the inmate committee to ascertain their safety in the population is done often. Offers of a transfer to another institution, voluntary or not, is one of the methods most often used. But sometimes the inmate has burned so many bridges throughout their career in crime that they cannot be held safely at any facility in the general population. Some present such a

**"Even in the Segregation Unit, there are predators that still look for their prey."**

high degree of danger to staff members and other cons that they have to be shuffled around from one prison to the next across the country.

Even inside the Segregation Unit, the cons still act like cons and will assault, threaten, or extort the weaker inmates. This is why they cannot be out on the range together or in the exercise yard together. They have to be out of their cells one at a time for their own protection and the protection of the other inmates and staff members. Even in the Segregation Unit, there are predators that still look for their prey.

## Assault a Guard to Get Sent to Segregation

Sometimes a con wants to go to the Hole but doesn't want to be seen and labeled as a (PC) protective custody inmate, so they will punch a guard in the face and be admitted that way. Now he looks like a badass to his peers because he assaulted a guard, but it was just a cowardly cover-up for his own protection. Most segregation is by choice and their own actions, not some barbaric plot by the CSC to confine or isolate. The CSC does not have "solitary confinement" and "the Hole" does not mean a hole. In most prisons, the Hole is much larger, cleaner, and brighter than the regular ranges in the general population and those within it have it better than the general prison population. There stress level is lower because they don't have to be looking over their shoulder all of the time wondering if this is the day they get killed over their crimes or their debt.

You could build another prison to house the incompatibles and have another segregation unit within that only for it to fill up and have the same problem. There is never going to be a solution to this kind of human dynamic that is going to satisfy the critics at any level. The only absolute solution is that those involved in violent criminal acts against another person stop. Everyone knows this will never happen, regardless of the conviction and efforts of our available applied rehabilitation strategies.

Kingston Penitentiary was a protective custody prison before it closed on September 30, 2013. It housed offenders who could not be kept in general population due to the nature of their crimes and other issues that would endanger their lives. Yet even though the cons incarcerated within KP were there under the same circumstances, they would still prey upon each other. KP also had a segregation unit and within their segregation unit was a protective custody range.

This is something that you just can't get away from by putting a different name on the term Segregation while at the same time trying to manage people who live their lives bent upon harming others around them.

## Keeping the Lid On

## This is How We're Going to Play This

In February 1990, a con in 1 Block was "acting out" – the politically correct label for violence that the CSC bestowed had upon it. He fought all the way to Segregation and injured several officers. Fixed point alarms and Personal Portable Alarms (PPAs) were activated, but no one responded to help. Officers were kicked and punched as they struggled to get control of this guy. He was maced and finally brought into Segregation. The con was seen by the nurse within 10 minutes of entering Segregation. The injured officers went to the institutional hospital for treatment.

Up to that time, no one except the officers involved knew that the alarms had been activated as the guard in the Central Control Room was not on his post. He left the Control Centre and was standing at the Main Gate awaiting his relief as it was near the end of his shift. No one acknowledged the alarms nor deployed any help. The relieving officer discovered the alarms going off when he went down into the basement control centre to take over the post.

The negligent guard walked out the front door and went home. This guard who was not on his post, was one of the "good guys to have around when there was trouble." He was later promoted to supervisor.

I wanted the con charged criminally with several counts of Assault Peace Officer but one of the Unit Managers had other ideas. This Unit Manager was the puppet master of the prison who had a long reputation of intimidation and harassment of the staff. He had done his bit on the "island of misfit toys" a few years prior for harassing his staff members. After "doing his time," he returned to the same institution in the same position over the same staff members that he had victimized.

There was no recognition of the harm caused by this man and no restoration of his many victims' self-worth. There was no protection at all from being re-victimized as the CSC just ticked off another of their boxes and expected these predators to act differently just because they did their time on the Island. Just like they expected to inmates to act differently after doing time in segregation.

But he had learned to hone his tactics of corruption and manipulation to a fine point. He now used his subordinates, who were eager for promotion, protection, or perks, to do the dirty work for him.

He made it very clear to me that "I would suffer" if I pursued criminal charges against the con for Assault Peace Officer. He threatened me with removal from the IERT Team and suspension from my job.

## Keep It Quiet and Pretend It Never Happened

I couldn't understand where he was coming from with this and after a heated back and forth, he told me that the con "got worse than he gave." I didn't understand what he meant by that remark until sometime later as it was kept very quiet by all those involved. After we got the guy in Segregation some of the staff on duty there decided to tune him up in retaliation for the assaulting officers. Now I know what he meant by "got worse than he gave." So instead of reporting the staff who assaulted the con he tried to muzzle the staff who were victims of the assault to protect his cronies in the Segregation Unit.

This is the way he operated all of his corrupt career.

Now the staff in Segregation owed him for having covered up their criminal acts for them. The main player in the "got worse than he gave" situation was promoted to supervisor sometime later.

Both the coward at the Control Centre and the thug in the Segregation Unit were eventually promoted to supervisors, largely on the recommendation of the corrupt Unit Manager. This is the way Collins Bay Institution operated the entire time I was employed there. Promotions and medals for the lawbreakers.

The General Security Investigation reported: "The inquiry noted that a number of staff involved did not submit observation reports in respect of their activity in this matter." Selected staff members were threatened not to write reports as they may have implicated the staff in Segregation who gassed and laid a beating on the con. All of the printouts displaying the riot alarms and the PPAs that were activated in the cell block, and recorded in the Main Control Room, were mysteriously destroyed. The logbook from the Segregation Unit somehow went missing. Several medical reports completed by the nurse in the Health Care Centre for the staff members who were injured, disappeared.

Instead of addressing the individual staff who neglected their duty, the institutional management team issued a memo reminding "all staff of the importance of recording their **"Pretend it Never Happened"** observations and actions on observation reports, during incidents of this nature." —Quote from the Acting Warden, Memorandum file #3180-1 90-06-21.

In the aftermath of the assaults, the offender was issued with only two charge forms under the CCRA, "Inmate Offence and Notification of Charge" CSC/SCC 222 R-88-05. Both of these charges were for "Assaults or threatens to assault another person". In the tick box on the charge form there is a section for "physical evidence". This box was checked "no". The injury reports kept at the Institutional Hospital were all missing and the Officers that were assaulted were not called to testify about their injuries. There was a finding of guilty but the con only spent five days in segregation for the assaults and the sentence was suspended. Some months later, this same inmate overdosed on drugs. I applied first aid/CPR and saved his life. As was the culture in that period of time I received no recognition for that life saving act.

The walls and fences constructed around our Canadian Prisons are not just to keep the cons Inside. But to keep the truth Inside as well.

Integrity, Courage and Honour Inside the Chaos.

In the 1980s and 1990s, this is the way some assaults on staff were handled. Keep it quiet and pretend it never happened. The Commissioner at that time would never release a statement to the media about staff assaults. The cover-ups were intended to convince the Canadian public that these criminal acts simply did not happen in our prison system. They had to pretend that their Mission was well established and that only positive interaction between "offenders" and staff took place.

Today, if a staff member is assaulted on the Inside, its front-page news. Assaults, weapons charges, drugs, and other contraband seizures as well as drone sightings moving contraband into the prison are in the paper almost weekly. These serious criminal charges are now pursued through the court system rather than dealing with them through an internal charge under the CCRA.

This is what should have been done years ago but was not because the Commissioner wanted to present a different picture of what went on behind his walls. A criminal conviction carries more weight than an internal discipline charge in the eyes of the Parole Board and in the Court system when sentencing for further convictions is being considered. The consequences of a further criminal charge are more severe than having your TV taken away for a week or having the inmate sign a behavioral contract as their punishment.

# PART 20

## Illegal Arms Possession

> Staff have been placed on tower duty although they had never had a rifle training course.
>
> A woodworking instructor at Archambault Institution stated that "quite a few times I went to work on the tower with a weapon although I was never taught how to handle it…
>
> I was only taught how to put the bullets in and get them out."
>
> —*MacGuigan Report* (1977), para 264

### Armed Clerks and Plumbers in 1991

When contract negotiations between the Union and the CSC extend over a year without any movement, the Union would call for action at the workplace. This usually takes place in the form of an information picket. The main road to the institution would be blocked by the picketers walking back and forth, impeding vehicles and personnel. These actions would be rotational so you would not know which prison would be picketed on any given day.

They usually employed this action at the prisons located in the city proper or other heavily trafficked ones where there would be the greatest visibility to the public. So, Kingston Penitentiary and Collins Bay would get hit with pickets more often than the prisons in the outlying areas.

The managers absolutely hated this tactic as they were forced to remain at the prisons, sometimes for days at a time, and they would have to have daily contact with the cons. Often, the managers had to sleep on mattresses in an office or a meeting room. This is not what they signed up for. Some of the managers that I had experience with usually avoided up close day-to-day contact with inmates.

During the months of September and October 1991, support staff such as maintenance personnel, office staff, cooks and teachers were pressed by their managers into working areas of the institution that they were in no way qualified to do. The managers at Collins Bay used non-Correctional staff members on armed posts such as mobile patrol, towers, and main gate control.

### "Placing an untrained plumber, carpenter or clerk in an armed tower post with a fully loaded AR-15 rifle and a revolver is a deliberate act of negligence."

These staff members had no training in Use of Force or Firearms and yet they were in a tower overlooking the exercise yard with inmates in it, with a loaded revolver and a high-powered rifle at their disposal should they need it.

This was an unacceptable risk. If the cons saw this, they might take advantage of the situation to grab a hostage, along with all the weapons inside the tower and what would the office clerk do should the inmates make a break for the wall?

Some staff members willingly performed these duties to advance their careers or did so out of fear of retribution from their supervisor. Either reason chosen meant they were still committing a criminal offence to be in possession and control of loaded firearms without a Peace Officer designation and up-to-date training. Placing an untrained plumber, carpenter, or clerk in an armed tower post with a fully loaded AR-15 rifle and a revolver is a serious act of criminal negligence.

As well, those without Peace Officer status have no authority to possess firearms and it is a criminal act for them to do so.

*Commissioner's Directives: 567 Use of firearms*

4    *The Institutional Head, or Director of a Correctional Learning Centre where applicable, will have procedures in place to ensure that:*

a.    *Every staff member issued a firearm or assigned to an armed post is properly trained and qualified to the National Training Standards.*

5.    *Staff who may be required to use firearms in the course of their duties will qualify in the use of firearms utilized in their specific institution according to the national Training Standards.*

6.    *Staff not qualified on a given type of firearm will not be issued that type of firearm during an emergency or be deployed to a post where that type of firearms assigned until such time as they have been qualified.*

These people were given firearms without any training, without lawful authority, without Peace Officer Status under the *Criminal Code* and told to enforce the law. This was not within the scope of their duties as government employees.

I remember being relieved in the South West Tower on 31 October 1991 by a plumber and asking him if he was weapons and Use of Force certified.

His reply was that he "didn't remember."

## Management Violations of CSC Policy

These people are intimidated and/or threatened by their institutional managers to commit acts that clearly violate CSC Policy, *Commissioner's Directives,* and the *Criminal Code* of Canada, and that challenge any sense of morality and integrity that they may have possessed. The staff members who bow to this pressure do so because they fear the very real reprisals from their manager for standing up against them. Or they do it because they want to be remembered for that promotion or acting assignment. They do it mainly because it's all about their survival in this kind of broken and corrupted workplace environment.

The CSC speak of their core values and how relationships among staff are based on openness, trust, and mutual respect. It speaks to staff members to emphasize interpersonal skills, maturity, good judgment, effective communication, and teamwork. One entire section deals with accountability and yet these words were undeniably meaningless within the CSC in my time.

Even the CSC managers who were staffing posts within the walls and on the perimeter were carrying a revolver on their hips, a semi-automatic rifle or in charge of a post with several loaded firearms being present without having the required training to do so, in breach of CSC Policy. And yet these are the same people who would take an officer off a post if they were not up to date on their annual refresher training and quote for them the very Directives that they themselves violated with impunity.

Herein lies the very core of how the CSC worked in those days. This is only one very serious example of a truly corrupt and poisoned work environment where the weak-willed are manipulated into committing criminal acts by their morally bankrupt supervisors. Just like a criminal organization.

## Systemic Management Manipulation

This is not an isolated incident but a systemic and dynamic use of intimidation to control the actions of staff members. Those who stand up to these acts and respect CSC policy and the law are labeled troublemakers, slapped with a terminal rank, and will have no career future within the CSC.

If you do follow blindly and accept the gratuities offered for selling yourself out you may get a better position, but you are now indentured to the system in order to keep your perks. You have been manipulated once and that one act can be held over your head in order to have you do more and more for them.

Just like the cons, who will try to corrupt a staff member into lugging drugs and other contraband into the prison, you are never off the hook to them. You don't want to go back down Inside and do the shift work again, walk the ranges again, and get your daily abuse from cons. You don't want to be exposed to the day-to-day violence again so you swallow any integrity you may have and tell yourself it's the cost of a better job, the price you pay for your pension and benefits, a safer work environment, and better mental and physical health. You sell out for the sake of a better future and your own personal survival.

I found this blog article in the *Waterloo Region Advocate* dated September 12, 2013, and headlined:

### Top Down Corruption, Correctional Services Canada and Ashley Smith[19]

*One of the definitions of corruption is "riddled with errors". Therefore, calling an institution corrupt could refer to criminal matters such as "on the take", or taking bribes or in this case simply corrupt as in rotten or as in riddled with errors. It is beginning to become obvious that the brain trust at the top of some organizations aren't there because they are smarter than their colleagues or more knowledgeable. They are there because they have convinced their* superiors that they are "company men or women".

*They will follow orders even immoral and possibly illegal ones if necessary. They are not rats, snitches, or whistleblowers; no matter what. As these people ascend the corporate or government ladder, they make sure that the people coming up below the share their organizational view. Their raises and promotions rely on blind loyalty and obedience. Upon*

[19] Alan Marshall, "Top Down Corruption, Correctional Services and Ashley Smith," *Waterloo Region Advocate,* September 13, 2013. Accessed November 10, 2020, http://waterlooregionadvocate.blogspot.com/2013/.

*this altar, right and wrong loses its importance. Keep in mind that despite so called progressive attitudes you can only sacrifice human beings' rights and dignity by viewing them as less than human. How else do you rationalize an inmate strangling themself to the point of turning purple as merely "acting out?"*

*....The Deputy Warden for Grand Valley tried to defend the management plan for Ashley Smith. This so-called plan endorsed by both the warden and allegedly Correctional Services Canada basically said to ignore a strangling inmate until the point of death (non-breathing). The Deputy, under pressure from her warden and CSC claims she did not know that her memos, critical of guards, would lead to Ashley Smith's death. The Smith family lawyer also accused her of throwing the guards under the bus after Ashley's death. All in all, it is a damning indictment of theoretical decision making at the top causing havoc and tragedy at ground level.*

This was written by someone who was on the Outside looking in at the CSC and how it operates. And despite of all the bad publicity over the years, the CSC continued to operate in the same manner as was reported in the Mark McGuigan Report* from the 70s and still doing it with impunity.

These facts were further reiterated by the Justice Arbour investigation into the events at *P4W*. In keeping with one of the recommendations from the Arbour Inquiry, a training course called "CSC and the Law" was established because, as I mentioned, most CSC Staff did not know the law and its application within the Correctional environment. While

---

* 1977 "Report of the House of Commons Justice Committee's Sub-Committee on the Penitentiary System in Canada" (known as the "MacGuigan Report"), describes significant inquiries and other studies made of the Canadian Correctional System, with particular emphasis on the issues raised by the Sub-Committee. It concludes with a consideration of the major themes of those studies and inquiries, and an analysis of possible areas that may merit further study.

true in some cases, in others, the law was well-known yet simply ignored as no repercussions came from not following it.[20]

I was tasked with teaching "CSC and the Law" while at the Regional Correctional Staff College. But still, even after all that, the law means nothing without enforcement and the CSC has enjoyed a long reputation of not policing themselves.

Chances are, this will be demonstrated once again in the next "Sensational Incident".

## Misfit Guards Isolated

> Being given extensive powers, peace officers are compelled to exercise such powers lawfully. They must act on reasonable grounds, without abuse of their powers; furthermore, the power to act is in some instances coupled with an obligation to act, and peace officers can be held criminally responsible for a failure to intervene in certain situations.

*—Commissioner's Directive No. 003* (1992)[21]

Protective Custody (PC) guards are the ones who cannot get along well with the cons and other staff members. Some have demonstrated violence or threats of violence, actual assault, and death threats towards other officers and other staff members. They often have been transferred around from one prison to another due to their behavioural issues. They are often put on a security post that isolates them from the staff and cons. They are placed in posts such as the towers, mobile patrol, the control centres and electronic gates. Preferably out of sight of and out of contact with the public as well as the cons and other staff. These posts are often seen as a break from day-to-day inmate contact and some of the staff enjoy

---

[20] This was proven again and again and continued to be proven in the Coroner's Inquest into the Ashley Smith murder.

[21] Correctional Service Canada, "Peace Officer Designations, Annex A," *Commissioner's Directive No. 003,* (November 1, 1992), modified June 30, 2007, www.csc-scc.gc.ca/politiques-et-lois/003-cd-eng.shtml#AnnexA.

them. But when the misfit toys take up the majority of these posts, it creates conflict. Some staff members were relegated to these posts due to a legitimate injury or other tangible issue and that was accepted among the officers.

I remember one PC guard who worked at the Main Gate all the time as he could not get along with anyone down Inside, cons or staff. He was a misfit toy who was passed around for one workplace to another. This particular guy was quite proud and vocal in his creativity with respect to his expressive forms of racial hatred.

One of the women who worked in a department close to the Main Gate was Inuit and so the target of his racial hatred. He drew a picture depicting her coming out of an igloo and captioned it as her new office. He proudly displayed this for everyone to see on the inside of the bulletproof glass that he was hiding behind. I took it away from him and gave it to the supervisor in charge. Of course, nothing was ever done about it. At least he didn't call me out to the lower parking lot over ratting him out. He wasn't the type to show up anyway.

The CSC was showcasing the jails to an international contingent of prison staff and management. As they queued up in the front lobby and signed in, this same guy starts piping up with the "N-word" about the representatives and how they are probably all on the dole in the country where they were from. Of course, no one could see him as he was throwing out his comments from behind the tinted glass, but I could hear him as I was standing in front of the guests signing then into the institution.

## Same Pay, Less Risk

The prison management tried to say that some of these posts do not require the guard to be current in use of force, firearms, First Aid/CPR and firefighting. This kind of thinking places the safety of the entire prison in jeopardy but it would save money on refresher training.

If that is the case, I often wondered why should frontline staff suffer more potential for violence during the day-to-day risk that comes with inmate contact when the PC guards have considerably less stress and risk for the same amount of pay?

Their pay was never reduced because they avoided inmate contact and the potential for them using any means of force was greatly reduced or eliminated altogether. The pay level was also protected by the employment contract so it couldn't be modified to reflect the elimination of hazardous duties. They could not even fire a weapon from one of the gun ports on their post because they had not re-qualified on firearms and use of force in years, despite *Commissioner's Directives* requiring annual re-certification. If a firearm is on the post, then you require annual certification.

I witnessed some staff just walk away from a situation and say that they were not certified to help out in any way.

I remember having to subdue a con in the main corridor in order to prevent him from assaulting another inmate. While attempting to gain physical control over this con, a PC guard walked right on by me while I was wrestling on the floor with him. He didn't even look at me. I called out to him by name to help out and he still kept on going in the other direction. Do these cowards not have a duty under the *Criminal Code* to act in these circumstances? Does management not have a duty to address these acts of cowardice?

Yet to neglect all of this was a direct violation of the Commissioners Directives and their duty to the preservation of life as a Peace Officer.

# PART 21

## Inmate's Guide to Crisis Negotiation

> Each maximum and medium security penitentiary must have a tactical unit of staff trained to deal with hostage-taking and other crises.
>
> —*MacGuigan Report* (1977), Recommendation 16

The CSC puts their own spin on descriptive terminology including replacement of the term "Hostage Negotiator" for "Crisis Negotiator". The term "Crisis Negotiator" doesn't sound as negative or violent as the word "Hostage Negotiator". The word "crisis" does not conjure up the image of someone holding a knife to a person's throat. It could mean that there is not enough bacon to go around in the cons' dining hall at breakfast.

The term "crisis" can be applied to any number of things, so it's a much broader and softer term than the word "hostage", which can only be applied to one thing. It just works better and sounds kinder and gentler written that way in the *Crisis Management Manual*.

If you have been selected as a Crisis Negotiator and completed your training in this area you are given a *Crisis Negotiation Manual* rather than a Hostage Negotiation Manual. Those selected staff are given a numbered copy of this tool, designated with their name in it for their use and study.

There was an area inside Collins Bay where the cons held their group meetings in the evenings. These meetings often included citizens from the community as participants. It was very much like a classroom setting with blackboards, tables and chairs and the inmates that attended these meetings were, for the most part, unsupervised. A guard would walk down the hallway every hour and maybe look in the window at them if they did their walk at all. Once the group was over, the cons returned to their ranges for the night.

One morning, I was going down that same hallway to open up the Institutional School for the day. When I passed the Group Rooms, I noticed a large three-ring binder on a table inside one of the empty rooms. The binder was a *Crisis Negotiation Manual*!

It contained the entire Crisis Management Model with details of negotiation tactics and the roles and responsibilities for every key player from the Institutional level right up to National Headquarters staff members. It also identified these members by name, position, and contact number in order for the negotiator to be able to speak to these people directly as a resource.

The entire Use of Force Management Model, grantable and non-grantable demands, specialized equipment, and services available from the CSC, the local police, and other Justice Partners, SMEAC forms, negotiation tactics, it was all in there:

- *The RCMP "I" Division on-call technician*
- *After Hours OPP Communication Centre*
- *The Penitentiary Squad*
- *Technical Support – Hostage-Taking RCMP*
- *Equipment available such as Fibre Optic Device*
- *Night Vision Optics*
- *Negotiators Telephone System*
- *Miniature Body Transmitters*
- *Frequency Synthesized VHF-FM Receiver*
- *Tactical Audio Recovery Kit*

….the list goes on.

It also had the name of the person that it was issued to printed on the inside cover. The designated owner did not even report the loss of his manual.

A document with this degree of sensitive information was to be nowhere near where the cons, nor any unauthorized person for that matter could get a look at it, yet here it was found down in the very bowels of the institution.

You can be sure the cons had copied every single page inside that book and now had them safely hidden inside the prison before giving up this valuable tool. If the owner reported it missing, and it was suspected that the cons did have it, there would be a major lockdown and a massive institutional search to recover it. This would piss off the cons and cause more trouble for them than they needed so they could just photocopy it and give up the original without any hassle or disruption to their routine and yet still hold on to a very valuable document.

This negotiation tool was classified 'Secret' and was now separated from its designated owner. It was not even reported missing and was in the hands of those who could do a great deal of damage with the knowledge recorded within it.

**"There was no investigation because the CSC did what was easy, not what was right."**

I have this vision of a hostage-taking within the institution and the cons thumbing their way through their copy of the *Crisis Negotiation Manual* to keep several steps ahead of the Crisis Negotiator throughout the ordeal.

The *Crisis Negotiation Manual* that I found should have been fingerprinted to determine whether or not it was in the possession of the inmates. All inmate fingerprints are on file and if they discovered that even one inmate left behind a fingerprint on it then they would have known beyond a doubt that they indeed had it in their hands and exactly who they were. But there was no fingerprinting done, and there was no investigation because the CSC did what was easy, not what was right. The manual was given back to its designated owner.

That was the end of it.

I remember being involved in a Crisis Management exercise that was staged as a mock hostage taking. The crisis manager was a new Deputy Warden who was putting the Contingency Plan into activation. He was ordering all of these resolution tactics up to and including sniper placement.

Well, the CSC has no snipers, they never did in my time.

The CSC had no Specialized Team trained in hostage rescue tactics as the *MacGuigan Report* recommended.

The CSC rely, for the most part, upon their Crisis Negotiation Team Members who will bring to the incident, and use, the same Crisis Negotiation Manual that the cons now have in their possession.

The new manager had no operational experience at the Institutional level and had no way of knowing what resources were available to him inside the prison and outside during a sensational incident like a hostage taking. It was fortunate for everyone that this was not an actual hostage taking and that he was not in charge of resolving it. He was later promoted and left the Institution for another Region.

# PART 22

## Institutional Emergency Response Teams (IERT)

"Each maximum and medium security penitentiary must have a tactical unit of staff trained to deal with hostage-taking and other crises."

— *MacGuigan Report* (1977), Recommendation 16

As the result of a hostage-taking in British Columbia Penitentiary on June 14, 1975, an intensive investigation was completed, and the *MacGuigan Report* was release in 1977. One of the recommendations that came from this report was that the CSC formally train an Institutional Emergency Response Team (IERT) for each prison.

During this particular hostage-taking, a group of untrained staff members entered the inner perimeter of the hostage scene armed with revolvers. Several people were shot and a female hostage, a Classification Officer, was shot through the heart and killed. After this tragic incident, the commander of the team that stormed the scene deliberately mixed up the revolvers so that no one would be able to determine who fired the lethal shot that killed their fellow staff member.

This was not the first time that officers and staff members were killed by friendly fire from the untrained and undisciplined line staff. It has happened at least three times within the CSC.

In each medium and maximum prison there is now a contingent of volunteer frontline officers who have been trained to be Emergency Response Team Members.

Medium security prisons have a 15-member team while the Max prisons have a 20-member complement. The Collins Bay Team also looks after Frontenac Institution, a minimum camp located on the same grounds as the main prison. The Joyceville Team looks after Pittsburgh Institution, also a minimum located on the same grounds. The Millhaven Team took care of Bath Institution next door to them until it was reclassified as medium security and they got their own team.

To be a member of the Emergency Response Team you are required to attend a 10-day Basic training course at the Regional Correctional Staff College. But before that you have to be approved by the current members of the Team and the Institutional Management.

## No IERT Selection Protocol or Criteria

In the day, approval for membership usually meant that you played hockey with and or bought the whisky for the current Team Members. This was the systemic selection process for IERT nationwide at the time.

When the Team required new members, they would simply ask around among their friends and drinking buddies if they wanted in. No one else at the Institution would even know that vacancies on the Team existed let alone have the opportunity to apply to them. Women were very much excluded from the IERT membership in those days, that was the culture then and up to the time I left CSC.

I applied for membership on the Emergency Response Team because I felt that I could contribute through my extensive experience in law enforcement and the training I received there, even though I was not one of the people who fit the mold of an IERT member in that period of time. I was not a guard, and I didn't travel in the same circles as the other team members, and I did not conduct myself on the job as some of them did. But the co-ordinator of the team insisted that I become a member much to the dislike of some of the established people on that team.

Several times, the Team was deployed, and I was not called in with the rest of the members because I was not one of them.

After a few incidents where I demonstrated extensive knowledge, leadership and skill I was accepted and in a short period of time became the Team Leader until I left the Service for the Toronto Police.

CSC did not have a nationally sanctioned recruitment policy for the selection of IERT members. There were simply no selection criteria to be met at all in order to become a member. It was an old boys club in every sense and with no selection protocol to work from, and great many poor choices were made in the appointment of new Team Members.

When I was Team Leader at CBI, I changed all that and made it a fair and transparent process. This began with a poster displayed within the institution advising of a vacancy to be filled on the Team. Any interested officer would submit their desire to join in writing to the Coordinator of Correctional Operations and at the closing date, the submissions would be turned over to the Team Leader.

At the next training day, a round table would be held among the current members to discuss what the "Strikers" would bring to the Team and each member would have the chance to speak about the officers on the list and their ability to perform the tasks of a Team member.

Once a decision was made, the Strikers would be rank ordered, and the list would be returned to the CCO with the results. Successful Strikers would be notified of those results.

I remember on one training day we were to select new team members and a woman's name appeared on the list of Strikers. One of our redneck guards stood up and loudly exclaimed that if a woman got on the Team there would be fifteen resignations handed in the next day. I calmly told him that there would only be one resignation submitted if a woman got on the team and that it would be his.

It was always a good plan to have an active list of Strikers on hand should we lose current team members due to a transfer or a promotion. One year, we lost five team members, a third of our team to promotions and transfers.

The current selection list would be active for one year and once that expired, we would start over once again with active recruitment to make the process fair. I submitted my Team Member Selection Protocol Guideline to National Headquarters for consideration… it was ignored.

# Notes: A Critical Tool for Evidence Gathering

When I began working as an IERT Member I always carried a notebook with me to record the events that the team was involved in. I soon began to carry my notebook with me during my regular workdays. My notebook was one of the ones I used as an Auxiliary OPP Officer with the cover removed so it could not be identified as a police notebook. Of course, I paid the price for using such a tool by having the staff and supervisors criticize it.

In the 1990s, the CSC decided that they would also issue a notebook to its officers. So, they did.

But that's all they did.

In every police service in Canada and at the Ontario Police College (OPC) a great deal of time and training is devoted to making your notes as a critical tool in evidence gathering. Your notes are always the main target of great scrutiny at a trial, so you had better know how to record your observations in the way that meets the high expectations of a courtroom.

The Correctional Service of Canada felt that they met these high standards simply by handing out these little green books without any formal instruction to the user whatsoever. Most of these notebooks were thrown into the staff member's locker and never used.

Included with these little green notebooks was a plastic laminated card CSC/SCC 1032(91-05). This card titled "Charter of Rights" contained, in French and English, the arrest warning that police are duty bound to read and explain to anyone whom they take into custody. It also contained the "Police Warning" about not having to say anything that may be used as evidence against them. It goes on to advise of their right to obtain legal counsel.

Again, the Ontario Police College, RCMP Depot Training Centre, Toronto Police College, and the OPP Police College spend a great deal of time training on the *Charter of Rights* as it is applied to arrest and detention.

The CSC handed out plastic laminated cards.

My notebooks, which I still have in my possession to this day, and utilized to write this book, have been beneficial throughout the years as evidence gathered to protect myself and other staff members against the corruption I have faced from the one sided and careless CSC investigations.

But, in the prison system, producing my notes as evidence did not carry the same weight that my notes as a police officer did in a courtroom because in those days, most often, the results of a CSC investigation were pre-determined before the hard evidence was even examined.

# PART 23

## Cell Block 1 Riot – March 28, 1991

## "Yard Up For Sure!"

### Criminal Code of Canada

67. A person who is

(a)   a justice, mayor or sheriff, or the lawful deputy of a mayor or sheriff,

(b)   a warden or deputy warden of a prison, or

(c)   the institutional head of a penitentiary, as those expressions are defined in subsection 2(1) of the *Corrections and Conditional Release Act* or that person's deputy, who receives notice that, at any place within the jurisdiction of the person, twelve or more persons are unlawfully and riotously assembled together shall go to that place and, after approaching as near as is safe, if the person is satisfied that a riot is in progress, shall command silence and thereupon make or cause to be made in a loud voice a proclamation in the following words or to the like effect:

*"Her Majesty the Queen charges and commands all persons being assembled immediately to disperse and peaceably to depart to their habitations or to their lawful business on the pain of being guilty of an offence for which, on conviction, they may be sentenced to imprisonment for life. GOD SAVE THE QUEEN."*

64. A Riot is an unlawful assembly which has begun to disturb the peace tumultuously.

There was a large-scale riot in 1 Block, or the Ghetto as it's called, in the evening of March 28, 1991. This was the first real taste of a full-blown riot of this scope that Collins Bay had ever experienced. Of course, regardless of the number of cons actively involved in this riot or the amount of damage done to the cell block, it was still labeled an "Isolated Incident" by the Institutional Management Team. The word "riot" was just not used in the Canadian prison system in the '80s and '90s.

One Block is one of the original cell blocks built in the 1930s. It had a capacity of 123 inmates in its cells on four tiers of thirty-three cells each. The tiers or "ranges" are numbered A, B, C& D. A and C are on the left hand side of the cell block with B/D on the right hand side. The main entrance to the cell block is a door off of "the Strip", which is a very long hallway that runs from the Main Entrance of the prison to three-quarters of the length of the walled structure of the prison itself. The upper Tiers, C and D have a long catwalk that runs the length of the cell block. At end of the cell block is a barred walkway that is secured at all times except when being cleaned. It serves as an emergency fire exit. This is where the high-pressure fire hoses are kept in a locked cabinet. A long duct passageway runs between A/C and B/D and contains all of the plumbing and electrical access to the individual cells. This duct is locked at all times except when services are required.

*Dave Woodhouse*

The length of Cell Block One is 242 feet and the width is 65 feet 10 inches.

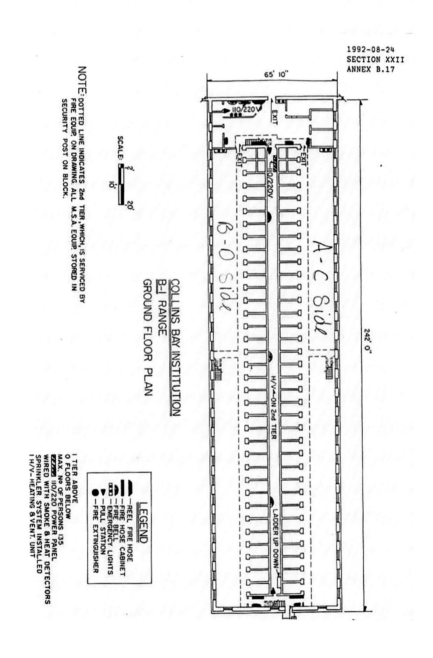

148

The cell block was in the process of being newly decorated using colours that were deemed "neutral" and "calming". The scaffolding that the painters were using to paint the two-tiered ranges was chained to a metal staircase so the cons could not move it or damage it. The chains securing the scaffolding are large and thick, almost like the anchor chains on a large boat with a heavy-duty padlock in place to keep them secure.

The cons got into the brew that night and decided it would be fun to set fires in the cellblock. Why you set a fire to a building that you are locked inside of has always been a mystery to me but, in my experience, it happens all the time in prison riots.

The boys smashed up and flooded, set fires, and tore down all the scaffolding. They used the lengths of metal pipe from the scaffold to smash more windows, toilets and sinks as well as use the broken metal pipes as weapons. With the windows broken out in the summer you would think the mosquitos would feast on the cons and in the winter they would freeze. But that really doesn't happen because the windows are the first things to be repaired as soon as possible once we gain back control of the prison. The cost for this is covered by the Canadian taxpayer along with the repairs for the rest of the physical damage caused and to replace the washers, dryers, refrigerators, lockers, toilets, sinks, bedding, microwave, shelving, plumbing and electrical.

The Institutional Emergency Response Team (IERT) was called in to deal with this "isolated incident".

The cons that were drunk on brew really were a sad sight staggering around the range. Homemade brew can be really potent stuff depending on how it's made, and the impairment can be enhanced even more when you down some pills with it.

As the IERT moved down the range you can hear the following orders being shouted by someone and recorded by the video camera: **"Anyone who doesn't want to get blasted with water get in your fuckin' cells, shut the fuckin' door, and everything will be all right!"**

The investigation team had a field day with this after hearing it on the video tape recording and felt that the IERT member who issued this order was very unprofessional. It took a while to make them realize that it was a con yelling these orders at his fellow inmates and not a staff member.

The Team was deployed down the range on the A/C side and began to remove the barricades of beds, washers and dryers, lockers, refrigerators, and freezers. These barricades had to be removed to gain access to the range and in order to remove the drunk inmates one at a time to Segregation for them to sober up.

Being a double-tiered range, the IERT was divided into two parts having Team Two securing the upper C-Range while Team One worked on the bottom A-Range. It's not only about getting the cons safely back into their cells and regaining control of the prison but also to ensure that this was not just a cover-up or a stall tactic for a murder or an escape attempt. So, the cons all have to be secured, counted, and seen by the nursing staff to make sure they are all there, alive and uninjured.

One of the cons decided that there was still some fight left in him and to prove it he stood up and ran toward the back of the range. He searched through the debris until he found a length of pipe that he wanted and then ran up the stairs to the second tier and attacked the members of Response Team Two.

The team on the second tier had their backs to him and did not see him coming at them with his pipe held in both hands and raised above his head to strike them. Any warnings shouted at the Team Members could not be heard because of the noise on the range and because of the riot helmets restricting their hearing. I was the Response Team Member on A-Range holding the shotgun and saw the inmate attacking. So, I fired a round from my shotgun directly at him. The con caught a load of pellets, dropped his bar, ran down the stairs and lay face down on the range with his hands behind his head. The Warden was standing right behind me when I fired the shot. The CSC was using #4 Bird Shot at that time and, due to the distance and the light weight of the ammunition, the con was not injured by the pellets, none of them even broke the skin.

After that, the cell block got a lot quieter, and the remainder of the cons went into their cells. This isolated disturbance (Riot) was at an end… for now.

The Warden was standing behind the Response Team the entire time while this cell block riot was going down. The Warden, as the Crisis Manager, is not to be anywhere near the scene, inner or outer perimeter. Taking him hostage or harming him gives the rioters that much more power. The Crisis Manager was to be inside the Crisis Management Center with the rest of the Crisis Management Team far away from the scene, never down inside the prison during an emergency such as this.

Since I fired the shot though, I was the one put through the wringer and to this day I firmly believe that shot, applied to save my Team Members from being attacked, ended any career aspirations that I may have had within the CSC under that Commissioner. This belief of mine was confirmed for me years later by a Unit Manager.

In the military this kind of treatment is called being Terminal Ranked.

The people who conducted the internal investigation simply did not know the law with respect to the use of force in the defence of the person. I had later found that this was a common and systemic issue with CSC investigators and with many of the management teams. They did not know the law, and this has been proven time and time again, much to the embarrassment of the CSC, when their work is examined by experienced outside agencies like police, a coroner's inquests, and the Justice Arbour Commission as an example.

If you shot a con in those days, you may as well have followed up with a shot directly to your own head as you are now dead to the Correctional Service of Canada.

In the aftermath, when the ringleaders were placed in Segregation two of them went to work plotting a murder...

This conspiracy to commit murder took place on May 1, 1991, in the Segregation Unit where an officer had intercepted a handwritten note between two cons. These were the same cons that were involved in the Cell Block One riot just months earlier on March 28. In the handwritten note the cons used their own names. Their names are blocked out in this copy.

I GOT SOMEBODY TO PUT 2" SHANKS, 2 MASKS AND TWO PAIRS OF RUBBER GLOVES NEAR THE YARD, TODAY AFTER WORK, HE'LL PUT IT THERE FOR SURE, NAME UNKNOWN, SOLID GUY, SO THAT WE'LL FISH FOR IT TOMMOROW AND PACK IT WITH US, WE'LL — AT YARD, DO WHAT WE SAID AND GO ON WITH THE PLAN, JUST HOPE WE DON'T GET PINCHED FOR FUCK ALL,

"GERONIMO"OOOOOOOOOO

O.K, THE GUY THREW THE STUFF THEIR NOW, SO FAR SO GOOD, ALL WE GOT TO DO IS FISH FOR IT, I THINK IT'S BETWEEN THE TWO FENCES,
YARD UP FOR SURE ·

The officers searched the exercise yard in Segregation and returned with: *"a balaclava and hidden inside was a 'Rambo' type knife approx. 6–7 inches in length."* (Quoted from the report of the officer who recovered the weapon)

The old Segregation/ Disassociation cells were located in 2 Block on A-range. Two Block was one of the original cell blocks built and it was a mirror image of 1 Block. The initial two cells on the range were converted into showers and after those came the cells proper. Directly across from the open barred cells is the Officers office.

When the riot in 1 Block was put down, the principal instigators were placed into Segregation immediately after but were not transferred out to another prison as should have happened.

The officers in Segregation openly discussed the events of the night of the riot as it was a sensational incident for Collins Bay to have experienced at that period in time. So, my name was often brought up in the conversations as the one who fired the shot at the inmate. The cons could easily overhear all the talk that took place in that office due to their proximity. So, all of the cons in the Segregation Unit knew who fired the shotgun that night – including the con who was shot.

The events of that night are not the only things that the guards talk about in front of the cons. Every shift of every day the guards spend their time talking and gossiping about other staff members. Often this is done around the inmates so they have a direct pipeline into the personal lives of the vulnerable guards and staff. This provides useful information that can be exploited to blackmail the staff.

If a guard is having financial trouble for instance, that may be the vehicle to coerce them into accepting money from an inmate or their associate thus putting them on the hook to lug drugs or turn a blind eye to an event on the Inside or to influence a parole officer into writing a favourable report. This kind of manipulation by the cons is done more often than people think. The same method is used by the guards and the CSC managers to control other staff members, just like in a criminal organization.

It would appear that the cons now wanted some payback for the night of the riot, and it wasn't hard for them to identify who I was as I often worked the Segregation unit on all shifts; another astonishing example of the complete lack of common sense that was systemic in the CSC in those days.

Why would the prison management team permit an officer to work in the same cell block that housed the inmate whom he had recently shot?

They had a motive, they had a letter of intent in both of their handwriting, and they arranged for a weapon to be delivered into their hands. Now, they had a method to carry out my murder.

I was never informed that I was their target.

The Management Team decided that this was a 'need to know' situation and I, in their thinking, did not need to know. Part of their thinking was that I would have insisted that they be charged criminally for conspiracy to commit murder and Collins Bay did not need a second Sensational Incident within a couple of months.

After the cons' plot was discovered one of them was witnessed saying: *"This proves that you cocksuckers need your fucking heads cut off and you would have if I'd had gotten my wish... We had the right idea, too bad the pigs found out!"* (Quoted from the officer's report dated 02 May 1991.)

The cons were soon transferred to a Maximum Security Prison.

No criminal charges of conspiracy to commit murder were even considered by the management team at Collins Bay Institution. They never reported to or even consulted with the Penitentiary Squad about the event for their advice even though it was their duty to do so. I only found out that I was their intended target years after the fact. If it had not been for the officer intercepting their note by chance, I would be dead.

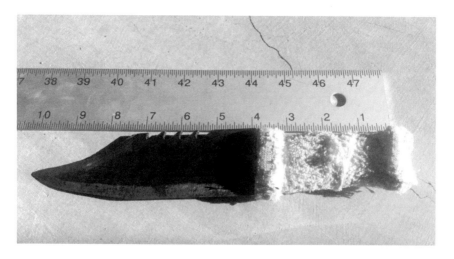

The weapon destined for my murder

In the aftermath of the riot that night where thousands of dollars in damage was done to the cell block, an inmate attacked officers with a weapon and a firearm was discharged at that inmate. You would think that all of this would be reported to the police. It was not.

*Commissioner's Directive 567-5*
Responsibilities:

4. "The Institutional Head, or Director of a Correctional Learning and Development Centre where applicable, will have procedures in place to ensure that:

g. The police department having jurisdiction is immediately notified when a firearm has been discharged other than accidentally or for training purposes."[22]

This was another reason that no criminal action was taken when the cons' plot to kill me was discovered. A police investigation would have caused me to be interviewed by the Joint Forces Penitentiary Squad (Police officers from different services assigned to investigate crimes within Kingston and area Penitentiaries) and it would have been determined that I discharged a firearm at an inmate on the night of the riot and that this act was not reported to them as required by the Correctional Service of Canada's *Commissioner's Directives*.

I was never interviewed by the Penitentiary Squad over my discharge of a firearm as a use of force, over the riot or over the con's assault on the officers with the metal bar. And the handwritten note, intercepted in the act **"The lid was on and firmly in place to keep that information behind the walls."** of being passed between the two authors, containing their conspiracy to commit murder along with the corroborating evidence of the weapons and disguises found in the yard, all of this was kept on the Inside. The lid was on and firmly in place to keep that information behind the walls.

This was how the CSC did its business in those days and they did this often and at the expense of their staff members.

---

[22] Correctional Service of Canada, *Commissioner's Directive 567-5 – Use of Firearms*, Ottawa, Modified 2018-12-10, www.csc-scc.gc.ca/acts-and-regulations/567-5-cd-en.shtml.

I remember, as an Auxiliary OPP Officer once sitting in a marked police car outside the home of a Warden to protect him as he had received a death threat from a con. But I was a CX-1 not a Warden; my life was of no value to the Service. The indifference, ignorance and neglect continually displayed by our managers at all levels of CSC is the direct cause of the failure of their Mission and the deplorable morale of its employees. At that time, the CSC was the very definition of a 'poisoned' work environment encompassing every aspect of the term.

You would think that this would be the end of that Sensational Incident, but there was much more to come yet…

\*   \*   \*

In the aftermath of the riot of March 27–28, 1991, the *Commissioner's Directive 600, Management of Emergencies,* memo from the Deputy Commissioner dated January 1990, file #192–5, required that the staff members involved receive a Post-Traumatic Stress Debriefing.

This Commissioner's Directive was not followed after the 1Block riot as was often the case after a Sensational Incident such as this one. That would have cost money.

A few days after the riot, the Institutional psychologist scheduled a debriefing on April 3, 1991, at 15:00 hrs in the boardroom on the third floor of the prison. The staff members who were required to go were ordered not to attend but to perform cell searches instead. This was in keeping with the "Least Restrictive Measures" policy that the CSC developed in order to get the prison back on operational routine as soon as possible after a "major incident" like a riot. The goal of "least restrictive measures" simply means not to inconvenience the cons any further than necessary. I stood up at that shift meeting and asked when the officers could be expected to be relieved for the scheduled debriefing.

I was ignored.

The needs of the staff and compliance with Commissioner's Directives were never a management priority in the 1980s and 1990s. Trying to save money at the expense of uniformed staff members and their health and safety was.

Getting the searches over quickly so the cons could be let out of their cells as soon as possible was the main goal, the only goal. "Least Restrictive Measures" was another over-used buzzword that surfaced in the 1990s and is still used to this day. This was the managers' main intent after the cons destroyed their own cell block and tried to assault or kill staff members.

The stress debriefing was not rescheduled after that. It would have cost overtime to backfill the many staff members who were required to attend.

So, I filed a Grievance Presentation through the Public Service of Canada. Grievance number Ont-91-160-440.

Lesser measures and polite requests for them to do their duty by their own staff members and the Commissioner's Directives were simply ignored by the Collins Bay Institution management team. I always gave them the opportunity to do the right thing before making things more formal.

The Grievance was heard by the Deputy Warden Management Services on May 6, 1991. It was upheld, and the very first Post-traumatic Stress Debriefing for Collins Bay Institution Staff Members was held at Westlake Hall on January 21, 1992,… *ten months after the Riot took place.*

It wasn't much good ten months after the ordeal and was only initiated due to my grievance.

In the Management Decision on my grievance, it stated: "However, once the completed inquiry arrives, I will schedule a briefing with staff."

They were awaiting the outcome of the investigation before attending to the immediate welfare of their staff.

The "Inquiry" report that the Deputy Warden was waiting to see is no longer in existence as the CSC destroys these kinds of embarrassing reports as part of their vetting process. The CSC has never taken the opportunity to learn from their history; they just want their sad history to go away.

A formal Grievance Presentation had to be pursued in order to get the senior managers of Collins Bay Institution to do their duty toward their own staff members who performed their jobs with courage and professionalism on the night of a major prison riot. This is not an exception, but common practice in the CSC. But for me filing a formal grievance, it never would have been done. This was another reason I achieved Terminal Rank early in my career. To the management team at Collins Bay Institution, I was a troublemaker.

*     *     *

The weapon smuggling into the Segregation Unit took place on more than one occasion and it was all documented. In a second incident, a con had made similar arrangements with the inmates in the general population to place a homemade knife within the segregation exercise yard. The inmates do not go through the trouble of arranging to have knives smuggled into the segregation unit to use them to butter their toast. These knives are meant for a murder.

This weapon too was intercepted by chance alone. Most of the arrangements for weapons and drug smuggling into the Segregation yard was through the open windows of 2 Block located just above their exercise yard. The cons would stand outside in the yard and make their needs known to their friends on the second floor. The 2 Block cons would simply drop the items into the yard through the open window. So, heavy mesh screens were fastened to the 2 Block windows that overlooked the segregation yard. But the mesh was not tight enough to prevent the shivs and drugs from being passed through. The institutional management team thought that was good enough though.

Of course, the senior management types who make these decisions do not work down Inside with the cons; they are not at risk. They are separated by physical distance, electronic gates, bulletproof glass, and armed control posts. Very often the decision makers do not even know what the ranges and cellblocks even look like down Inside.

I was forced to make a complaint to Labour Canada after going through all of the low-level resolution methods without any tangible effect. An investigator from Labour Canada was sent into the prison and looked at all the reports from past incidents. He then went out into the yard to see the physical layout. There happened to be a "fishing line" for passing contraband, made up from the lengths of string tied together from a floor mop hanging down from 2 Block into the Segregation Yard. When he looked up at the windows of 2 Block to see where the string was coming from, he caught a handful of gravel in the face from the cons tossing it down at him. He then left the Institution and wrote up an order for the windows to be secured in such a way that they could not be opened.

The window frames were then welded shut to prevent them from opening. The cons made a formal complaint that they were not getting enough fresh air because four out of the fourteen windows on the range were welded shut. But cons being cons, they just smashed the window glass when they wanted to throw contraband weapons and drugs down to their friends in the Segregation Yard.

So, the institution placed a tightly woven metal mesh screen over the old windows. That way the cons could still get their fresh air.

But they left a four-inch gap at the bottom of the screens. Room enough to traffic contraband weapons and drugs down to the boys in Segregation.

It was years in the future when they finally resolved this issue by constructing a separate segregation building, physically removed from the other cell blocks.

# PART 24

## Riot in the Gym – April 11, 1997

During lockdowns and major institutional disturbances like murders and riots or if there is information that dangerous contraband items such as a large drug cache or weapons are within the walls, a major search will be conducted called an Exceptional Search. In the past, the managers would sometimes order the ranges to be cleared of inmates by having them wait in the gym or yard until the search is completed.

This ploy will often backfire if the cons take offence to the search. They will smash up the gym and or refuse to return from the yard until their demands are met. The advantage of damaging the gym rather than their cell block is that none of their cell effects are smashed or burnt up and anything that they do destroy in the gym will be replaced in a short period of time with brand new equipment, fresh paint and window glass. And the chances of anyone being charged criminally for the damage that they cause is very slim.

The 2 Block cons were required to go into the gym for the morning as their cells were being searched. As a result of the search, a large amount of heroin was found inside the hollowed-out portions of some marker pens in a con's cell.

12:00hrs:

In the afternoon, the cons were getting bored and restless, so they decided to stage a non-violent protest because their lunch was late. That peaceful protest lasted just over an hour before things changed. They began to smash up the lower weight room using the heavy weightlifting equipment.

Then, as seems to be the case in every riot, they started setting fires to the very building that they were locked inside of and smashing the glass out of all of the windows.

The cons really liked to set fires. This is just a universal thing that they all do in every prison where there is an "extreme event" (new politically correct term to replace the word Riot) on the go. But they are always locked inside the cell block, cell, range or building that they set on fire. And then they start screaming that the cell block is burning, and they want out.

13:03hrs:

I was ordered to activate the Emergency Response Team to deal with this… "Isolated Disturbance, Extreme Event, Contained Incident."

The cons took the 45-pound Olympic bars from the weight room and used them as battering rams to breach the metal bars on the windows of the gym. This gave them access to "U" shaped area outside between the gym, the Strip and Cell Block 1. This was an anatomical dead space, unused for anything and nothing was within that space but a couple of garbage pails. From here they could simply climb up on the roof or even go over or through the ten-foot-high fence topped with razor wire.

They made their way easily into this area from the gym once they peeled the window bars back. Then they passed an Olympic weight bar and some aluminum baseball bats to the cons across the way in 1 Block while trying to induce them to join in on their fun.

The Olympic weight bars are a great tool for destruction and were now being used to ram their way through the east wall of the weight room into the prison yard proper. They are in essence a large heavy battering ram that can be wielded by one or more inmates with the end result being the great destruction of government property.

I recommended to the Crisis Manager that the remainder of the prison be locked down and all of the other cons secured in their cells. We now had two areas of the prison rioting and I did not want it spreading to any more parts of the institution.

I deployed a contingent of Team Members outside in the yard at the fenced in area between 1 Block and the gym in order to keep the cons contained in that space.

I deployed a second unit to 1 Block to keep those cons isolated there. We now had three separate locations in the prison beginning to riot, the gym, one block and the outside area between the gym and one block. All of the cons armed with aluminum baseball bats and at least one 45-pound Olympic weight bar per group.

13:30hrs:

A warning shot was fired from the 12-gauge shot gun to try to contain them inside the gym. At this time, only two cons were in the yard area outside of the gym working on peeling the window bars off the building. As the shot went off, the cons never even flinched or looked toward the sound. They just continued with their smashing and assisting the other cons to pour out of the gym.

You could hear them shouting "Fuck you!" and "Do it!" after being given oral warnings that the shotgun would be used.

A second warning shot was fired with the same result... they just ignored it. The inmates all know just how far they can go with their destruction before "the shit gets real" for them. Having possession of a "CSC Crisis Management Manual" is a handy tool for them to plan and coordinate their prison riots and hostage takings.

The inmates have their faces covered with torn bed sheets to avoid identification and to try to beat the effects of the gas. Many have blue cotton blankets draped around them because they had used their winter coats for other purposes while inside the gym.

They are armed with aluminum baseball bats, weight bars, hockey sticks, and one con even has a hammer. They are wearing the hockey helmets, gloves, and knee and elbow pads from the gym, so the hockey gear allowed them to be equipped in a similar fashion as the Response Team Members.

Broken glass litters the yard now as all of the windows in the gym and in 1 Block have been smashed from the buildings. Some cons get together and simply use their strength in numbers to peel up the window bars on the gym as more and more cons pour out of the building. White smoke was now streaming from the broken windows of the gym and covering the yard area making it hard to see them at some points.

14:00hrs:

A "203" expulsion round was fired into the area from the gas gun. This is a short-range CN Gas deterrent. But this simply blows back in the faces of the Riot Team Members as it is composed of a micro pulverized dust and is easily influenced by the prevailing wind and the distance to the target.

A gas grenade was tossed in to keep them back from the 1 Block windows so they can't pass in any more weapons. The grenade didn't detonate as it had expired eight years ago.

The cons just laughed at our ineffectual efforts to contain them and go back to consulting their Crisis Management Manual to see what tactic we may try on them next.

14:07hrs:

The 1 Block A/C side cons are now rioting. We can hear them using the weight bar and aluminum bats to smash their cell block to pieces. They jammed the locks on the range with debris so we could not use the keys to open the doors. If one of their fires gets out of control, we cannot get them out.

14:16hrs:

The gym cons are still pouring out the windows and continuing their battering attack on the inside wall of the weight room.

They are rioting in three locations now: the gym the yard and 1 Block.

I recommend to the Crisis Manager that all non-essential staff be accounted for and then evacuated from the prison. The risk of losing containment is getting higher by the moment.

The Crisis Management Team on the second floor of the prison are trying to have the Crisis Negotiators establish a dialogue with the rioting inmates. The cons just keep telling them to "fuck off!"

The non-violent Crisis Intervention Strategies are not working today with this crowd.

I called for the use of Defense Technology Skat Shells for the gas gun but there were none of these munitions in our prison armoury. These are fired from the 37mm gas gun, and the round contains five separate sub-munitions that scatter and deploy the gas over a greater area. The prison armourer didn't feel that we would ever need them, so he just didn't keep them on hand.

Many of the prison managers truly did not believe that their Correctional Clients were capable of these acts of violence and so did not properly prepare their Response Teams with the equipment and training they required in order to deal with an actual, full-on, prison riot such as the one we had on our hands right now.

Back then, the Wardens in the Ontario region did not even know that they were required by law to read aloud the "Riot Act" to the cons when violence of this scale was taking place within their Institution.

There was a great fear that officially declaring a Riot within the Prison walls and reading the "Riot Act" as prescribed by the law, would give those responsible for containing the violence and putting it down more power to act and use force. There was a great systemic fear among the prison managers that this power would be abused and exceeded by the Response Team. They did not want a free-for-all of force being used on the cons and did not trust their Riot Team members to use restraint. This fear is not without good reason as there are past examples of loose cannons doing stupid things during prison riots.

I had kept the loose cannons off of our Response Team but there were

**"We can't have a perfect system that locks up dangerous people and never have a riot or murder. It's naive and foolish to believe otherwise."**

still some within the rank and file of guards who I had to keep an eye on throughout all of this.

It had been so long since a major riot took place with an Institution in the Ontario Region that many of the prison managers had not experienced one in their careers. Some prison managers came from a non-custodial background and may have read about the violence an inmate committed that was recorded in their file in the course of their duties as report writers but had never really experienced this level of physical violence and destruction firsthand.

Reading over reports and watching videos about prison riots is no substitute for being in the thick of it. We can't have a perfect system that locks up dangerous people and never have a riot or murder. It's naive and foolish to believe otherwise.

We were now greatly outnumbered so I requested the assistance of Joyceville Institution's Emergency Response Team. I told them to bring with them tear gas that works... lots of tear gas.

We had to hold the Prison on three rioting fronts until they arrived, while being greatly outnumbered and holding nothing but wooden sticks in our hands against aluminum baseball bats and Olympic weight bars. And there was no way that we would have been permitted to resort to using a shotgun directly against rioting inmates.

There were staff members standing on chairs on the Strip looking out of the windows trying to see the action. I recommended to the Crisis Manager that those people remove themselves from that location immediately as we are firing warning shots in that very direction with the shotgun.

The 1 Block cons were now using the weight bars to try to breach the fire door at the end of the cell block. If they got through that, they would then have the run of the entire prison yard.

I recommended to the Crisis Manager that a large service vehicle or front-end loader be parked against that door to reinforce it as we can see the metal begin to buckle outward with the repeated strikes from their heavy weight bars.

The gym was still on fire and the city of Kingston Fire & Rescue were just outside the walls, but they couldn't enter the prison while the cons were rioting (isolated disturbance times three now).

14:25hrs:

I asked to have the water shut off in 1 Block. The Crisis Manager replied, "I thought it was shut off." The cons are using the fire hose and directing it at the entrance to the range to keep the staff from seeing what they are doing and from trying to repair the jammed lock.

With the second hose they are spraying the Riot Team in the yard through the broken windows.

Inmates using the fire hose on the Response Team Members

14:34hrs:

The Warden asks me over the radio how long before we get the cons back inside the building?

The 1 Block A/C side cons have broken through the barriers at the back of their range and now have access to B/D side of the cell block. The entire cell block is now in riot, and we are outnumbered even further.

I am hoping that the Joyceville Team is on their way.

A large front end loader is driven up to the fire exit door of 1 block and the bucket is placed against the door to keep them from getting through it.

15:43hrs:

We toss in two more gas grenades over the fence between one block and the gym. They too fail to detonate. We are running out of our useless expired tear gas that won't detonate because it's so old.

15:47hrs:

An evacuation plan is established for the IERT should the cons attack the fence as we are outnumbered, have no tear gas that works and certainly will not get permission from the Crisis Manager to defend ourselves using our only shotgun.

16:34hrs:

The Joyceville Emergency Response Team Arrives. I immediately deploy the working tear gas munitions that we asked them to bring. The Skat Shells are fired down 1 Block A Range and the cons abandon their attempt to breach the window bars and the back door.

We also got some tear gas delivered for the Regional Correctional Staff College, but those munitions were well beyond their expiration dates and useless to the situation.

The arrival of the Joyceville Response Team was well-timed because the violence was rapidly escalating to the point where further containment was becoming a problem without resorting to the use of firearms. The situation in the yard was deteriorating and the possibility of losing that containment area was impending. More and more inmates were entering the yard from the gym, mostly to avoid the smoke from the fires that they started themselves.

In the area outside between the gym and 1 Block we form a line with the combined Riot Team Members in front of the fence facing the cons. This show of force acted as the final deterrent to de-escalate the situation.

The cons were now having second thoughts once they saw the Riot Team Members deployed in strength and ready to act.

16:40hrs:

Most of the cons were now back inside the gym. They were removed one at a time, searched and escorted back to their cell block. Many of them had chocolate smeared all over their faces. They had broken into an office in the gym that contained chocolate bars being sold to raise money for an event they were having in the summer. They were trying to guzzle down all they could for fear of having us take their stolen candy away from them.

Once the gym was emptied of cons, the Response Teams swept the area, putting out fires and searching for more of them that maybe hiding, injured or dead.

They had covered the CCTV cameras located high up on the gym walls. They did this by getting their winter coats wet to add weight to them in order to throw them up to that height to drape the video cameras. When they cover the cameras, it means they don't want us seeing and recording what they are doing… and that's usually a murder.

There were several holes on the back wall of the weight room from their efforts to get through. Every window, office, toilet, and sink has been smashed. Smoke, fire, and water damage was everywhere and burning debris littered the gym floor.

17:00hrs:

We entered Cell Block 1, locked them up and counted them.

The prison nurse and a doctor as well as the Citizens Advisory Committee went from cell to cell to ask them if they are all right.

Some of the cells locking bars were badly damaged, so the doors had to be secured using padlocks and heavy chains.

Again, once the cons saw the Team Members out in the yard between 1 Block and the gym, in force and ready to act, they knew their fun was over and when we showed up at their cell block door they immediately went into their cells. It's my extensive experience having been involved in many prison riots that it's not very often the cons will challenge the Riot Team once we approach them directly. The only ones to do so are usually drunk or high and not much of a threat.

The CSC relied heavily upon negotiation to resolve these acts of violence. Sometimes it worked if it was one inmate acting out and he was contained to a cell or a range. In my experience as a Riot Team Leader for many years and throughout many prison riots, that when the cons get together in numbers and begin to destroy all that they see, setting fires along the way and arming themselves with weapons, all the prolonged negotiation attempts are achieving is to give the cons more time for them to destroy. The longer this goes on the more likelihood that someone is going to be gravely injured or killed.

Later in the night, we performed several cell extractions in order to transfer some of the cons involved in the riot to Millhaven Institution.

03:10hrs:

We left Millhaven and returned to Collins Bay to stand down for the night. It was another long day in the life of a Response Team Member responsible for restoring order on the inside of the Gladiator School.

There was considerable damage to the gym and its roof due to the fire, smoke, water, and the use of the weight bars upon the building. One Block was also a mess with thousands of dollars in damage done to it. One thing that was not damaged throughout the whole riot was Cell Block 2 where the cons who started the rioting lived. Their cells and their possessions were not damaged by fire, smoke, water, or tear gas. Their windows were not smashed out and their plumbing and heating system still worked for them.

The Warden hired ServiceMaster to come in and clean it all up before allowing the local newspaper to tour through the next day and take photographs. The broken exercise equipment was all replaced with brand new, the walls were patched and painted and the trashed items and appliances on the ranges were replaced along with all of their broken windows and screens.

The following was taken from our local newspaper, printed on the day after the riot:

Saturday, April 12, 1997

THE KINGSTON WHIG STANDARD

Front page news

"Prisoners smash walls, set fires in riot"

"Costly uprising at Collins Bay Institution ends peacefully"

"Damage to one area of Collins Bay prisons estimated at more than $35,000 after a six-hour riot by convicts."

"....20 rampaging inmates who had trashed their cell block agreed to return to their cells peacefully, said a prison spokeswoman..."

"(Staff) **didn't have to use force,**" she said.[23]

"Cruisers ringed the perimeter, and police officers armed with shotguns kept watch for any signs of escape". "At the height of the disturbance, there appeared to be more than 30 officers on hand."

Several of the photographs show fire and police with police dogs present at the front of the institution.

Other photographs showed the trashed ranges with the flooding and the gym with someone pressure washing the walls to remove the smoke and scorch marks. Still another showed the back weight room with the many holes puncturing the wall from the Olympic weight bars being used as a battering ram.

"**But,**" the Deputy Warden said, "**the rioting inmates were contained to the building at all times.**"

"**They were never really loose in the yard.**"

---

[23] DW: Bold emphasis is mine.

**"Shots were fired by a guard in the gym area early in the disturbance"**

**"They did work because inmates were trying to get out of the area... and they backed off,"** she said.

This is what was reported to the public by the Deputy Warden the day after the riot. Maybe she was speaking of a different riot at a different prison than the one I attended that day.

## Cleaning Up for Guests

I remember once speaking to an international guest touring our Correctional Service of Canada facilities. In the late 1990s, the Service sponsored the exchange of representatives from other countries to visit the CSC and tour some of the facilities. Good in a way because the institutions had never been so clean.

Within the prisons, there is an inmate welfare system to cover those who decide not to work while they are Inside. So, sometimes they have to hire out the cleaning services to local contractors. Late at night when the offenders were locked up, you would see an army of professional cleaners and painters move through the institutions hitting all the areas the visitors were expected to see.

This method of presenting to the public is the common strategy used after a riot. When the fires have been put out, the blood mopped up, and the debris swept and shoveled away, teams of private outside cleaners come in to do the rest before allowing the press to come in and see the aftermath, as was the case in the riot of April 11, 1997.

It's all part of the façade that Corrections puts on to make fools out of the staff and public. This is often the case when the Commissioner comes for a visit. The institution is dressed up and looking its best for him/her and the community to see.

One of these VIPs I spoke with was an employee from another country who held a high rank within their Correctional system. This person saw beyond the new paint and fresh floor wax. This person told me that the Correctional Service of Canada claimed to them that it was the best in the world. The officer agreed with that statement and went on to say that we, meaning their organization, would be the best in the world too if they had the budget to work with that Canada does.

I admired the officer for being so straightforward. Canada must be a very wealthy country indeed if we can afford to keep our prisoners in comfortable luxury.

# PART 25

## Cell Block 1 Riot – November 17, 1998

18:00 hrs:

At the Regional Correctional Staff College there is a gym and weight room, which all staff members are permitted to use. You sign in at the desk in the front entrance and sign out once you are finished.

In the early evening on the above date, I was in the process of signing out at the front desk when I saw my Warden in the lounge attending a meeting. I saw him look down at his pager and then approach the desk to use the phone. I stood back at a respectful distance and watched his face as he listened with the phone up to his ear. After years of watching the cons closely you get to be very good at reading body language.

The warden was giving off some telling clues, so I stuck around to save him an additional phone call. When he finished his call, he looked up and saw me. He called me over and ordered me to activate the Emergency Response Team as the 1 Block cons were lighting fires.

It began at 17:45 when the 1 Block cons on A/C side pushed four garbage pails with their contents on fire into the vestibule of the cell block toward the office of the guards. I remember the same occurrence took place on "A Night in The Ghetto" some years prior.

The staff activated the emergency alarms and tried to put the fires out. A container of liquid was thrown by a con and when it made contact with the flaming garbage pails it caused an exploding fireball. The 1 Block Officers managed to lock the barriers to the ranges in order to contain the violence. The fires were then put out by the staff members.

The A/C cons began to barricade the entrance to the range, arming themselves and smashing the lights and windows.

By 19:00 hrs, the remainder of the prison was in lockdown so that the 1 Block cons did not have the opportunity to induce the other cons to join them in their frenzied destruction of government property.

19:33hrs:

The Emergency Response Team has been activated and we met in our Ready Room for a briefing and a plan of action.

I wrote the Team Member designations and assignments on the white board in our ready room and advised them of the current situation in 1 Block. The 1 Block A/C cons had barricaded the entrance to the range with washing machines and dryers, metal bed frames and mattresses, freezers, and lockers. B/D side had done the same with the addition of draping bed sheets over the windows so no one could see what they were doing. This, in my extensive experience, is always a bad sign because what they don't want you see is often a murder. I wasn't far off the mark in this prediction.

19:39hrs:

I met with the Crisis Manager (Warden) and a number of other managers in the third-floor boardroom now designated as the "Crisis Management Centre". I had to present my plan to the Crisis Manager on how I intended to deal with our current "Major Disturbance" (Riot).

This Plan must be written out in detail on an official form called SMEAC[24], containing:

- the kinds of equipment that we intend to use from tear gas to firearms
- our strategy to retake the cell block

---

[24] SMEAC is Situation, Mission, Execution, Administration, and Communication.

- an explanation in detail regarding the use of force levels that may be applied
- names of the nurses on duty are included and a note that we have consulted with them to determine if any inmates in 1 Block had a medical issue concerning them being exposed to tear gas.

I must explain in detail the effects of every chemical agent that I requested because very often the Crisis Manager and his entire Crisis Management Team do not know what these devices can do. He wants to know if they have the potential to cause a fire or if a con can be hurt by any discharge from the gas gun or the gas grenades that we intend to use.

This has to be approved and signed off by the Crisis Manager, and I am required to keep a copy on my person throughout the Riot as my permission slip to have authority to act and to get the equipment that I need to put down this Riot.

If the situation changes, we must complete a new form by doing it all over again. With such a prolonged crisis as a riot, and with the inherent conditions of a riot being dynamic, it was not uncommon for me to be compelled to resubmit or to update many of these SMEAC forms to resolve one event.

The first priority is to contain the cons on A/C side of 1 Block, so they don't break through to B/D side and we have twice the number of inmates to deal with. This had recently taken place in our last riot. The more participants the cons can muster, the more damage they can do and the more danger to life they pose.

20:41hrs:

We are going to contaminate the dead space at the end of 1 Block with Tear Gas to prevent them from smashing through the metal bars that separate the ranges and joining the cons on the other side of the Cell Block. As we proceed down the duct in between the two ranges, we find out that the cons have already ripped off the steel bars at the end of A/C side. They were now working on the bars on B/D side. The only hope of stopping them was using the gas to keep them away from destroying those metal containment bars.

When we enter Cell Block One, I see a guard in this area who had no business being there. I gave a very direct and detailed briefing to the Co-Ordinator Correctional Operations some time ago as to why he should not be anywhere near a crisis situation. Before entering the ducts to deploy the gas this same guard tells me that he has already been down there and had opened the door to see if the cons breached the area, they had indeed been in this area at the time he took it upon himself to open the door.

If they went through the door that he opened for them, they would then have access to the entire cell block and then the remainder of the prison. This guard decided to open this door without permission and jeopardized the safety of the entire prison. I needed this guy to completely remove himself from that area of the prison. I didn't want him interfering again and risking the safety of the whole jail. I asked one of the managers to give him a job away from the action and to make sure that he remained there until the riot was over and most importantly, not let him go anywhere near the prison armory.

Just as we were about to apply Mark 9 Mace under the door at the end of the range we heard a cheer go up from the cons… they had just broken through the barriers to B/D side and now the entire Cell Block is in riot. We were too late to apply the gas and we are now greatly outnumbered.

I ordered gas saturation of the area anyway in order to keep them out of there, so they don't attack the fire door leading to the outside of the cell block.

Because the inmates outnumbered us, I asked the crisis manager to request that the Joyceville Emergency Response Team be called upon to reinforce our team members.

21:55 hrs:

I met again with the Crisis Manager to report the current situation in Block.

The SMEAC action plan has to be updated.

Now that the cons had control of dead space at the back of the range, they were working on breeching the metal fire exit door in order to get into the yard just like they did in the Riot of April 11, 1997. Once again, I ordered a front-end loader to park against the fire door to try to prevent them from smashing it open and getting out of the cell block and into the prison yard. If that happened, we would lose the entire prison. We must hold the door until the loader could be driven from the garage to the back of the cell block and be positioned against it.

It was decided by the Management Team, without our input, that a Team Member with a 12-gauge shotgun would stand outside the fire door exit on the east end of 1 Block until we got the door properly secured.

I had some serious concerns with this decision as it placed the Team Member out in the open with a firearm and his only retreat option was to run away from the cons should they get out.

He was instructed by the Crisis Management Team to fire a warning shot if they got through the door and into the yard.

Our experiences with firing warning shots were that the cons generally ignore them. They know just how far they can go before the shit gets real. If the cons breached the door and began to exit the Cell Block into the yard it will be in numbers. Just what was he supposed to do if they rushed him? If the cons attack him, he will be forced to shoot them to defend his life and a shotgun only contains so many rounds.

If they get him, they get his gun, an institutional radio, and a team member as a hostage, if they don't kill him outright first. They placed that team member in a position not only dangerous to himself but to the cons as well should they get out of the cellblock.

This plan was a disaster in the making on many fronts.

I explained the tactical repercussions of leaving him out in the yard alone with a loaded gun. I recommended to them that the team member place himself on the roof of the school building overlooking the fire door and that an additional armed officer go with him to watch his back. That way he would have a better vantage point and he also had an escape route should they get through the fire door. I felt like saying... please leave the tactical deployment to those with extensive experience in that area. This kind of armchair tactical thinking had been done in the past during extreme events. Too many people without experience and training had input into what use of force options would be used with disastrous results just as the *MacGuigan Report* clearly stated.

Back in 1 Block the cons had removed the vertical locking bars from some of the cells. These are solid steel bars about one metre in length and are very heavy. They were using these to destroy the concrete walls of their cellblock.

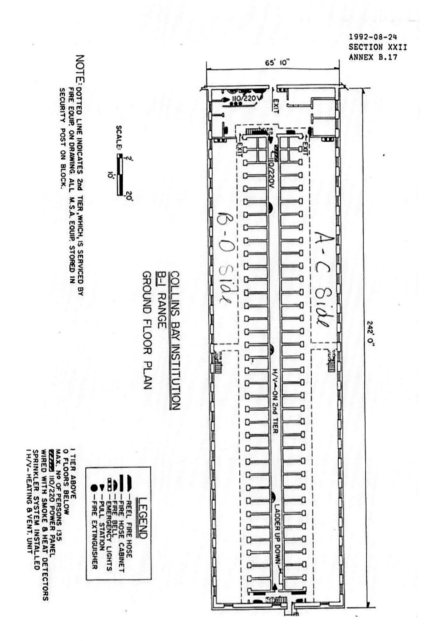

COLLINS BAY INSTITUTION
B-1 RANGE
GROUND FLOOR PLAN

NOTE: DOTTED LINE INDICATES 2nd TIER, WHICH, IS SERVICED BY
FIRE EQUIP. ON DRAWING, ALL M.S.A. EQUIP. STORED IN
SECURITY POST ON BLOCK.

SCALE:

LEGEND

— REEL FIRE HOSE
— FIRE HOSE CABINET
— FIRE BELL
— EMERGENCY LIGHTS
— PULL STATION
— FIRE EXTINGUISHER

I — TIER ABOVE
O — FLOORS BELOW
MAX. No OF PERSONS 135
— 110/220 POWER PANEL
WIRED WITH SMOKE & HEAT DETECTORS
SPRINKLER SYSTEM INSTALLED
I H/V — HEATING & VENT. UNIT

"While my Blood Drips from My Hands onto the Floor."

In order to limit their access to the fire door the Crisis Manager approved the use and deployment of a CN Gas Grenade into that area. CN is a more powerful kind of tear gas than the aerosol Mace or pepper spray, which we had been using and has more intense and longer lasting effects. An effect that I would soon be experiencing much to my discomfort.

This grenade is called a #98 Tactical Discharge (formally called a 109 Pocket Grenade). It has 25.5g of solid CN content which, when burned, emits a cloud of tear gas. It is called a "pocket grenade" due to its small size.

We had to deploy this grenade through the window at the back of the cell block. The window was about two metres from the ground, barred, and thanks to the cons' efforts, no longer has glass in it.

The cons in the area that are still trying to break through the fire door were given an oral warning that the gas was going to be used and to vacate that area. Of course, the cons are notorious for not doing what they are told so they just continued.

I knelt down and cupped my hands together to boost my team member up to the window to have him to toss in the grenade. He stood on my knee with one foot, and I boosted his other foot up to the window with my hands. But I was forced to drop him down unexpectedly. The shards of glass trapped in the treads of his boots cut into my hands and my knees.

We switched positions and he was able to get me up to the window without being cut himself. The grenade was deployed, and the cons abandoned their attempt to breach the fire door.

The Author deploying a gas grenade

The tear gas was so potent that almost two hours after being deployed it was still very effective in keeping everyone out of that area.

While making my way back inside the prison to the Institutional Health Care Centre to have my hands bandaged, one of the junior managers stopped me in the hallway and started to advise me how he thought I should be dealing with this "Major Disturbance" as the Institutional Response Team Leader. This manager had no experience with IERT tactics or Use of Force situations or the deployment of Chemical Agents and had never experienced a prison riot in his entire career. I listened respectfully to his advice while my blood drips from my hands on the floor and started to pool by his feet. He was so intent upon giving his advice that he didn't notice me bleeding all over the floor. He finally looked down, saw the pool of blood, went pale, turned, and walked away. This event was all being recorded by the video camera person.

For the remainder of the Riot, I can be seen in the video recordings with my hands bandaged. I have the scars from that night still on my hands and legs today. The other scars that I have from past riots are in my head.

The Author with his hands cut and bandaged

22:27 hrs:

The SMEAC Plan has to be revised once again to include the Joyceville Response Team. Once the Joyceville Team arrived, I quickly briefed them on the situation and assigned the mission to our combined Teams. I choose to enter B/D side first because this is where they were draping the windows so we could not see in and that's always bad news in these circumstances. Only someone with extensive experience dealing with riots and knowledge of how the inmates think in these situations would be able to conclude this.

As the riot played out, circumstances proved that this was a lifesaving decision.

We entered 1 Block B/D side with one quarter of the Team on the upper tier D-Range, and the remainder, the larger number of team members, on the bottom of B-Range. Both Range barriers were blocked with mattresses, washing machines, dryers, beds, fridges, freezers, and lockers.

I used a megaphone and ordered the cons...

"ATTENTION ONE BLOCK OFFENDERS, ATTENTION ONE BLOCK OFFENDERS. THIS IS THE LEADER OF THE RESPONSE TEAM. THIS IS A DIRECT ORDER TO GO PEACEFULLY TO

YOUR CELLS OR CHEMICAL AGENTS AND PHYSICAL FORCE WILL BE USED TO MAKE YOU COMPLY WITH MY LAWFUL ORDERS. GO TO YOUR CELLS NOW!"

The Author giving direct orders to the rioting inmates.

I told the guard holding the keys to *"Open this door now!"* and pointed to the main entrance door on B/D side. The guard holding the keys to the Range door was the one I told the manager not to allow back down Inside earlier, yet here he was once again, in the thick of it. Now I have to watch out for him on top of trying to put down this riot.

I stepped aside to give the video camera operator some instruction, then turned back to the cellblock door. The guard was just standing there with the keys in his hand staring blankly.

I asked, "Why didn't you open this door?" Maybe he saw something that I didn't that would have made him cautious.

He just stood there staring blankly back at me. He was experiencing audio exclusion from the weight of the stress of this situation and didn't even hear the orders I gave to him.

I ordered him in a loud voice to *"Open! This! Door! Now!"* That seemed to shake him out of it.

He unlocked the door and got out of the way.

The first thing we see is an inmates' blood-covered hand reaching out through the bars of the cell block door and his voice pleading, *"Help me get out! I've been stabbed!"*

I immediately ordered a dynamic assault upon the Cell Block.

He was begging us over and over to… *"Open the door please!"*

The cons were throwing typewriter-sized pieces of broken concrete at us.

The Team Members were throwing their combined weight against the barrier door trying to push back the barricades and debris so we could get in.

I ordered a 203-expulsion gas munition to be fired through the gap in the debris to keep the cons back from their side of the barricade as they are pushing back on the door.

The effect of the tear gas drives them away.

We finally we got the door open enough to reach in and pull the injured con out of the cell block and into the safety of the vestibule. He was placed on a stretcher and the nurse, and two officers took him to the Institutional Hospital.

A few days after the riot, a manager approached me and advised me that I had no business or authority to order a dynamic assault upon the cell block. That upon seeing the wounded inmate begging for his life I should have withdrawn the team and reported it to the Crisis Manager immediately for consultation and had a new SMEAC form completed. He was another manager with no experience in the Use of Force, Crisis Management, IERT Tactics, the Law and had never been near a Riot in his entire career. He was not even at the Institution on that night, but he saw the video recordings of the riot and thought that he was now an expert on the subject.

I just walked away from him.

There was also criticism from a manager about how I was dressed that night. Under my IERT uniform I wore a white turtleneck sweater. I wore this distinctly visible garment because the rest of our IERT uniforms are all black and or grey so everyone looks alike. There was nothing on our uniforms that distinguishes the Team Leader from the Team Members. Every response Team Member present at that Riot knew that the guy with the white collar was the overall Team Leader. This prevents confusion as to who is in charge and who is authorized to give orders to the Response Teams. This was not the only time that, as an IERT Team Leader, I got into trouble with the inexperienced decision makers over what I was wearing during a response.

More gas was fired down the range to keep the cons away from the barricade. The floor was wet from the firehose discharge and the flooding from all of the sinks and toilets that were smashed. They were still throwing debris at us from farther down the range and off the second tier of the cell block. We were using our shields to deflect away the concrete and broken shards of toilets being thrown at us.

The Joyceville Team Leader shouted, *"We are taking this range!"* as we burst through their barricade and into the Cell Block.

The Response Team Entering One Block

There were no lights on so all we had were our flashlights to see with. You could see the occasional brilliant flash of white light from the muzzle discharge of the Gas Gun, which illuminated the entire Range for a brief second. The intense light created by the muzzle flashes, the smoke from the fires, the cons running here and there, and the large-scale debris field down the range all combined to create a surreal battlefield. Our night vision was challenged briefly by the blinding flashes of light and often the Team members paused their advance momentarily until they could see properly once again.

A gas-powered generator was brought in, and floodlights were put in place after the Cell Block was secured. We dared not turn the electricity back on with all the flooding due to the threat of electrocution.

All power to the Cell Block had to be shut off as the cons will often electrically wire the range bars and cell doors so that when you step in the water and touch those bars you get shocked. They did this at the end of the B/D Range, but their man trap was discovered and disassembled before the power was turned back on. Only someone with extensive on the ground experience dealing with prison riots would know about these hazards and how to deal with them.

After the response Teams got established on the Range, the B/D cons all went into their cells and the doors were locked. It took maybe twenty minutes to accomplish this part of the mission from the time we breached the door.

We moved to the back of B/D Range into the passageway to A/C side.

This area was heavily contaminated with CN Gas and pepper spray. I had my Gas Mask with me but was not wearing it. With my mask on I cannot have my orders to the Team Members heard. It's like trying to be understood while shouting with your head under water. The internal communication devices in our Riot Helmets never worked because the radio connectors were not compatible with our Institutional radios. As a result of this neglected radio communication issue, the Team Leaders often did not wear their gas mask.

Over my many years with the ERT, I was exposed to our different varieties of Tear Gas more times than I would have liked so I thought that I could just tough it out.

I was wrong.

I had to place the Riot Team on standby while I rapidly left the Range to decontaminate. I went into the staff washroom in 1 Block to get access to some fresh water not thinking that the water to the Cell Block was currently turned off. So, I ran across the Strip to the 2 Block washroom only to find another team member there with his head in the sink trying to decontaminate too.

As a last resort, I chose to use the toilet water. But when I lifted the lid, I changed my mind after seeing what was in there. Eventually, I got to wash the gas contamination off, and I returned to our Riot.

We continued down the back of B Range and through to A/C side.

The cons on that side went into their cells without offering us any opposition; they knew that it was over.

The damage to the empty cells on One Block-A Range was so severe that they were never occupied again. We removed all the barriers that the cons placed in the doorways being ever wary of the water on the floor and more electrical man traps throughout the task. There were large pieces of masonry smashed from the very walls of the range and scattered around the Cell Block. These are what they were throwing at us from the second tier of the range.

Every washer, dryer, freezer, bed frame, microwave oven, locker, table, chair, desk, toilet, and sink were smashed and piled up in a great barricade in front of the main door to the range. The pile of debris was so large that it reached to the second floor of the range. It was all now just scrap metal items now that would have to be replaced.

Heavy metal-barred door frames were twisted and rendered useless.

All the spent chemical munitions were picked up and counted as some of the fuses in the pyrotechnic grenades can be made into zip guns with very little modification or effort. (This bit of technical knowledge about the gas grenades was completely unknown to most in the CSC. Even those who taught Chemical Agents at the Staff College for years had no idea that you could easily make a zip gun or an IED from a spent gas grenade fuse.) An inmate count was performed to make sure that everyone was accounted for and alive.

Gas-powered generators and floodlights were brought onto the range to give us some light while a thorough search was performed looking for more electrical man traps before turning the main power back on. Large fans were positioned throughout the cell block to clear the chemical agent from the Ranges.

The nurse went from cell to cell to see that more inmates were not injured. The Citizens Advisory Committee walked the Ranges to witness the damage and speak with the cons to see if they were all right.

The fact that the line staff and civilians walked the Ranges just after the riot without any gas mask protection was testament that the Ranges were no longer contaminated with Tear Gas.

23:40 hrs:

The Crisis Manager was advised that 1 Block was now secured, and an inmate count was being taken.

The inmates did thousands of dollars in damage to the cellblock but none of the inmates that participated in the Riot were charged with a criminal offence.

Many in the field of Corrections in Canada just don't realize that what the IERT do is battle. We go toe to toe with some of the worst nightmares that the criminal underbelly of this world has produced. We did it voluntarily with a courage, integrity and honor that the CSC absolutely refused to formally recognize.

This is combat in the truest sense of the word. We go into situations where the people that you have to contain and arrest will kill you outright if you give them an opening to do so. You will be stabbed, beaten with iron bars and aluminum baseball bats, set on fire, electrocuted, held hostage, tortured, and fucked up the ass with a metal bar if they get hold of you under these conditions. The CSC would never admit that their correctional clients had the will and ability to commit these acts against another human being. Yet the commission of these acts of violence is precisely the reason that they are incarcerated in the first place.

This is no different from combat in the military with respect to the high degree of battle stress because it's the same stressors and the same direct danger to your life. But unlike the military rules of engaging an enemy combatant in battle, they don't have official "CSC Approved Target Areas" to strike, and they don't fight the enemy with wooden sticks.

But senior managers just didn't see this. They were of the mind that the cons are just some good old boys who never had the same opportunities as others in society and they don't really mean what they do. That's the way that you are expected to think when you are 200 km away from a rioting prison and you yourself are never in any direct danger.

The senior managers at NHQ who view these recordings have the great luxury of sitting back in their padded chairs in a nicely appointed office with their popcorn, viewing the work that we risked our very lives to do while they record on their notepads what they think we were doing wrong. Passing judgment even though they themselves have never been in a riot, have no experience in the Use of Force, have never used force in an Institutional environment, don't know the Law, have never used Chemical Agents, or even experienced the effects of it. This is my extensive experience throughout my many years working for the Correctional Service of Canada speaking.

The CSC has absolutely no intentions of acknowledging the actions of their own staff members on the night of the riot, staff members who saved the life of an inmate, prevented the prison riot from spreading further and saved their entire prison from even more destruction. This is what working for the CSC was like in those years. Yet we continued to do our duty to the best of our abilities even though there was no recognition and no effective mental health treatment to help us recover from such extreme violence. The men and women who did this work still suffer from PTSD symptoms to this day.

How can you possibly go home after your shift to try and relax when you find that you have to pick brain matter out of the treads in your boots. Brain matter that belonged to the con who just got his head stamped flat by another inmate that day? This is what it is really like to work on the Inside.

Every Riot that I was responsible for putting down, as the Emergency Response Team Leader, was permitted to happen because of the belief in, and the pressure from above to adhere to their Crisis Intervention Strategy, which relies heavily upon negotiation.

There is a time and place for negotiation and if applied properly can achieve the required outcome, that of a peaceful resolution. But many strict factors must be in play for that to happen. When dealing with the cons one on one there is a much better chance of achieving your goal. If you are trying to apply it to a large mob of convicted criminals who are intoxicated on home brew and smashing the hell out of your prison, you are fooling yourself and placing the entire prison in jeopardy.

Each time I have witnessed the deployment of these misplaced intervention strategies under those circumstances, the only result was to give the cons the time they required to gain and hold large tracts of prison real estate to occupy and destroy. Or, as in the case of the forceable confinement and rape of a clerk at Kingston Penitentiary, they gave the con all the time that he required to rape her repeatedly. Only when he was through with her did he surrender.

There was no hostage rescue team or hostage rescue training in the CSC, the very environment that you would expect a hostage taking to take place. The CSC didn't even put preventative measures in place such as intelligence gathering should such a hostage occurrence happen in the future. Even to suggest that the CSC invest in this kind of tactical training and advanced information gathering and planning would result in you being looked at by the management teams as a complete idiot. The CSC, at that time, would not even consider a discussion on such a topic.

They relied upon negotiation as being the main tool in crisis resolution and only deployed the pointed end of the stick as a last resort when there was blood on the floors.

And when the cons have a copy of your Crisis Negotiators Manual in their hands, then all the intervention strategies you're banking on are completely useless.

The CSC needs to know their clients.

In the investigation report that followed, the main concern was all about the welfare of the cons, not the staff and not the thousands of dollars in damage done to the cell blocks.

There was one section of a report that was a small paragraph onto itself in large bold and capital lettering…

*"REVIEW OF EMERGENCY RESPONSE TEAM TAPES.*

*THERE IS NO SECTION OF EITHER TAPE WHERE INMATES ARE SEEN IN A NUDE CONDITION."*

At that time, the deliberately anonymous and mysterious people at National Headquarters who reviewed the tapes of cell extractions, involuntary transfers, riots, or any recordings where force may have been used on a con got very upset if they saw a naked inmate on the recording. All of these new measures were put into place to avoid any video tape recordings of naked inmates. The IERT had to carry blankets and paper gowns with them in future responses to cover the inmate should he or she choose to take their clothes off at any time, and they did this often for some reason. Our video recorder did not have the black dot editor to cover a con's ass or dick for the sake of providing a comfort zone for those at National Headquarters who viewed the tapes.

I approached NHQ with a proposal that questions or concerns that the unidentified viewers may have while evaluating the video tapes of IERT activity be directed at the Team Leaders who are able to address any questions that they may have. It seems like such a commonsense approach to take in these matters. But this suggestion too was ignored.

The G-Rated version National Headquarters had was a very different one from our X-Rated Institutional world. And those working at Headquarters did not want to see the real-world environment that we worked in. Their image of a convicted criminal was not based in reality. It was steeped in the Mission that speaks to the belief that they all have the "potential to become law-abiding citizens" no matter what the long-term intention is that the convicted may hold about the direction that they have chosen for their lives.

Their fear of seeing nude inmates on video recordings is derived from the Arbour Commission's damming report where the IERT intervention at the Prison for Women showed female inmates being strip searched on camera by the male IERT from Kingston Penitentiary.

Anyone viewing those tapes would be shocked and appalled. It was totally out of line to have an all-male Response Team perform the strip searches, but the P4W Management Team created the perfect storm for that to happen. P4W had a fully trained IERT comprised entirely of women officers at the time. But P4W management never thought they would be needed so they did not supply their Response Team with the scale of issue safety equipment and uniforms required to do the job. So, as a last resort, the all-male Response Team from Kingston Penitentiary was called in.

Just as some of the Institutions within the Region did not keep current their supply of Chemical Agents, CSC management nationwide truly felt they would never be needed, and that Interpersonal Skills Training and Crisis Negotiators were all that was required to bring order back to their prisons. They truly did not know, or more likely did not want to acknowledge, the potential for violence that our correctional clients possessed.

## Real Performance Issues

> Members of the "Millennial Generation" and "Generation Z" appear to care more than older workers about certain intangible rewards such as career advancement, skill training, social connections, and company purpose (Smith & Aaker, 2013). Similarly, the newest generation of workers strive to work where they feel that their input makes a difference.
>
> —*Compensation and Benefits Review,*
> Harvard University[25]

## Lack of Recognition

One systemic issue I had with most senior managers within the CSC concerned the lack of recognition for staff members who performed an outstanding job or demonstrated courage in the face of life-threatening sensational incidents.

Time and time again I submitted written requests to have staff members recognized only to have these requests completely ignored by senior managers at the institutional level, regional level, and right on through to National Headquarters.

Absolutely no response at all.

---

[25] Anais Thibault-Landry, Allan Schweyer, and Ashley V. Whillans, "Winning the War for Talent: Modern Motivational Methods for Attracting and Retaining Employees," *Compensation & Benefits Review* 49, no. 4 (September 2017): 230–246.

At the institutional level I found that many managers would not acknowledge an award nomination if they themselves had never been nominated or received a Service Award. It was an ego thing with many of them in that it couldn't appear that someone else's performance looked better than theirs. And bringing further attention to a sensational incident is not in the best interest of CSC management even if that attention awards a staff member for outstanding performance.

Very often, the Warden would not acknowledge a staff member's actions until maybe after the security investigation had been completed and the report returned to the Institution. Many managers did not have the courage to stand up for their staff and reward them after the event because it was safer for them to await the results of the investigation so the manager would not look bad if that investigation identified a "performance issue".

The security investigation report would not be read by anyone at the institutional level unless some problem was identified that required further action or redress on behalf of a manager.

In a year's time, the staff member would be forgotten and their performance on that day never officially recognized.

This is yet another way in which many staff are systemically undervalued and marginalized by the CSC at the institutional level right through to National Headquarters.

The reason for the systemic neglect by the service is that the CSC did not want to officially recognize acts of bravery committed by officers because they wanted the public to believe that such acts are never necessary within their idealistic world of 'meaningful interaction' between staff and inmates.

## Outstanding Performance by a Volunteer Team

I nominated a couple of staff members from the Joyceville Institutional Response Team for acts of Bravery for rescuing an offender who had been stabbed down-range during the largest riot in the history of Collins Bay Institution. I took it upon myself to nominate them in an email I wrote to the Deputy Warden while at the same time asking for Certificates of Appreciation for all of the Team Members involved. It was – you guessed it – ignored.

I submitted the formal nomination forms outlining the details involved in an act of bravery. I waited six months for a response. None came. I resubmitted the forms with a letter attached this time. Waited another month, nothing. I contacted National Headquarters looking for a response. I wrote a letter to the Deputy Commissioner of the Ontario Region.[26] When I finally received a response, it was curt and to the effect that acts like those described in the nomination were part of an officer's day-to-day duties and would not be recognized as being exceptional.

I wrote back to the contrary:

> A major Institutional Riot was taking place and these officers were part of a Volunteer Team that suppressed that riot and saved an inmate's life as well as stopping the widespread destruction of government property.

This was not good enough to sway the minds of those who have never been in a riot, even though their actions clearly went beyond what the Primary and Secondary Considerations listed below stipulated. So, I wrote a letter of commendation as the Response Team Leader and had it placed on their files. This was the only recognition that they received.

The CSC is always promoting the value of Teamwork within their organization. The IERT embodies that value yet got no formal acknowledgment for it from the very people who should be recognizing and awarding it.

*Correctional Service of Canada Guidelines for the CSC Awards Program*[27]

Commissioner's Awards Citation for Bravery

Primary Considerations:

  A.  A person puts his or her life in danger

---

[26] This was not an exceptional chain of events. This was the norm within the Correctional Service of Canada throughout that time whenever a sensational incident would go down.

[27] As of the time I made the initial application. The criteria used in 2021 are substantially similar.

B. The purpose of the act was to save life, to protect a person from serious injury or to protect property

C. The act was beyond the normal call of duty, and

D. The act was neither imperious nor needlessly dangerous

Secondary Considerations:

A. The degree of risk (e.g., possible death or serious injury)

B. Duration of risk

C. Voluntary nature of the act

D. Extent of training for specific action

E. Effectiveness of act

F. Nature of the background of circumstances and

G. Extent of physical, emotional, or mental stress on nominee

H. Reflection on the Service.

It was always my practice to submit a request through the *Access to Information Act* to see the original security investigation and have a copy provided to me. Only after several internal requests to see the report were ignored did I resort to making an application via the *Access to Information Act,* and having to pay for it, in order to see it.

It's in the best interest of every staff member involved in a sensational incident to obtain a copy of the CSC investigation. The copy you receive will be heavily vetted but you, having been there and witnessed the incident, will be able to fill in the blanks and fill in the truths.

You also have the right to see the original investigation un-vetted. Often, you only get to view it in the presence of a manager, and you may make notes from it. I have had the manager present try to stop me from making notes from the original copy, though they have no authority to do that.

After reviewing the investigation report and seeing that there was nothing in it that may embarrass a manager, I would then write up a letter of commendation and walk it into the Warden's office to be signed. I then photocopied the original and walked it over to the Records Office to have it placed on the staff member's personnel file and then gave the staff member a copy. All this work for a fucking piece of paper that does not cost the CSC a single cent.

The CSC did not want to recognize the heroic actions of volunteer IERT Officers because that would be tantamount to admitting that those actions were required in the first place. It would require them admitting that these violent sensational incidents actually took place within the idyllic walls and fences of the dream world that is the perception of National Headquarters and the false images of 'meaningful interaction' between staff and inmates presented to the Canadian public.

## Memorandum

**Date:** April 11, 1999
**Subject:** *IERT RESPONSE TO CELL BLOCK RIOT, 17 NOVEMBER 1998*

**From:**

Name: Dave Woodhouse

Emergency Response Team Leader

Collins Bay Institution
Phone number:

**To:**

Name:

Deputy Commissioner, Ontario Region

☐ Enclosures      ☑ Attachments

Notes:

Dear

Thank you for attending the funeral service for last Thursday. It is always a morale booster to have a Senior representative of the Service present at such occasions.

While at the Staff College last week picking up the flags for the service, I noticed a new addition to the honors wall along the corridor to the classrooms. It is a large plaque intended to recognize Officers who have saved the life of another person. At the present time it is devoid of names. The instructions at the bottom of the plaque are to direct any nominations of those Officers deserving of the award to the Wardens or to yourself.

On November 17th 1998, Collins Bay Institution experienced one of the most harmful riots in the history of the Institution. As the Emergency Response Team Leader it was my responsibility to try to contain the disturbance and bring it under control.

I have worked at Collins Bay for the majority of my sixteen years in the Service. Most of that time I have been a Response Team Member and Leader. I have experienced many a crisis during that time and have been witness to much of the trauma associated with them.

This particular response effected me in a way that no others have. As I told the investigating team from National Headquarters " this one took a year off of my life". I am still exploring the reasons for some of the feelings that I am struggling with. I know all too well of the damage that post traumatic stress can do to a person. This incident was the first time that I experienced doubt in my ability to lead the Response Team. I divulged these feelings to Chris Van Duyse, the Team Leader from Joyceville Institution. Chris remained at my side throughout the riot and was a major source of assistance and motivation for me. A prime example of the benifits of peer counseling.

When the crisis manager ordered an assault upon the cellblock the first thing we were met with when we opened the door to the range was Offender reaching out to us through the bars. His hands and body were covered with blood and he was pleading with us to get him off of the range. He had suffered numerous life threatening stab wounds.

The number of Offenders on the cellblock was eighty seven. They were boiling cooking oil on the range to throw at us. They were armed with home made knives and heavy locking bars that they ripped from the cells. As the door was opened they threw large pieces of concrete down at us from the upper tier.

Upon seeing Offender condition, I immediately ordered the door opened and the offender be removed from the range.

Dispite the barrage of projectiles being thrown at the door, Officer from Joyceville Institution put everyting he had into hammering down the barricades that the Offenders had erected to defeat our access.

Officer Van Duyse reached into the range and pulled Offender to safety. Offender was placed on a stretcher and evacuated to the hospital.

As you can see by the attached recommendations I have already nominated both of these Officers for awards for bravery for their actions in saving the life of Offender

In the past I have recommended other response Team Members for awards. Unfortunately there seems to be the perception that because the Officers are Response Team Members they do not merit such recognition because they are trained and equipped to perform these kinds of hazardous duties. In the words of the award committee " it's part of their job".

The awards committee does not seen to realize that Response team Members are **volunteers.**

The ten-day basic IERT training program is just that, a basic. It is very much the same training in arrest and control procedures given to Correctional Officer Recruits. There is no tactical training offered on how to defeat a cellblock riot or how to rescue a hostage. This craft comes from the experience of seasoned Team members and leaders.

In my many years experience with the Emergency Response Team I have yet to see a Team

Member be officially recognized for an act of courage or heroism.

I have always felt that motivation involves the application of incentives which encourage a certain positive pattern of behaviour and attitude, and contrubutes to the accomplishment of organizational goals. Perhaps now is the time to recognize and honor the efforts of Response Team members for their contribututution as an integral part of the crisis management team.

I am asking you to work with me to recognize the courageous action   these two Officers took  to save the life of Offender▬▬▬▬on that night.

*Dave Woodhouse*

Dave Woodhouse

The above memo to the Deputy Commissioner was never acted upon.

# PART 26

## Riot at Millhaven

> We have had undermanned, professionally inadequate and often exhausted custodial staffs who have spent an unacceptably high proportion of their time presiding over destructive riots and smashups by inmates whom they are neither trained nor motivated to control properly, all at the taxpayer's expense.
>
> —*MacGuigan Report* (1977), paragraph 276

### Prelude to a Riot

It has been my extensive experience as a Team Leader and being tasked to put down many a prison riot that the actual cause of a riot is not what most people expect. Often, it's assumed that the cons riot because they want to draw attention to a grievance or they want better food, better medical care, cable TV, or something tangible. But in my experience, the cons very rarely cause a disturbance with a goal in mind. Often, the riot begins with a couple of cons smashing things up on the range just because they feel like it or because they are drunk, high, or just bored.

When this begins, the other inmates will join in out of loyalty or just for the fun of smashing up. Or some will go quietly into their cells because they don't want any part in what's to come.

The range is locked down to prevent it from spreading and the negotiators are called in to get to the bottom of things. By the time the crisis management machine gets up and running, the cons have had lots of time to decide if they want to continue rioting or go into their cells. If they choose to continue with their party, the negotiators will try to make contact with them. If the cons choose to talk with them, they will be asked what this is all about. More often than not, the rioting inmates don't have an answer to that question. The negotiators will ask them what it will take for them to go quietly into their cells. Now the cons are given an option. Now they have to think about what they would like. Often, they don't have an answer and have to go and ask the other inmates.

It's very fortunate for the staff that the rioting cons don't have a plan. It's usually a spontaneous event, and they have not put any real thought into preparing for their riot.

Preparations include, but are not limited to, gathering food supplies, water, soap, and items useful for barricading the range doors, relocating the hockey, baseball, and weight-lifting equipment from the gym to the cell block to use as weapons and stealing gasoline from the garage for firebombs. Using coat hangers to wire the barred doors shut. Taking hostages. When in full riot, the cons will use the fire hose against staff members who are trying to gain access to the cell block. They will flood the range and then hotwire the metal bar doors with electricity to shock the unlucky guard who touches the door. They also like to set fires.

Often, the Crisis Manager will want the utilities turned off to prevent this from happening. From my experience, I prefer the cons to have their water and power on up to the moment that we are about to enter the cell block in force.

Another advantage of maintaining their water supply is that if their fires get out of hand, they can put it out themselves because very often we can't get into the cell block do it for them.

They are spraying the barriers and windows with high pressure water hoses to keep staff at bay, their music is up to its highest volume, they may still have light if they haven't smashed all the lighting fixtures.

Once the Team is in place, then it's time to cut off all these utilities – suddenly and without warning.

Their music is now off, the lights are out, and their water hoses are useless. In the sudden quiet and darkness, I can make clear my verbal orders over the loudspeaker. Now the Team applies gas if needed and enters the range.

The cons often don't have a Plan B when you do this. They have nothing to fall back on, so it's over for them at that point. They have lost their water and electricity and the team is now through the door. At this point, they very often go into their cells without the Team having to apply any further force to get control of the cell block.

## A Full-on Major Disturbance (Riot)

**"Well, you pick your battles. I was already the pariah for deterring the party."**

On February 11, 1997, the beginnings of a large-scale riot at Millhaven Institution were in the making. The cons in various sections of the prison were involved in setting fires, collecting weapons, threatening staff, and smashing their ranges and cells and causing massive damage to the prison. Water was everywhere as the cons flooded the cells out by smashing their toilets. They smashed through the walls from one cell into another. This went on for days.

Three other Riot Teams within the Ontario Region were called in to augment the one already stationed at the prison. The mission was to get back control of the prison and to transfer the ringleaders and certain participants to a Special Handling Unit in Quebec (the SHU as it was known).

The cell blocks and ranges were littered with broken glass, partially burned bed sheets, mattresses, and cell effects. Food, urine, and feces were tossed out the broken cell windows onto the Ranges.

A number of the inmate ringleaders were identified for transfer and were removed from their cells and placed on a bus with the Riot Team Members present on board for security. We were all escorted to the Ontario Quebec boarder by the Ontario Provincial Police with a helicopter and police dog teams in accompaniment. Upon reaching the Province of Quebec, their provincial police completed the escort to the prison.

Once at the institution, the cons were admitted, and the Riot Teams were free to return to Ontario.

At that point, there was a contingent of guards who decided to remain in Quebec for another day as they wanted to party. Beer was less expensive in Quebec and available at every corner store. I was opposed to this and pointed out that the biggest riot in the prison's history was still going on and to leave the prison without a riot team would be irresponsible of us. Anyway, how could anyone go out to party in Quebec sporting their Riot Team uniforms?

Then they pulled out the Collective Agreement and started quoting that the travel distance exceeded the maximum number of kilometers traveled in one day and that they were entitled, by this agreement, to remain there in a hotel overnight at the government's expense. They could get their beer at any corner store in Quebec and party at the hotel without worrying about being out in their riot uniforms in public.

It came down to a show of hands. Some chose to remain and others to return. The overall supervisor consented to a stop to pick up beer as to cushion the blow of those missing out on the party. Well, you pick your battles. I was already the pariah for deterring the party.

On the way back home along Highway 401, one of the team members decided to give the bus driver a beer. Bad enough to offer it to him as he's driving along a series 400 highway with a bus full of Peace Officers, but the driver took it.

When they passed him a second one, I took it away from him. So twice in one night I'm the asshole. I wondered at the judgment of the bus driver drinking beer as he was driving down the 401. Here you have a person who is dependent on their driver's licence to make his living and is risking that as well as the lives of his passengers and others on the highway by sucking down a beer while driving down one of Canada's busiest major highways.

## Major Disturbance Investigation

The use of additional Riot Team members from other prisons continued at Millhaven for a few days after the major disturbance (riot). When it was all over, the Warden convened an investigation in accordance with policy after a major disturbance.

The team tasked to do the investigation really gave me the third degree for my alleged actions the night after the interprovincial transfer took place. According to their accusations and the video evidence that the investigators had, I had assaulted a con.

### "Irrefutable video recorded evidence."

They really worked me over as being the Team Leader and not setting an example for the other team members, using words like 'disgraceful' and 'criminal' and 'suspension'. I sat and listened to their accusations and when they were finished, I told them that I wasn't even there on the night this incident took place.

That got them really fired up. They had the videotaped evidence of me. They set up the video, and I watched it with them. They pointed me out and identified me by the #1 on my riot helmet, stabbing their fingers at the image on the screen repeatedly. How could I deny my guilt when confronted with such irrefutable evidence?

I asked them to take a close look at the Riot Team member in question with the #1 on his helmet and then take a close look at me. The guard in the video was much larger and heavier than I with a great beer gut hanging out over his belt. I got up and left, leaving them to ponder that bit of factual "irrefutable evidence".

I noticed that one of the investigators was a supervisor who was present during the riot and actively involved in the decision-making on that night. It was clearly a conflict of interest according to policy, but he was their safety net, in place to make sure that the investigation went the way CSC wanted it to.

After interviewing a few more people, it was determined that some of the former Riot Team Members took it upon themselves to hop onto the overtime gravy train, don some Riot Team Member uniforms and go off to Millhaven without permission.

The term "riot", as defined by section 64 of the *Criminal Code,* is "an unlawful assembly that has begun to disturb the peace tumultuously."

The CSC at all levels of management are very reluctant to use the term "riot". They prefer to use softer terms like "isolated incident" or "localized disturbance" or "contained incident". Harsh words like Hostage Taking and Riot carry great weight within the CSC because they are terms to avoid. Even though the word Riot is clearly defined by Canadian law in the *Criminal Code* they prefer to use other less violent terms to describe the same thing.

This is not done by accident.

It has to do with the image that the CSC presents to the Canadian public and, more importantly, it has to do with money.

## Performance Bonuses vs. Sensational Incidents

Federal government executives have a bonus system based upon their performance objectives. This money is a part of their annual income and is awarded in degrees of percentage based on whether the manager met their performance objectives outlined for the year. The maximum percentage will be awarded to the manager who exceeded their performance standards rather than the one who simply meets them or falls below those expectations.

This performance bonus plays a big part in the executive's long-term retirement income because it is included in their five best years of income over their entire career. This five-year figure is what their retirement pensions will be calculated on. So, some managers have a vested interest in making sure that their performance standards are at least met at whatever the cost may be to others.

If you label a full-blown riot, as defined by Canadian law, as an "isolated incident" or a "minor or major disturbance", "a contained incident" then everyone on the prison executive looks good, and they all go home with their annual bonus. The definition of a riot under Canadian law is very different than the spin that some of the CSC managers put on it for their own benefit.

This is why the prison management team did whatever they could to keep down overtime costs. They want to come in under their budget in order to meet their performance objectives thus making themselves more money.

This bending of the law, this defining of the law by CSC managers has been going on for years. Although when their definition finally conflicts with the letter of the law as it is written in the *Criminal Code* it usually means a "Sensational Incident" has taken place. A "Sensational Incident" is something that has happened inside the walls of the prison that can no longer be contained by the label and spin that CSC bestows upon it to keep it hidden and to avoid calling it what it is. It has gone beyond the walls and into the criminal courts or to a Coroner's Jury.

The very first verdict of murder in the history of a Coroner's Inquest in Canada was returned against CSC in the death of Ashley Smith. The legal representatives for the CSC were striving for a verdict of death by misadventure or suicide to get their decision-makers off the hook rather than the precedent-making return of "murder".

I wonder – did the Grand Valley Management Team get their annual performance bonus that year?

# PART 27

## Incident at Kingston Penitentiary

"Deplorable defensive culture. Too often the approach was to deny error, defend against criticism, and to react without proper investigation of the truth."

—Arbour Commission Report (1996)

Here is an example to reinforce this scathing quote from Madam Justice Arbour.

On February 17, 1997, at 14:00 hrs, the Collins Bay Emergency Response Team was activated for the purpose of conducting an involuntary transfer of a con from Collins Bay to Kingston Penitentiary (KP). I was the Team Leader.

Once at KP, we were asked by the prison management team at the prison to escort an offender from the Segregation Unit to the Regional Treatment Centre (RTC). RTC is located within the walls of KP. The cell extraction and escort went without incident.

At the request of a KP Unit Manager, we remained at the prison. They had some security concerns and might require our assistance. At the time, the KP IERT Team was away from their institution on training, so this is why the CBI Team was being used.

At 18:00 hrs, I was instructed by the Crisis Managers to remove a con from his cell on the range and place him in the Segregation Unit. We performed the cell extraction and were required to use Chemical Mace on the con as he refused to co-operate and actively fought against the Team Members. He covered his face with plastic in an attempt to defeat the Mace. He tried to decontaminate himself by using the water in his toilet bowl, and he tried to attack the Team Members when they entered his cell. He was taken to Segregation, decontaminated, and placed into a cell there.

We were then contacted by the shift supervisor at Collins Bay telling us that we were required back at our own prison for some trouble they were now having. When we got back, we removed another CBI con and took him to the hospital at KP.

While back at KP again, we were instructed to return to the Segregation Unit to remove the KP con we had just placed there from our previous cell extraction. The Segregation staff had removed his handcuffs, and he was making a noose to try to do himself some harm.

Prior to positioning the Team for the cell extraction, we were given our instructions from the Acting Correctional Supervisor now acting as the Crisis Manager. Over the course of his instructions to us, he began referring to the inmate as a "N****r" on camera and with many witnesses present. And how we should "tune up this N****r" for acting out twice today.

These instructions from the supervisor were all videotaped as per the *Commissioner's Directives.* I leaned back out of the camera frame and began to make slashing motions across my throat and pressing my finger to my lips trying to get him to stop. He continued with his racist comments though.

When the instructions were over and the camera was turned off, I asked him, "What do you think you're doing talking like that?"

He told me, "I don't give a fuck."

So, we went in and took the noose away from the con. He was compliant and so we had no use of force issues to deal with concerning him. He was placed back in the cell and the team withdrew.

KP staff members were watching him on the video monitor in his cell and saw him making a show of holding up something to the camera too small to see on the monitor. Then he made slashing motions across his wrist with the object. I turned to a staff member who was earlier identified as "doctor".

I asked him how he wanted to proceed with the inmate. Did he want us to place him in a four-point restraint, Posey Body Belt or escort him to the Regional Treatment Centre for more intense observation? I was looking for direction on how to proceed with this inmate and his single-minded determination to harm himself. The only intervention strategy the doctor advised was placing him on suicide watch.

We entered the cell and took away a straightened staple that he was using to try to harm himself. As the team left the Segregation Range, the video recording officer remained outside the con's cell, still filming him.

This was the end of our involvement in IERT activity while at KP.

All interaction with this con and the CBI IERT Team were video recorded, and the reports were submitted in full before the end of the day.

But for the racist comments made by the Kingston Penitentiary Acting Supervisor, this was a non-issue IERT intervention.

The cell extractions performed by the Collins Bay Institution that day were all routine. No inmates, staff, or team members were injured. Every action with respect to IERT deployment and use of force was completely and professionally executed and all documents submitted in full and on time.

Then, on February 19, I began to receive email requests from managers at Kingston Penitentiary about the cell extractions we performed for them on February 17.

March 3, 1997:

More and more questions and opinions arrived via email from the managers at KP. Unsolicited opinions and armchair quarterback criticism from people who have never done the job and were clearly fishing for something – anything.

I still didn't know what this was all about, and they were not about to tell me the intent of their queries. The Management Team at Kingston Penitentiary even had their own Response Team Members review the videotapes of the Collins Bay Team's cell extractions in order to critique our work that day. This had never been done before in the history of the IERT. Would a CSC manager go behind the back of another CSC manager to have their work scrutinized by their peers? Probably.

I answered all their questions in a three-page report and referred them many times to the video recordings and the detailed Plan of Action and Use of Force reports that were submitted while we were at KP.

But the questions kept coming, and I didn't know why as this was very much out of the ordinary. They seemed to be digging, looking for something without being specific as to just what they wanted.

I finally asked if this was part of a fact-finding that I was not made aware of. I was told that it was not, but my years of experience told me differently. I knew I was being lied to and the streams of email evidence suggested that the KP Managers were casting a large net trying to catch someone up in it.

Then the bombshell came.

**"As usual, and against all policy, the request was flatly refused at all levels, so I had to pay my fee and go through Access to Information to see these recordings."**

An eight-page investigation report (File#1382-4) was completed and sent to the Deputy Warden of Kingston Penitentiary from the Regional IERT Trainer as per her request. The report went into great depth about the videotaping of the events, the way the Team Leader gave his verbal orders to the inmate, the way the Team Leader was dressed, the handcuffing technique used by the Team Leader, the strip search conducted by the Team, the video camera battery running down and on and on …

Smelling a rat, I requested to see this report and all the video recordings of the IERT actions conducted by the Collins Bay Team while at KP that day. Of course, as usual and against all policy, the request was flatly refused at all levels, so I had to pay my fee and go through Access to Information to see these recordings even though:

*Commissioner's Directive 060*
*Protection and Sharing of Information*

Infractions:

d. Fail to disclose, where appropriate, any information which they have an obligation to share.

Months later, myself and the Team Members who were present that day at Kingston Penitentiary were asked to attend the Regional Correctional Staff College to view the tapes. We were escorted into a small, secluded storage room off the gym by the Regional IERT Trainer. There was a TV and videotape player on a portable stand placed in the storage room for us to view the tapes.

The door was closed, and we were all crammed together shoulder to shoulder into this small room standing around the TV. We watched all the cell extractions and could still not see what the KP Managers were looking at to cause them so much concern with the Collins Bay Response Team. The supervisor calling the con the N-word was on the tape but that was no surprise to us as we all witnessed that event.

Finally, at the end of the last tape, after the IERT Team had moved off of the range and with the camera still recording at the con's cell door in Segregation we saw what all of the secrecy and attempted diversion was about.

A KP guard was standing in front of the cell door and the con was swearing at him. Suddenly, the guard exploded at him in a long-winded retort. We thought the supervisor's racist language was bad, but it had nothing on this guy.

Each sentence began with the N-word and ended with it. It just kept going on and on. It ended only when the camera stopped recording because the battery died. Our Team was not witness to this and was not even present on the Range when it happened. Upon hearing and seeing the video recording of the guard's racial outburst, myself and my Team Members recoiled physically from the monitor.

We were shocked.

The Trainer just hung his head. This was the Regional IERT Trainer who completed the report requested by the deputy warden at KP. In his report there was only a small and vague reference on page five to these grossly offensive racial statements uttered by the KP staff that stated: *"Background language/comments were not made by the CBI IERT team and cannot be expected to be controlled by them."* This was the only reference in the entire official investigation report to the racial name-calling by the KP Supervisor and the guard.

In this case, you had a manager and a guard throwing around racist insults about an inmate while being recorded on videotape. The KP Management staff closed its ranks and tried to divert attention away from their own racist staff members and put it on to the Collins Bay Emergency Response Team for the work they did for them that day.

It was obvious to anyone in possession of the full facts in issue that it was not what the CBI ERT Team Leader was wearing that day that was the cause for their covert investigation.

In that entire eight-page report, there was no mention of the Kingston Penitentiary racist Acting Correctional Supervisor and the racist guard calling the con the N-word repeatedly.

I was the lowest ranking officer involved that day, so I was the target of their attempt to cover up and divert the attention away from their own staff member and their own manager. I was forced to protect myself and my Team from the path of the bus that we were shoved under by the Senior Management Team at Kingston Penitentiary.

The Acting Correctional Supervisor at KP who was recorded on video calling the inmate the N-word was promoted to a full Correctional Supervisor and transferred to Collins Bay Institution shortly after that incident. Soon after his promotion and transfer, he received an Exemplary Service Medal because the CSC "recognizes employees of the Canadian Correctional Service who have served in an exemplary manner, characterized by good conduct."

About a year after arriving at CBI, he was transferred yet again to another maximum-security prison within the region. He retired from there with his medal and a full pension. Yet before he left Collins Bay, he managed to do even more damage.

The Deputy Warden of Kingston Penitentiary who initiated the investigation was also transferred to Collins Bay Institution soon after that incident.

The frontline guard at KP who also called the inmate the N-word while being recorded on videotape was given a "no inmate contact" post checking the vehicles that come into the prison. Straight days, weekends off, and no reduction in rank or pay level.

As usual, when things go wrong, the first step is to close ranks and protect the managers while offering up the heads of the lowest ranking officers involved using whatever underhanded means they can muster to achieve that goal. Many of the low-ranking staff members who are victims of this kind of systemic corruption do not even try to defend themselves from it. They do this out of fear of their supervisors and managers and the reprisals that will come back at them. They also know full well that regardless of the evidence in their favour, they are not going to be treated with even a modicum of fairness.

In all the internal investigations and fact-findings conducted by Managers of the CSC that I have ever read, there was nothing in any of those reports that even remotely suggested any acts of wrongdoing by a Correctional Service of Canada manager at any level.

# PART 28

## Murder in the Kitchen

> "Staff involved indicated that the inmates were applying
> appropriate first aid."
>
> —Board of Investigation Report[28]

The last time I saw an offender die from stab wounds, was in the prison
kitchen at Collins Bay on May 1, 1999. The victim worked on the food
line and an argument took place over an egg. It cost him his life.

I was working in 4 Block located just across the Strip from the main
kitchen entrance. Four Block A-range is where the inmates who worked
in the kitchen all lived. Because 4 Block had solid metal doors rather than
open metal bar doors, each one could be unlocked with a key rather than
having to spin the locking wheel to open up as was done in 1 Block and
2 Block. Also, the kitchen inmates had to go to work earlier than the rest
of the prison population, and it was much easier to release them from just
one cell block rather than many.

I was sitting in an alcove that jutted out onto the Strip so I could
observe inmate movement on that corridor and watch the meal parade.
Not many cons were in the queue for breakfast as it was a Sunday morning,

---

[28] Dated: 2000/07/05, File #1410-2-393, page iv.

and they prefer to sleep in on weekends unless bacon is being served on the line. There is an officer stationed at the end of the strip where the cons enter the dining hall, and their job is to monitor the meal parade. Usually, it's quiet on the weekend mornings but today there was suddenly a lot of noise coming from the main kitchen and the Kitchen Riot Alarm was activated at 08:08. You expect the sounds of pots and pans falling to the floor and loud voices but today was different; there was an uncharacteristic urgency to the voices.

I picked up the radio with the intention of going over to check it out. Just as I approached the door, I heard a broadcast from an officer in the kitchen saying that someone had been stabbed.

I reached down to the electronic control panel and secured the metal barriers to both the ranges in 4 Block and then to the barrier across the Strip to prevent any movement. I crossed the hall to the main kitchen door. These actions locked me inside with all the cons. Once again, I found myself locked inside the prison kitchen, greatly outnumbered by the inmates, with several large knives out in the open.

But I was always one of the officers who went toward the trouble rather than in the opposite direction. One of the Food Service officers let me into the kitchen proper. As I approached the food preparation area, I saw a con I'd known for several years being supported upright by two other offenders.

He was clutching his hands to his throat with a look of terror on his face. His mouth was open and gasping for air like a fish out of water. There was a white towel wrapped around his neck that was covered in blood. He was drenched in blood from his neck down to his pants. All the other cons who worked in the kitchen were running around in a panic; some were trying to get out.

I radioed for an ambulance. Then I asked one of the Food Service officers "Who did this?" He pointed to an offender standing in front of a large floor-mounted kitchen steam kettle. He told me, "He was the one who did it." I asked him what the con's name was and he told me. I walked over to the kettle and noticed a large eight-inch yellow-handled kitchen knife on the table in front of the con. It was still wet from being recently cleaned.

I placed myself between the con and the knife. I asked him his name and he told me. I said, "Looks like we are going to the hole." He said, "Okay, Boss." Then he asked me "Am I going to be charged?" I cautioned him that I didn't know at this time, but it would be best that he does not speak to anyone about what went on here until he got some legal advice. I handcuffed him behind his back and escorted him to the Segregation unit.

## A Very Calm Suspect

Once in segregation, I had him strip down and took all his clothing for evidence. Before searching him, I asked him if he had anything on him as it's best to just give it up to me now because I didn't want any surprises. He told me that he was clean and that he wasn't "packing", meaning carrying a weapon. Considering the amount of blood I saw on the con who was stabbed, there was very little blood on the con I had just arrested.

He had on a white vinyl apron that extended from the top of his chest to just below his knees. The apron was wet like it had just been washed or freshly rinsed. There was some blood on the underside of his right arm and some small drops on his running shoes. I had him hold out his hands with his arms extended fully. I was looking for telltale blood on his hands or under his fingernails. Blood is sticky outside the human body and when it dries out it's tough to wash off especially if you are in a hurry to rid yourself of it as evidence. I was also looking for defensive wounds. His hands were clean of blood but what was most disturbing to me was that they were rock steady as he held them out rigid in front of himself.

You would think that a person suspected of committing a murder just a few moments before, would be a little more pumped up due to the adrenalin rush. Or he would at least show some signs of coming down from that chemical dump and the physical exertion of the act. There was nothing like that from this guy; he was perfectly calm in his demeanor, mentally and physically. I admit in that moment, in light of this behavior, I began to doubt if I had the right guy.

I collected up his clothing in a paper bag with the intention of securing it in an evidence locker and completing an incident report on what I just witnessed. But as I left the Segregation unit, I glanced toward the main entrance of the prison located at the top of the Strip. The victim of the stabbing was on a stretcher with three other cons gathered closely around him. This was a bad scene as these cons were only two doors away from freedom and standing over a man who was just seriously assaulted.

## A Duty to Protect Life

I changed my plans and cleared the cons out of the lobby and away from the victim. I turned and looked down at the injured man and noticed stab wounds on either side of his face along the jawline. There was another at the point of his chin. It struck me that he wasn't bleeding. He was lying face up with his head back, mouth and eyes wide open. He also wasn't breathing.

All that the guards had done for him while standing around was place a pair of leg irons on him. I turned to one of the two guards and asked, "Where is the trauma bag?" If the wounded man was lying on a hospital stretcher there should be a large orange trauma bag available that is normally left right on top of the gurney. I told one of the officers to go and get the bag, as we had to go to work on the inmate right away. He never moved; he just stood there and looked at me. The guards had removed the trauma bag from the gurney and left it behind on the floor of the Institutional hospital.

None of them moved to help. I asked them all, "What do you think you're doing?" They told me they were waiting for the ambulance. They all just stood there watching this guy without lifting a finger to help him. I started to run back down the Strip to get the trauma bag when one of the guards said that the ambulance had arrived.

I rode with the victim in the back of the ambulance and performed CPR on him while the paramedic breathed for him using a resuscitation bag. One of the guards who was standing at the Main Gate post watching it all and doing nothing to help, rode in the front of the ambulance. I witnessed additional stab wounds on the victim's chest. One was mid-thorax above his mediastinum and one just to the right of that at the level of his clavicle.

Once in the Emergency Department at the hospital, the inmate was quickly examined but there was nothing to be done for him at that point.

The bottom line with respect to the duty of a Peace Officer is the preservation of life. This duty was completely ignored by all the guards at the Main Gate that day. Not one of them lifted a finger to provide emergency first aid to the victim.

## Ticking Off the Box – The Post Traumatic Stress Debrief

To demonstrate the profound foolishness of the manager on duty that day, he ordered everyone who was witness to any aspect of the murder to attend a post-traumatic stress debriefing together. After many years of being neglected this was finally made mandatory in the CSC for anyone who has been subjected to intense stress like witnessing a murder. It is supposed to give the staff member the opportunity to express any feelings of trauma they may have experienced over the incident. The supervisor decided that the debriefing would take place en masse rather than, as it is supposed to be conducted, in private with the Institutional Psychologist. In his mind, the debriefing would go faster, and it would not involve the cost of overtime to the service if those involved were debriefed all at the same time.

Everyone involved met in the boardroom on the third floor of the prison with the Institutional Psychologist. Everyone had the opportunity to tell what they experienced that morning. They all stated what they saw and what they did in front of the other witnesses in a round table format. This was done before the staff members had the chance to submit their written reports, or even make any notes on the murder. Witnesses to a murder are not permitted to sit around a table and openly discuss what they saw and what they did in front of the other witnesses before writing their up statement or before being interviewed by the police.

Also, given the kind of poisoned environment that we work in, no one is going to admit experiencing any emotional difficulties about the murder in an open room full of their peers. Any display of weakness voiced by a staff member in that room on that day would be spread around the prison and be used against them by some of their peers the very next day.

This botched PTSD debriefing was cut short as the police wanted to interview the witnesses. But it saved the Institution overtime money and the supervisor got to tick the box on his report saying that all involved had their stress debriefing.

A couple of years later, the accused inmate was tried and convicted of this, his second murder. I had left Corrections by that time and was I working for the Toronto Police Service and had to come back to Kingston to testify at his trail.

All three of the guards who stood and watched the offender die that day have since been promoted and each has been given an Exemplary Service Medal.

One of the guards involved in this sensational incident was later promoted and given charge of all the firearms, ammunition, and chemical agents at a maximum-security institution. This, after having assaulted two separate staff membes and threatened death and bodily harm towards another while at Collins Bay.

When the internal investigation was completed, the only mention of their violation of duty was to state that the con was going to die of his injuries anyway, so it really didn't make any difference that the staff did not provide emergency first aid to him.

Nothing was said to the people who neglected their duty that day and nothing was said to the people who did a good job.

The investigation went on to say that they didn't identify an issue with the cons providing emergency first aid to the mortally wounded inmate. The guards who didn't want to get their hands bloody thought the cons were doing a good job and let them continue. But –

- The guards are the ones who have first aid and CPR training, not the cons.
- It's the guards' duty to protect life, not the cons.
- The guards are the ones being paid to do that job, not the cons
- It is the guards' duty to protect evidence of a murder and not let the inmates tamper with it.

The guards involved in this neglect of duty were not even spoken to about their lack of obligation to human life. This was a very serious violation of their oath toward the preservation of life, yet it meant nothing to them or to the senior management of the prison.

"Of concern was the area of First Aid and CPR. It appeared that the inmates had taken over the administration of First Aid. However, staff involved indicated the inmates were applying appropriate First Aid and as was later discovered, due to the severity of the wounds, any application of First Aid would have been futile".

Board of Investigation Report [29]

I remember the next day, sitting at the morning briefing with the staff and institutional managers, listening to some of the "good guys to have around" boasting of the heroic acts they performed on the day of the murder.

I also remember being the first officer on the scene, arresting the murderer, handcuffing him, and taking him to segregation, searching him to recover evidence of the crime, performing emergency first aid and CPR on the victim, and riding with him in the ambulance while performing chest compressions.

I remember watching him die.

I remember arriving at the hospital only to be ordered to return to the prison immediately by taxi to lead the Emergency Response Team to perform cell extractions and involuntary inmate transfers to a maximum-security prison.

I don't recall any of the "good guys to have around" being anywhere near these events with the exception of them watching safely from behind bullet-proof glass and steel bars in the control centres or standing idly by on the Strip smoking and providing comment on all the action going on around them.

The keeper on duty that day calling the shots was the one formerly from Kingston Penitentiary that had called the inmate a "n****r" while being videotaped.

For me, this Sensational Incident was the last straw. I pictured myself being on the next stretcher, having the guards standing around me not lifting a finger to help, afraid to get their hands bloody, watching me die. I placed into motion the events that would get me out of prison.

---

[29] Executive Summary dated: 2000/07/05 File #1410-2-393, page iv. Performance Assurance Sector, Correctional Service of Canada. Accountability, Integrity, Openness.

# PART 29

## Remembering Tyrone Conn

"His death was a logical consequence of his life."[30]

—Lynden MacIntyre, *Who Killed Ty Conn*

The escape of a notorious con one night from Collins Bay Institution on November 5, 1991, was a prime example of the way in which this system was so corrupted back then.

There was mass publicity generated from Tyrone Conn's escape from Kingston Penitentiary in 1999, but very little was known of his escape from Collins Bay prior to that in 1991.

I had known Tyrone Conn for a few years as he lived in 3 Block, the cell block that I was assigned to. He was a quiet and low-profile con but he had a lengthy history of escape. I got along well with him and indeed liked him. But I also knew his history of ingratiating himself to the staff so he would be permitted freedoms within the prison that should not have been granted to a man with his escape risk history. Again, and not for the last time his method of getting on the good side of staff members would be his foundation for planning and executing successful escapes.

---

[30] Lynden MacIntyre and T. Burke, *Who Killed Ty Conn* (Toronto: Viking Canada, 2000).

He was twenty-four at the time of this escape and had a sentence of seventeen years for armed robbery and use of a firearm to commit and escape lawful custody.

Tyrone Conn put a great deal of planning into his escape from Collins Bay and had used a lookout while he was cutting through the metal bars in the upstairs washroom in 3 Block using a Dremel tool. Yes, cons have Dremel tools for their "hobby craft work".

The noise of this power tool in operation was masked by the lookout using a power sander to strip away the old paint and varnish on the officer's office windows downstairs. This con had "volunteered" to refinish the woodwork in the office for the staff. With the CSC being all about rehabilitation, the con was allowed to do this even though it was totally out of character for him. The communication code between the two of them was that when Tyrone Conn was upstairs cutting the bars and heard the power sanding tool stop running, that was the signal that an officer was going up on a patrol and to stop using his Dremel Tool on the window bars. Tyrone Conn had cut an "X" shaped section out of the window bars and removed any trace of the metal shavings that may have given away his work. The cuts were so precise that you were unable to tell the bars were compromised without actually touching them, as I later found out.

## "All Clear From The Mobile"

On the night of his escape, I arrived for my midnight shift early, and as I was walking into the prison, I noticed that the Mobile Patrol vehicle was parked at the Main Gate entrance. The officer on the mobile post was sitting inside the gate with a coffee in hand and his feet up on a desk. I walked down the Strip to the Keepers Hall just as an alarm sounded on the perimeter fence atop of the West Wall also known as Sector #9.

The guard on mobile patrol radioed "all clear from the mobile". This officer, who was supposed to be in the vehicle, was still sitting on his ass at the Main Gate with a coffee in his hand and lied about it being "all clear". He was supposed to be in the vehicle for the duration of his shift until relieved by the officer on the midnight shift. He was not on his assigned post during the escape. Had he been doing the minimum of his job he could have prevented this escape. He simply looked out the window of the Main Gate at that portion of the wall identified by the alarm and thought this effort was good enough.

The officer in the Southwest Tower, overlooking the area on the wall where the alarm was activated asked over the radio, "Did some in the construction crew leave a ladder against the wall?"

The supervisor looked at me. I looked at him.

I got up, grabbed a radio, and ran up toward the Main Gate and the exit to the West Yard. I found a homemade ladder against the West wall (Sector 9) across from the family visiting trailers. I removed the ladder from the wall.

The escaping inmate had placed his ladder directly under a burned-out light on the top of the wall. That broken light was reported to the security office over four months prior to his escape and was not replaced until the day after he went over the wall.

The ladder that Conn used was constructed using the support brackets from several of the metal shelves that are located in the cleaner's closet on the ranges. Conn had removed the rear support brackets from the storage shelves and then secured the shelves themselves directly to the wall with screws to support them. That way, no one would know that the rear vertical supports were missing. Because of the con job that he did on the staff members, he was rarely searched or even suspected so he was able to move these metre-long metal supports around the Institution and locate them in strategic places ready to be assembled into his ladder.

To gather the length he needed to get over the wall, he took two rear vertical supports from several different shelves located in other cell blocks. For ladder rungs, Conn used pre-cut sections of scrap oak lumber that were used to make government office furniture. The scrap lumber was discarded in the hopper behind the woodworking shop. Holes were drilled into the oak ladder rungs using a stolen cordless drill and then the rungs were bolted onto the vertical supports. In addition, Conn added a standoff extension at the top of the ladder so that it would stand out a couple of feet from the top of the wall to avoid the sensors located there, thus not activating the alarm until he was actually on the top of the wall. I found the drill, extra pre-drilled oak rungs and the box of bolts and nuts outside of his cell block in a gym bag.

Once atop the wall, he used a length of electrical extension cord to lower himself down the other side to freedom. He put his extension cord to two uses. He initially used it to climb down from the second-floor cell block washroom window where he had cut through the bars. He looped the cord through the bars and hung on just outside the window. While hanging there, he replaced the "X" shaped section of the bars he had cut out back into the window frame. He then lowered himself down and simply pulled the cord through the bars after him. The cord was used once again to climb down from the top of the West wall.

Exterior view of 3 Block

The cord was left behind, dangling on the outside of the West wall.

Once the escape was discovered, the mobile officer got off his ass and actually drove by Tyrone Conn as he lay down hiding on the ground at the bottom of the outside of the wall. The guard did not see him lying on the ground and he did not see the extension cord still hanging from the top of the wall as he drove by. Once again, the Mobile Patrol guard stated over the radio that this section of wall was clear. Conn got up on his feet once the patrol vehicle had passed and ran across Bath Road at the front of the prison and then behind some retail stores on the north side directly across from the prison. He then followed the railroad tracks running east and west to get to where he wanted to go. It was reported by the investigation team that they suspected someone had picked him up in a vehicle at a prearranged meeting place.

## Gone Fishing

In searching his cell after all the excitement died down, I found a book about cold weather survival, and on his calendar for that date he had written "gone fishing".

Prior to his escape, he had spent a few days in one of the family visiting trailers by himself. Some select cons were permitted to stay in the trailers by themselves. They called that a "solo" trailer visit. It remains a mystery to this day as to who granted a high escape risk inmate like Tyrone Conn time in the trailer by himself. This was not something examined in the internal investigation.

It was there that he got down the routine of the night patrols in the yard and the fact that the light on top of the wall was burned out. The ladder was placed directly under this light fixture, which was located directly across from the very trailer he stayed in.

## No Firearm State of Readiness

In the meantime, another officer entered the Main Gate Control Post and reported to me that he saw the escaping inmate running north across Bath Road as he was driving in for work. As both mobile vehicles were being used, I got into a private vehicle with another officer and searched for the con as instructed in the Escape Plan located at the Main Gate Control Centre. This action was sanctioned by the Keeper via a radio broadcast. We had a revolver and a 12-gauge shotgun, which we obtained from a sealed cabinet at the Main Gate.

The cabinet was locked with a heavy plastic numbered seal to prevent people from tampering with the firearms inside it. These weapons and ammunition were supposed to be in a state of readiness to deploy in just such an emergency. On this night, these weapons were not in a state of readiness.

After searching the perimeter for a short time, we came back to the Main Gate Control Centre to return the weapons. I set down the shotgun on the counter after unloading it and the barrel fell off. The magazine cap that secures the barrel was missing. It was found on the floor in the vehicle that we were using. It was not properly attached to the gun in the first place.

Firearms are supposed to be inspected and maintained for readiness in emergencies. This was often not the case at that time in history because the institutional security equipment maintenance officer was not the most diligent in his duties. This was the same person who kept the stockpile of useless, expired chemical agents that failed to detonate when we deployed them in a riot.

## Suddenly, A New Escape Plan Appears

There is a sealed envelope at the main gate that is only to be opened when an escape is in progress. It is the Contingency Plan that instructs the officers on how and where to deploy resources during an escape. Oddly enough it's called the "Contingency Plan Escape Plan". I had asked the Correctional Supervisor over the radio, "Has the escape plan been activated?" He replied that it was.

Knowing just how the Correctional Service of Canada operates, I photocopied that "escape plan" after the dust settled that night. I had learned many years ago that this is what you have to do to in order to protect yourself from the corruption in the Corruptional Service of Canada.

The next day, I noticed that the Escape Plan at the Main Gate was now contained in a nice new, clean envelope, not the beat up one from the night before.

It was a good thing I had copied the original plan on the night of Tyrone Conns' escape because overnight, the plan that was acted upon by officers performing their lawful duty during the escape, was removed and a back-dated and modified replacement plan was substituted in order to cover up the criminal acts of a manager on duty that night.

The replacement plan was quite different than the original one and implicated a number of frontline officers for not following the plan the way it instructed them to.

This new replacement plan failed to have the signature of the current Warden at the bottom of the document. In fact, the new plan had no authorization signature affixed to it at all. The plan that I had in my possession, and acted upon the night of the escape, was dated 1987/88 and signed by the Warden of that period in time.

> **"Destroying evidence relating to an escape from a federal prison is a Criminal Act."**

There had been a recent escape in the same year just months prior to that of Inmate Conn's. An inmate by the name of Woods went over the wall. The investigation team looking into the Woods escape was asking why the Contingency Plans and the Escape Plans were so out of date. The outdated plans had been identified and reported to the Collins Bay management team long before Conn's escape. But the plan was never updated until after the dust settled on the very night Tyrone Conn went over the wall. The management team had been caught once already having an outdated Escape Plan and they did not intend for it to happen again, so it was quickly replaced before the investigation team arrived and examined it.

## Disappearing Evidence

The Institutional Senior Duty Officer was called into the prison on the night of the escape. The Regional Headquarters Duty Officer instructed the Senior Duty Officer at Collins Bay to "confiscate all tapes" as per CSC Policy. The voice recording tape that copies all radio transmissions was removed by the Correctional Supervisor on duty that night a full half-hour before the Institutional Senior Duty Officer arrived to do so. This voice recording tape was cut from its' spools and destroyed.

A half hour later, the Senior Duty Officer removed only one videotape from Monitor #1. There are four monitors with a designated videotape for each. The remaining three videotapes of the actual escape were not seized as evidence and were subsequently taped over… erased, destroyed.

The continuity of documents and recordings are to be safeguarded to ensure that the courts and the decision-makers have the best evidence possible at their disposal. CSC policy at that time was in place for the proper disposition of documents and evidence relating to an escape and other serious matters in the institutions. But in this case, you had a public servant, acting in an official capacity that night, who breached the standard of responsibility expected, in a marked departure from the norm and contrary to the public good.

## Management Coverup

A few days later, when the two investigators arrived to interview the officers about their actions on the night of the escape, I brought in my copy of the original Escape Plan in an envelope and placed it on the table in front of the investigation team.

The investigators began to accuse me and some of the other officers of not following the instructions contained in the bogus replacement plan. I then opened up the envelope, brought out the original plan from the night of the escape, the plan that was actioned on that night, and I advised them of the coverup.

The investigators never even considered the condition of the envelope that contained the bogus Escape Plan that they were handed when they requested it. It was in a brand new, pristine condition envelope without the wear and tear associated with being on a post, unopened for years.

The envelope containing the original unaltered orders was torn and repaired with tape. It had coffee stains on it and rips from being on the post for years. Yet they never questioned that.

**"The video tapes from the four (4) monitors were not seized in accordance with policy, as only the tape from Monitor Number 1 was seized. There is no logical explanation except lack of knowledge of policy or forgetfulness. *quoted from the report*"**

No investigation into who had replaced the original plan, the plan that was actioned on the night of the escape, was ever conducted or even considered. The list of suspects went too high up the Management Team ladder.

The resulting investigation report stated that they could not understand why the supervisor erased the recorded evidence relating to a prison escape other than maybe he was not trained in the proper recovery of this evidence. The following quote is from the investigation report:

But if you examine the orders, it will show that the only person authorized to remove these tapes is the "Senior Duty Officer". This order is in place to prevent criminal acts such as this from occurring.

The Correctional Supervisor on duty that night had no authority to do anything with those recordings. But he had to erase them to cover his actions of that night. Destroying evidence relating to an escape from a federal prison is a Criminal Act. Yet no criminal charges were forthcoming for this supervisor and the Pen Squad was not even informed that this took place.

This is how the CSC covers up and explains away the criminal acts of their managers.

## Turning a Blind Eye

They never turned their investigation toward discovering whoever replaced the original plan with their inept coverup plan. But it wasn't so inept in that it did accomplish their intent: that of focusing the investigation upon the actions of the lowest ranking officers on duty that night and taking the spotlight away from their managers and their actions on the night of the escape.

Nothing was mentioned in the investigation about how and where Conn got the battery-powered drill and ladder components. Nothing was said about why he was permitted solo time in a private family visiting unit and who authorized that stay, taking into consideration his history of escaping from prison.

As a result of the coverup, several officers were charged internally because shit flows downhill. No one above the level of junior supervisor was implicated in any wrongdoing, including the officer in charge that night who committed the criminal act of destroying the recorded evidence of the escape.

I was one of two officers who, acting upon the authority of the "escape plan", and *with permission* from the supervisor, pursued the escaping inmate off the property after getting a report of him being seen running north across the road from the prison as was our duty. Yet we were charged internally for abandoning our posts and leaving the property in pursuit of the escaping con. We were, in fact, disciplined for doing our lawful duty according to CSC Policy contained in the "Escape Plan" and the *Criminal Code* of Canada with respect to prisoner escape.

Further, we did not "abandon their posts" as we were accused, because we had just arrived at the institution for our midnight shift and were not even assigned to our posts yet.

## ATIP Request to See Investigation Report

The CSC Senior Management Team would not release the final internal investigation report or the one remaining videotape or the remaining remnant of the audio recordings that were not destroyed by the Keeper that night. The officers who were accused wanted to use that evidence in their defense. So, we all had to go through Access to Information (ATIP) to see it.

It has been my lengthy experience that the first approach the CSC uses is outright denial of access to General Security Investigation reports, even though there may be one sitting in the institution at the time and even though it is the right of the subject officer of the report to see the entire unvetted content of that report. And even though it's their duty to provide it upon request, this was just not done. So, we had to make a formal ATIP application to and await the production and vetting of this document. Sometimes this can take months.

We had no idea at that time that tapes had been deliberately destroyed. This information was well guarded and had it not been for our formal request through Access to Information we would never have known the machinations that the Collins Bay Institution Management Team went through to cover for one of their own.

## No Postponement While Waiting

On November 26, 1991, the unit manager from three block who conducted the fact-finding for the officer's disciplinary action refused to postpone that inquiry to await the release of the new intentionally undisclosed evidence because, "I have to wrap up my investigation before my transfer to the Prison for Woman."

As a matter of fact, the Unit Manager from 4 Block did postpone the disciplinary fact-finding for another officer involved in the same escape, to await the examination of the same evidence that we were all relying upon for our vindication. Our manager told us that he had examined the tape recording himself and admitted that it was incomplete.

We were denied our right to fair and equal treatment with respect to this sham of an investigation conducted by a manager who had already determined the outcome before examining the facts in evidence.

Months later, after making a formal written request through Access to Information and paying for that service, we finally got the opportunity to view the partial remaining videotape and to hear the partial radio transmission that it contained. They were mostly blank. We sat in an office with

> **"We sat in an office with a low -level manager as we listened to the salvaged remnants of the recordings, the manager just sat there with his head down."**

a low-level manager while we listened to the salvaged remnants of the recordings, the manager just sat there with his head down.

The Management Team at Collins Bay Institution and the Investigaton team did not tell the officers that the electronic evidence had been deliberately destroyed. Yet they proceeded in charging officers internally, based upon accusations and statements from the very supervisor who erased the tapes and based upon a very questionable internal investigation.

I told him that in light of this deliberately undisclosed evidence, the letters of discipline on the officer's files would now be removed.

He told me "No, that would not be happening."

So, as the lowest ranking officers involved, we were looking at the undercarriage of the bus once again.

*Commissioner's Directive 060*
*Protection and Sharing of Information*

An employee has committed an infraction, if they:

a.  fail to properly safeguard all documents, reports, directives, manuals, or other information of the Service

As well, the *Criminal Code* of Canada sec:25 (1) states that

"Everyone who is required or authorized by law to do anything in the administration or enforcement of the law (c) as a peace officer or public officer is, if he acts on reasonable grounds, justified in doing what he is required or authorized to do and in using as much force as necessary for that purpose." This includes taking action to capture an escaping inmate from a prison.

CSC Management did not appear to even know that this section of the *Criminal Code* existed or, if they did, they chose to ignore it.

## The Facts Speak for Themselves

The investigators tried to go after the officer in the Southwest Tower for not being observant and allowing the con to get as far as he did. But I had kept the report that I had written several months earlier stating that the lights on the West wall, where the con had set up his homemade ladder, were burned out. The broken light produced a blackout area directly under where he placed his ladder. The lights were repaired the day after the escape and before the investigating team arrived at the prison. The original report mysteriously went missing but I had kept a copy of that report and produced it as evidence, and that got the Tower Guard off the hook.

On the night of the escape, I was involved in a search performed on the cell block where Tyrone Conn lived. A homemade tool in the form of a wrench used for removing the bolts that secured the shelving units that he used to construct his ladder was found hidden in a cleaning closet on his range.

Conn had been issued a pass, which enabled him access to almost all areas of the institution despite his previous escape from other facilities and the recent escape from his Escorted Temporary Absence. With this pass, he was able to collect the material required to construct his ladder, steal a long extension cord, battery-powered drill, wooden ladder slats, nuts and bolts, vice grips, tape, and gloves without having to rely on other inmates to assist him in gathering his escape equipment, nor having to rely upon them to keep their mouths shut. None of the equipment he used was reported missing by the shops he took them from. The guards who worked in the cell block that he escaped from were not doing their security inspections of the window bars on the range.

From the Investigation Report:

> *There were suspicions about Conn's planned escape, but they were never shared with the Security Staff. There was never any follow-up with Unit Staff to suggest that Conn be watched more closely. Unfortunately, the information held by few, was not communicated effectively to staff with a need to know so that Conn could have been monitored more effectively.*

In the October 6, 1999, Security Investigation Report into Conn's escape from Kingston Penitentiary, many of these same issues were present and identified as contributing factors in his escape from KP.

Security Investigation #1410-2-395 stated:

> *Steps were taken by the Deputy Warden and the IPSO (Institutional Preventive Security Officer) to make staff aware of the risk posed by Conn in the form of shift briefings. The majority of staff interviewed claimed to have no knowledge of this risk posed by Conn or that any briefing specific to him had taken place.*

*It was clear to the Board of Investigation that middle managers spend little time in the Units with staff. Therefore, little is done to ensure that policies and procedures are implemented and carried out in a consistent manner.*

In the escape of offender Wood from Collins Bay, security issues were also identified and reported by the investigators, yet these recommendations were not acted upon. It is clear that some of these neglected issues contributed to the successful escape of inmate Tyrone Conn when his time came to get out of Collins Bay.

Many of these same security and information management issues were identified and reported in Conn's escape from Kingston Penitentiary. Tyrone Conn used the exact same methods as he had used in his past escapes. So, from Wood's escape to Conn's escapes (x2) nothing substantive was done by the CSC to prevent him from doing it over and over again.

While at Kingston Penitentiary in 1998, it was determined that Conn and two other offenders were planning escape and he was segregated to prevent that. He attempted to have a letter smuggled out of the prison by another inmate, addressed to his stepbrother, stating his intentions to escape.

He asked an ex-con in the community to send him maps of downtown Kingston, specifically the areas around the prison. He was able, once again, to obtain employment within the prison that gave him the freedom to go almost anywhere he chose to. He once again ingratiated himself to the staff members so they would let their guard down to his advantage.

He admitted to making what he described as a bulletproof vest using canvas from the shop he worked in, by sewing pouches in the vest and placing metal plates inside them. This was done in case he was spotted by a Tower guard and fired upon.

While at KP, Conn once again secured for himself all the equipment and freedom he required to make a successful bid for the wall.

Yet with all of these pre-indicating factors and more, the Management Team at KP still failed to take the steps required to prevent Conn's escape from this, a Maximum-Security Prison.

The CSC has a long and dismal reputation of not being able to learn from its history.

## What Happened to...

What happened to the Mobile Patrol guard, who was not on his post in the crucial seconds of the escape, sitting on his ass at the main gate. Then reporting over the radio that the section of the wall was clear even though he hadn't moved from the gate. Then, when he did get up and into the mobile patrol vehicle, he drove right past Tyrone Conn in the very act of escaping. He didn't even see the long extension cord dangling off the wall or the inmate laying on the ground as he drove by. Then reporting once again over the radio that all was clear. Nothing happened to this guard at that time... but, he was promoted to supervisor shortly after.

What about the indifferent security maintenance officer who couldn't be bothered to properly maintain the firearms or the chemical agents in a secured locker? He was never even interviewed by the Investigation Team.

What about the guard in the Main Control Centre who was supposed to be watching the monitors and did not acknowledge the fence alarm until 26 seconds after it was activated? He was off of his post, sitting up at the Main Gate having coffee with the rest of the guards and not even present in the Control Centre watching the monitors, as was his responsibility, when Conn went over the wall.

What about the person unknown who replaced the outdated escape plans at the Main Gate with augmented, unsigned, bogus backdated new ones written the day after the escape?

What happened to the supervisor who deliberately destroyed evidence related to this Criminal offence?

The list goes on...

Tyrone "Ty" Conn escaped from Collins Bay Institution that night and made his way to Ottawa to rob a bank and discharge a firearm.

He eventually surrendered to police, was charged and convicted once again, sent to Millhaven Maximum Penitentiary, then on to Kingston Penitentiary Maximum Security and escaped from there using the exact same *modus operandi* he used to escape from Collins Bay Institution. Yet no one seemed to notice that he was ramping up once again, using the same methods as he did in the recent past for escaping his prison. He was finally located in Toronto in a dingy basement apartment, surrounded by police, and turned a gun on himself and fired rather than return to prison.

The Correctional Service of Canada spent more effort trying to cover up their illegal and corrupt actions than to manage the workplace in a responsible ethical manner according to the law, their own Commissioners Directives and Core Values Statements. The Correctional Service of Canada does not learn from its past mistakes. This is their lengthy and humiliating legacy to the Public Service and to the people of Canada.

After learning the true facts of what happened to the voice and video recorded evidence of the Conn escape, I regrouped and gathered all the true, factual evidence into one rather large package and approached the Acting Warden with an appeal to have the disciplinary actions removed from the files of the officers who did their duty according to law and CSC Policy that night.

Below is the wording contained in the memo addressed to National Headquarters:

March 20, 1992

Memorandum File 3100-4 from the Acting Warden Collins Bay Institution to National Headquarters, Ottawa Ontario.

Security Investigation – Inmate Conn Escape

1. Attached you will find a memorandum in respect of Correctional Officer D. Woodhouse.
2. The portion of the inquiry pertaining to Mr. Woodhouse was verbally shared with him, at his request.
3. His memorandum is self-explanatory as he contends your report of his actions are inaccurate.
4. For your information and action.

The Acting Warden was not going to challenge the content of the investigation even though there was clear evidence of a cover-up. If the Acting Warden wanted to become a Warden, it's wise not to stick your neck out for your lowest ranking staff members. But he did, he said, forward the information package that challenged the report to National Headquarters.

There was no response from National Headquarters given in reply to my memorandum. National Headquarters did not respond to requests or inquiries from a CX-1 Level, Terminal Ranked Officer in those days.

National Headquarters felt that the results of their investigation produced their desired conclusion. Their lowest ranking employees were thrown under the bus.

During my writing of this book, I made an application to the CSC Access to Information & Privacy Division requesting a copy of the General Security Investigation into the Escape of Tyrone Conn.

File A-2019-00034
The reply I received was as follows:

*"We have carefully searched our records and did not identify any records regarding your request."*

Documents were destroyed 25 years after their creation and in accordance with the CSC's retention period."

The CSC destroys their investigation reports after a determined period of time. All CSC investigation reports need to be retained and archived for the purpose of education, training, and accountability in matters of in-custody deaths, suicides, murders, and escapes.

The record retention period had passed and any and all written and/or recorded material related to the escape has been destroyed.

The CSC as a whole from NHQ on down to the Institutional level truly despised anyone employed by them that challenged their corrupt acts. But if their reports were blatantly inaccurate and brought professional disparity to me and the members that I represented as Union President it was my right and duty to rebuke them.

The CSC required no help from me, or anyone to make them look bad, they did that all on their own in my time.

# PART 30

## Accountability, Integrity, Openness

> The office found CSC's investigation to be self-serving and not credible.
>
> I have recommended to the Minister of Public Safety that CSC should not investigate itself in rare circumstances involving riot, death or suicide or suicide in solitary confinement or death following a use of force intervention.[31]
>
> —Dr. Ivan Zinger, Correctional Investigator of Canada,
> June 2018

### Audit and Investigations Sector

You cannot expect a professional, fair, and thorough investigation of a Sensational Incident because the Correctional Service of Canada investigates itself. There were no professionally trained, experienced, impartial, and

---

[31] Office of the Correctional Investigator of Canada, *45th Annual Report to Parliament*, October 2018. Accessed October 30, 2020, www.oci-bec.gc.ca/cnt/rpt/pdf/annrpt/annrpt20172018-eng.pdf.

knowledgeable outside reliable agency that conducts investigations in the CSC in my time with them.

It has its own managers and staff do the investigations – managers and staff members who may be related to directly or indirectly, friends with, owe their careers or promotions to some of the people they are investigating. They cannot be impartial to someone who may have the potential to sit on a future board of selection for their promotion. Even when the CSC brings in managers from headquarters or other regions to conduct an investigation, there is still a great potential that some of the team members are not free from bias unless they disclose a conflict of interest.

This is part of the reason that the lowest ranking officers very often take the brunt of the blame. Those at the bottom can't be a threat or an influence on the higher ranks and they cannot defend themselves even in the light of overwhelming evidence because the CSC simply did what it pleased then with impunity.

Even the Office of the Correctional Investigator clearly saw and reported in his annual report 2017–2018 that the CSC should not be investigating itself.

At the time of this writing, the CSC contracts former, retired executive members to perform investigations for them. They are paid at the EX-2 level.

# PART 31

## Crime: Pulling a Gun on Your Colleague

While I was away from Collins Bay working at the Correctional Staff College on a "Rotational Developmental Assignment" as an instructor, I witnessed yet another very serious blunder by Correctional Service managers.

Collins Bay Institution required another firearms instructor to replace me in order to perform annual refresher training for the experienced staff. They recruited a guard who had a dismal reputation among his peers. He was constantly ridiculed about certain aspects in his personal life that he foolishly chose to disclose around the institution. This was a big mistake given the kind poisoned environment that he worked in. It was information that the staff used against him at every opportunity. He did not have the respect, trustworthiness, or maturity required to be a staff trainer inside this kind of dog-eat-dog workplace. That being said, I figured that a more experienced and respected senior officer would be with him and be able to keep tabs on him and take control of the situation that was inevitably going to happen.

I was very wrong.

I had warned the Coordinator of Correctional Operations that there would most certainly be some kind of Sensational Incident if this guard were placed in a position of authority on the Firearms Range over other staff members who did not respect him.

My warning was ignored.

While at the firing range, trying to perform refresher training, he was taunted throughout the day with the same ridicule and insults that he usually experienced within the prison.

On the drive back to the institution, at the end of the day, the two instructors were in the front of the van and the staff members being trained that day were sitting in the rear. The compartments were separated by a section of thin plexiglass and aluminum mesh. The van was commonly used for the transportation of inmates in the community.

One of the guards in the back made a comment about a public-school yard that they were driving past and related it to the junior instructor's relationship with a younger woman.

The junior instructor drew his service revolver, pointed it at the offending guard and uttered a threat. At that moment, the senior instructor should have stopped the van and had the junior instructor surrender his weapon. A criminal offence took place right under his nose and he failed to act upon it. He did not do his duty as a sworn Peace Officer in charge and directly witnessing an indictable offence.

**"As with most sensational incidents involving CSC, the scab on the surface is just a cover for the festering layers of infection beneath."**

After returning to the institution, the guard in the rear of the van called the police about the incident and the junior instructor was arrested and criminally charged.

The senior instructor was never disciplined about his neglect of duty in the face of this, a criminal act.

The accused guard was suspended from duty.

I spoke with the victim guard, and he agreed to withdraw the complaint after being reminded that he himself had been sometimes less than an exemplary officer throughout his career and no stranger to being the perpetrator of some outlandish things himself.

After speaking to his brother, a guard at another institution, he decided to proceed with the original charges simply to be vindictive toward the junior instructor.

The brother he had consulted with worked in another area prison and had himself been at the center of a front-page scandal involving the escort of an inmate to Northern Ontario whom he took out into the community and entertained on a boat cruise complete with alcohol and photos of the two together standing on the bow of the cruise boat. The incident and the photos were published on the front page of the local newspaper.

This was yet another Sensational Incident for CSC.

The accused guard was able to hire an independent investigator who interviewed the staff members that were on training that day as well as the Correctional manager, the senior officer instructor and myself.

The investigator was advised of my prior intervention attempt with the Correctional manager in which I cautioned him about the great potential for just such an incident to occur. Other factors, such as the senior training officer's neglect of duty in the face of a criminal act were discussed as well.

The other officers who attended the training that day gave witness statements to the harassment of the junior instructor by the complainant throughout the day and the fact that no attempt at intervention on behalf of the senior training officer was made to stop the teasing was also witnessed by the other guards.

The senior managers at the institution decided that the private investigator was overstepping the bounds of his mandate and denied him access to the prison. Any further staff interviews were to be conducted off-site.

A memo to me from the Deputy Warden dated 14 April 1999 stated:

*"The process that the private investigator followed in conducting their investigation is not consistent with CSC policy or expectations.*

*The document attached to the note to you does not appear to have been validated information or shared for verification. It appears to be a collection of rumours and hearsay information, without any indication that it can/is substantiated. Accordingly, I would ask your cooperation in returning the documentation, as well as any copies you have made, to me through the CCO's office."*

This is a true statement. CSC Investigations were "supposed to be shared with the person for verification" before the report is finalized. But in my extensive experience having contact with CSC investigations teams, this was never done for the staff member being interviewed. The CSC investigators simply got what they required and left. They did not "share for verification" with anyone before finalizing their report. This was part of their underhanded practice that has been going on in the CSC for years. And even after releasing their final report they would routinely refuse to permit the report being examined by those involved in the incident, forcing them to resort to applying to Access to Information at their own expense.

The managers at Collins Bay saw that their dirty laundry was being exposed and tried to shut it down by attempting to limit the scope of the investigation. But as with most sensational incidents involving CSC, the scab on the surface is just a cover for the festering layers of infection beneath. The deeper you go, the more layers of corruption you find.

Eventually, the accused officer was dismissed, but was reinstated at a later date and sent to another Institution to work.

# PART 32

## CSC Training

> The U.N. Standard Minimum Rules require that prior to entering service, personnel are to be given a course of training in their general and specific duties. During their career they are to maintain and improve their knowledge and professional capacity by attending courses of in-service training to be organized at suitable intervals . . . The Sub-Committee notes that Canada is therefore currently failing to carry out the standards of the U.N. Minimum Rules.
>
> —*MacGuigan Report* (1977), para 267

### Follow the Training Funds

There was often a great allocation of money placed into projects that would not even remotely aid the offender, the frontline staff worker, or to protect the public. For the most part, this was done to make it appear to the international correctional community that Canada is a leader in prison reform and research.

However, the frontline people who work directly with the inmates and who have the most impact upon them got very little in the way of training.

There were too many positions at National Headquarters that took up educational and training dollars that could have been applied at the institutional levels where it was needed the most and where it could have the most direct impact on offender rehabilitaion.

In my time with the CSC, very little money went toward the optimistic image of assisting the offender to become a law-abiding citizen. For the most part, there was no supportive benefit to the offenders' rehabilitation achieved by the advancement and training of people who had no direct interaction or influence on them.

Then, when the money starts to run out at the end of the fiscal

> **"The guards are treated as a simple commodity to be used up and replaced when the chronic stress and the compounded trauma of the day-to-day violence eventually damages you beyond repair."**

year the gloves come off and the battles begin. Department heads are in a predicament, with funds running low as a result of poor financial management throughout the season. So, the claw back starts, and it begins at the level of the guard staff:

- no funds for the purchase of new equipment
- no funds to keep the institutions running on a normal day-to-day basis
- no funds to give staff annual refresher training in First Aid, use of force, and firearms that is required by CSC National Policy.

Overtime for the guard staff has been a fact of business life in Corrections for years and it really eats up the budget. The rates of pay are established via contractual agreement between the Union, Management, and Treasury Board and can't be changed. If there is an emergency at the prison that requires staff members to remain on site for a prolonged period of time in order to deal with it, then it adds up in money spent on overtime. This is one of the reasons that great concessions are made to inmates to prevent them from staging a protest that will eventually lead to a riot. These violent actions cost money to regain control of the prison and money to repair all of the physical damage done to the prison.

The cuts to essential training and equipment were always targeted at the front line and the guard staff and yet at the same time one Commissioner took a Coast Guard icebreaker, the *Bernier*, out for a "Booze Cruise" costing the Canadian taxpayers $400 per person for the senior Correctional Service of Canada's managers to be entertained. That same Commissioner caused so much damage to his staff members across the country that myself and countless others still suffer from the way we were treated under his reign.

Indeed, whenever the budget gets tight, it is the frontlines across the country that suffer the most. The guards were treated as a simple commodity to be used up and replaced when the chronic stress and the compounded trauma of the day-to-day violence eventually damages you beyond repair.

# PART 33

## Issued Equipment in the CSC

The IERT equipment that was issued to us in the 80s'was very primitive, often used previously, hand-me-downs from past response team members. We each had a pair of green mechanics coveralls without any insignia, and a web-belt from the Army Surplus store. Our boots were also Army Surplus and often issued to us third hand. We each had a pair of baseball catcher shin guards and hockey elbow pads. The helmets were used and were so old that the face shields were often scratched to the point of being opaque and most of the styrofoam padding on the inside was missing. You also got a pair of Damascus Corporation brand "sap gloves".

Everything you were issued was sweat-stained and smelled bad from the years of accumulated perspiration from former team members. Our trusty wooden sticks were at our sides, some taped in places where they were cracked. A gas mask with no pouch to carry it in and our handcuffs completed the outfit.

This was the kit for the Institutional Emergency Response Teams within the Ontario Region at that time: used, shopworn, and dirty.

> Making very expensive nationwide purchases for useless
> items of equipment seemed to be the norm in those days.

## Trying to be Quiet? Try Velcro!

Yet another National Headquarters approved scale of equipment washout was the issue of a new IERT Uniform. Five years of research went into this project. Surveys were sent out to ERT team members requesting what they felt was required in a uniform.

The final product was nothing like what the survey returns suggested.

Heavy, lined cotton jackets with Velcro pocket closures were bought. One of the options that the teams were quite sure about was that no Velcro was to be used. Velcro makes too much noise when you are trying to be quiet. Reach into your pocket for an item of equipment and what do you hear? *R-r-r-rip!*

The coats were great for deployment in the cold temperatures of winter, but what do you wear in the summer months when you are only issued with a heavy, lined long-sleeved, winter type jacket.

The only thing we felt any confidence in were the boots and the belts.

In fact, when put to the Response Team, they all decided to scrap the Nationally issued and approved uniforms and buy our own for less than half the price of the CSC ones.

## 911 Rescue Knives

I remember the time when the IERT responded to a cell extraction and one of the team members used his own fixed-blade hunting knife that he carried in his boot to cut the clothing off the con, leaving marks on him from the blade. After years of attempting to have a 911 rescue knife on the scale of issue NHQ finally saw the light. They were issued to the Emergency Response Team initially and one was placed into each key safe in every cell block to cut down the cons that tried committed suicide by hanging.

Prior to that you stood in the cell with your arms wrapped around the con's legs trying to lift him up to take the pressure off his neck with nothing to cut him down with and no way to summon help without letting go of him.

At that time, some guards often carried their own concealed knife with them. It was not for the purpose of cutting down a hanging con, it was for their own so-called self-defence. Some of them used to stand around on the Strip and compare their knives in front of the cons. Some of these Rambos lost their knives in the prison and now the cons have them.

It was always my contention that the cons would simply take your knife away and use it on you if you decided to deploy it against them because in prison, you are always outnumbered.

## Stab-proof Vests Sat and Gathered Dust

Making very expensive nationwide purchases for useless items of equipment seemed to be the norm in those days. For example, the very expensive Point Blank S.T.A.R. Vest stab-proof body armour was all but useless to the IERT teams. Approximately $1,000 each based upon Security Manual Section "S" May 1993, these stab-proof body were so large and bulky that you were unable to get through a cell door with them on. You were unable to use your baton while wearing one because of their sheer bulk severely restricting your movement. You were unable to wear the NHQ-approved helmets when you had this body on because the high collar designed to protect your neck would not allow your helmet to fit onto your head. If you were able to force it down past the padding or even remove the protective padding, you could not turn your head from side to side. You could not use your handcuffing skills with these vests on because once you bent over or knelt down, it would ride up in your face so you couldn't see. You were a juggernaut who could move forward, backward and from side to side, that's all.

It was evident that no one who had practical experience with the IERT researched these purchases beforehand. These costly units remained in their bags on the shelves of the IERT ready room gathering dust for years.

I remember seeing some components of these stab-proof suits and the newly issued IERT uniforms in the local Army Surplus store located next to the prison some years later.

## Protective Gloves

> "The majority of injuries found on police, prison or security officer are to be found around the palm of the hand and forearm. These injuries are classed as 'defensive wounds' and can easily lead to irreparable injuries and rapid blood loss."

> —*Canadian Security*

"Slash and needle resistant gloves," *Canadian Security*, December 2, 2014, accessed March 19, 2021, www.canadiansecuritymag.com/slash-and-needle-resistant-gloves/.

Let me recount another example of senior management neglect that led to severe injuries. In the mid-1990s, a 'chair moistener' somewhere in the organization (I say "somewhere" because they were never identified) was looking at the issued equipment for the Emergency Response Team Members and decided to remove our protective gloves.

The Damascus safety gloves worn by response team members in the '80s and '90s were heavy grain leather gloves with lead dust sewn into the knuckles. The reason for using this particular type of glove was that the lead dust made the gloves flexible and protected the knuckles from strikes by baseball bats, pipes, hockey sticks, and any other weapon that a con may use to hit you, without limiting your ability to manipulate handcuffs, radio controls, and other equipment. They used to be issued to some police forces back in the '70s.

This inexperienced manager at NHQ or somewhere, somehow determined that these gloves, weighted in the knuckles with lead dust, would cause untold harm if the team member were to defend themselves by striking a con while wearing them. They couldn't allow the potential for that to happen, so the gloves were struck off the scale of issue and not replaced.

As these gloves were issued as an item of Safety Equipment, they should have been replaced immediately; exchange the old ones for new ones. They were not, and there was no intention to do so.

Being the advocate for the team in health and safety matters, I approached the Warden in writing about this issue. Nothing was done, it's out of their hands at the institutional level. Well, how about a pair of regular leather gloves for the time being, the ones they issue frontline staff members?

No, too much money.

All right, it was on to a formal complaint with Health and Safety the Union and Labour Canada to investigate.

**"Had the safety of a manager been in question, there would have been instant action and redress."**

In the meantime, while all of these lengthy formal resolution attempts were in motion, the largest riot in the history of Collins Bay Institution was under way on 17 November 1998.

The Response Team members had nothing to protect their hands during this riot. I can be seen in one of the video recordings of the riot speaking with a manager while blood dripped onto the floor from the cuts to my hands. I can later be seen briefing the Crisis Manager and the Riot Team Members with bandages on my hands. My hands were cut while boosting another team member up to a window to deploy a gas grenade. There was broken glass caught in the tread of his boots, and while assisting him up to the window by boosting him with my cupped hands I was cut on my hands, fingers, and on my legs. (see the photo in Part 25 Cell Block 1 Riot - November 17,1998)

Earlier that night when the Joyceville Response Team arrived I took note that all of their team members still had their Damascus safety gloves… it appears that they didn't get the memo.

In the aftermath, when I requested the name of the person at National Headquarters or wherever they were who was responsible for removing the gloves, my request was ignored.

**"Open and Honest Two-way Communication" is one of the values of the Service, but it didn't apply to the frontline staff in those days.**

*"Due to a couple of instances whereby IERT members injured their hands during incidents, new protective gloves to serve as replacement items* [were purchased].

*In addition, members have spoken with Labour Canada"* [with a formal complaint against the CSC].

—*Quote from Internal memo*

I was the one who initiated the formal complaint to Labour Canada order to get the proper protective equipment for my Team Members.

Much later (February 25, 1999), and after more and more complaints and injuries, the team members were finally issued with Hatch brand rappelling gloves as a replacement…a more expensive piece of equipment than the regular issued frisking gloves. This was the typical response we got from the Correctional Service of Canada Management Teams in most matters of health and safety where a frontline staff members safety was at risk. Had the health and safety of a manager been in peril, there would have been instant action and redress.

## The Real Tactics for Self-Defence

If you looked at the Self-Defence Arrest and Control study guide for officers and Emergency Response Team Members for that period, there is nowhere in the cadre of self-defence tactics that instructs you to *punch* a con.

In fact, that sort of personal self-defence was very much frowned upon in the CSC. They didn't want anyone defending themselves by actually having to strike a con with their hands because it would not look good to the inexperienced eyes of NHQ. That was why the self-defence training relied heavily upon wrist locks, twist locks, arm bars, and shoulder locks.

These tactics are not mastered easily or in a short period of time. It takes years of practice to become proficient in these methods of self-defence and to be able to use them effectively in an environment like a prison where the attack comes unannounced in the form of an ambush, gang attack or blitz assault – often with weapons.

The CSC provided no refresher training in self-defence, arrest and control, handcuffing, TAC-COM (tactical communication), situational awareness, emergency planning, or baton and shield. NHQ felt that the self-defence training given on your initial induction training was good for the remainder of your career.

None of these techniques were taught to me while I was at the Ontario Police College or at the Toronto Police College. They don't work in an active attacker situation against someone who is drunk, high, or seriously intent on killing you. They were approved by NHQ not for their effectiveness, but because these tactics were believed to lower the potential of harm to an inmate, not to give the staff member a fighting chance of defending themselves in one of the most hostile and brutal working environments that exists.

## CSC-Approved Baton Target Areas

While on the "10-Day Basic" emergency response team member training you learn to use 42-inch, 36-inch and 26-inch wooden batons, Riot Team Formations, Chemical Agents, riot shields, handcuffing, and Cell Extraction methods.

The CSC has "Approved Target" areas on the human body for striking with a baton. There are certain areas that you are not justified in striking with your wooden stick, according to CSC Policy.

The head, neck, and groin on men are the areas that you must not hit with a baton, so says National Headquarters. Those same areas plus

> **"Not many cons will stand still and allow you to target their "Approved Areas"; they are too busy trying to stab you or beat your head in with an aluminum baseball bat."**

the chest, are out of bounds on female inmates. The people at National Headquarters who constructed this policy have never been in a fight with a con and have absolutely no experience in the Use of Force and certainly no knowledge of the *Criminal Code* of Canada.

Many of these policy makers have never even been inside a prison except for a tour. Not many cons will stand still and allow you to target their "Approved Areas"; they are too busy trying to stab you or beat your head in with an aluminum baseball bat. And you can be sure that the cons do not have a policy or a law restricting where they can and cannot strike you or stab at you. This kind of foolish and antiquated thinking falls into the same realm as, "Why don't you just shoot the gun or knife out of his hand?"

As a Team Leader, I was in several prison riots in different prisons within the Ontario Region. I had actually used or ordered the use of force in an institutional environment many, many times. I gassed and handcuffed more than a few cons in my time. Had to fight for my life on more than one occasion against inmates that are intent upon killing me just for doing my job.

I was giving a demonstration to a few of the new team members who just completed their 10-Day Basic Emergency Response Team course the previous week. I had one officer dressed up in a Red Man Suit (a full body suit made from thick red foam padding) to role-play a con and have him attack a team member with a rubber knife. The team member had to stay within the boundary of a circle marked on the gym floor. The team member was to defend himself with a padded 42-inch baton against the attacking con using only the CSC-approved strikes and striking only in CSC-approved target areas.

The new team member was stabbed several times by the officer role-playing the con. Then I told a second team member and eventually a third to enter the ring so there were three on one trying to defend themselves from a knife attack against this one active attacker.

All they had to do was strike the role player once using a "CSC-Approved Baton Strike" in a "CSC-Approved" area of the body in order to win the contest. None of them were successful while using any of the "officially approved strikes and approved target areas" to save themselves. Eventually, all of the Riot Team Members had the opportunity to try out this role-play. None of the team members were successful in defending themselves, they were shocked.

The only one who was able to do so was the Team Leader – me – using a padded 26-inch baton and NOT using the CSC-approved strikes and target areas. You could see the looks of shock and confusion on the team member's faces when this practical demonstration was over.

What CSC Policy dictated and what they were trained to do and depended upon to defend themselves was not working for them at all in a real-life active combat situation. There are no such things as approved strikes and target areas on the human body when defending yourself from death or grievous bodily harm according to the *Criminal Code*. But the Correctional Service of Canada has a long and dismal history of trying to pit their political will against the *Criminal Code* with disastrous results (e.g., the Ashley Smith murder).

> "The reality is that you are dealing with people who will hurt you and even kill you without a second thought. They have had a lifetime of experience doing just that."

I told the group that if a con comes at you with a knife, "Take his fucking head off with your baton and forget about the CSC "Approved Target Areas."

The reality is that you are dealing with people who will hurt you and even kill you without a second thought. They have had a lifetime of experience doing just that. Fighting for your life does not mean following rules set up by people who have never had any experience using force or being in that kind of life-threatening situation as well as having no practical experienced knowledge of the law. The only rules that you follow in these circumstances are those of the *Criminal Code of Canada*.

I am sure that management would have shit themselves and immediately suspended me as Team Leader if it got back to them that this is what I told the team that day. This was the voice of real-life experience talking about defending your life against someone intent on killing you. This was the voice of someone who had more practical use of force experience and training both on the Inside and on the Outside than the armchair policy makers could ever fathom.

Back then it was a kinder, gentler Service and many believed that the cons were just misunderstood good old boys who truly didn't mean what they were doing and all you needed to defuse any violent situation was a kind word, a coffee, and a cigarette to share with them.

This was the philosophy of the CSC at that time under that Commissioner. "Non-violent Crisis Resolution" was the buzzword and National Headquarters truly believed that it worked in every situation.

Well, that only goes so far in dealing with some of the most violent criminals the world has to offer us who are confined inside our prisons today.

## Smoke Grenades

The Author instructing the deployment of chemical agents (tear gas).

We also had smoke grenades at our disposal for "outdoor use only". The suggested use of these devices at that time was to test the wind direction in the yard to see which way the gas would be carried when deployed. Or to mask the movements of the Response Team. That one never worked because although the cons can't see the team, the team can't see the cons either. This was a tactical suggestion from someone who was never involved in a prison riot.

One of my favourite tactics was to duct tape a small Pocket Tactical CN Grenade to a large 110 Smoke Grenade. When deployed, it would create huge billowing clouds of grey smoke with just a small taste of CN gas mixed in with it. The cons could see a great cloud of smoke and would be able to smell the CN gas and think it was all CN gas and move to avoid it. The Use of Force Report looked good in that you quelled a full-on riot with only one small CN gas grenade. Only someone with extensive experience in riot control tactics would know that.

Tactics like this and others were never taught to the Emergency Response Team Members on their 10-Day Basic Training because no one teaching them had any experience using gas grenades in a real prison riot. The "basics" that were taught were really only that, basic. Which was not much more than what was given to you on your initial induction training to become an officer.

## Wizard Piss

When pepper spray was initially introduced to CSC, the IERT members were given instruction on it first. This took place at the Correctional Staff College. The theory and application methods were done in the classroom, and the practical exposure to the spray was done outside to avoid having to evacuate the building due to gas contamination. The team members were to stand outside in front of a large stainless steel salad bowl borrowed from the mess hall and filled with cold water. You were sprayed in the face with pepper spray and permitted to decontaminate by plunging your face in the bowl and forcing your eyes open to wash out the irritant. No Sunlight dish detergent to wash with, clean clothes, nurse, and doctor examination for you; you are not an inmate.

When the third or fourth person had been sprayed and dipped, the bowl was beginning to fill up with lots of pepper spray-generated mucus. But it didn't matter to the person who had just been sprayed. They would have done anything to get their face into that cool water. There was an oil slick of pepper spray and snot covering the water in the salad bowl and all you were doing was to re-contaminate yourself again and again as you dipped your face in the bowl. Finally, someone had the idea to keep the hose running inside the salad bowl to have a constant flow of fresh cold water that would wash away the oily slick. Pepper spray and mace were sometimes called Wizard Piss because of their powerful ability to incapacitate.

There were no universal precautions in place for staff in the 1990s.

## Unrealistic Training in an Unreal World

Being taught these kind of impractical and inexperienced tactics is why people freeze up during an emergency. They were told by inexperienced people that the tactics and equipment they were trained with would get the job done. But most of the training proved to be unrealistic in the real world of a federal prison and the team members had nothing to fall back on.

Most of the IERT Team Tactics were approved by those who have never experienced a prison riot and never will experience a prison riot except from the safety of their padded chairs in front of a video screen one hour and fifty-five minutes away from the prisons they manage. We were once again sold a product by the CSC that was broken and/or just didn't exist in the first place.

To attempt to copy the riot control methods of the RCMP, OPP or the Toronto Police Service and then apply them to prison riots may sound like a good idea, but the environments and the participants are much different, requiring different methods and strategies.

Having extensive experience on the streets of Toronto and in the cell blocks and ranges of our federal prisons, I quickly learned that there is a vast difference in riot dynamics on the Inside than on the Outside.

But if you have a Team Leader with an experienced background who knows the prison environment and what to expect from the cons, then you stand a much better chance of gaining back control of your prison and saving the lives of those within it.

## One-time Only Training on Breathing Apparatus

SCBA – Self-Contained Breathing Apparatus – are available at all institutions and it is essential that staff members be properly trained in their use and deployment. Fire in a prison is a common occurrence. Either intentionally set or accidental, it causes massive structural damage and endangers the lives of everyone who works and lives on the Inside. The mandatory initial instruction is provided by the local fire department and takes place at the start of your induction training.

You are instructed and tested on inspecting the SCBA unit, the proper way to put it on, and in the environmental hazards associated with exposure to fire, smoke, and chemicals. In order for the device to function properly and protect the user from a potentially toxic gas exposure, the face seal of the mask must be secure and airtight.

A person who requires glasses cannot use the equipment, as the arms of the glasses break the seal between the mask and the face. To get around this a "Glasses Kit" is available. This kit is composed of a frame that fits on the inside of the mask and it contains lenses specific to the prescription of the user. CSC management did not purchase these kits because they did not know that they were a requirement. When I brought this to their attention and suggested that the kits be made available to the staff members who required them, I was ignored.

So, once again and not for the last time, I submitted a formal grievance and a complaint to Labour Canada, which was upheld, and a kit was purchased. But only one kit was purchased. They did not provide these kits for every officer or staff member who require one to accommodate their prescription glasses. So, more injuries on duty were reported due to smoke inhalation.

The same problem concerning a proper seal on the mask existed if the user had a beard. The institution issued a memo ordering that all staff who had the potential to use this equipment had to be "clean-shaven where the seal meets the face."

This was not the only safety issue that was identified with the use of this equipment. It was determined that when responding to fires in the institution, many staff members did not know how don the apparatus. Mostly because over the years they forgot how to use them. As a result, there were many smoke inhalation injuries reported because the staff was not even wearing the safety equipment before entering a smoke-filled range or cell. The CSC had determined that the initial training on this equipment was good enough and no refresher training was offered.

The matter was eventually brought before the Health and Safety Committee and the memo below was issued.

> *Memorandum # 565-1 27 May 1987*
> *from the Deputy Commissioner Ontario*
>
> *Use of Self-Contained Breathing Apparatus*
>
> 5.  *Further to our earlier discussions on the absolute need for staff to be familiar with the use of the above-noted, I am advised that in some Institutions.*
>
> 6.  *Most staff don't know how to handle the equipment.*
>
> 7.  *Training programs are almost nonexistent.*
>
> *Would you please determine the situation in your institution and, if necessary, take steps to ensure that staff are capable*

*in this area. Refresher training – once a year – would not be out of line on this one.*

## Basic Knowledge was Missing

Correctional officers have been employed for 15, 20, and even 27 years without receiving any training subsequent to their initial induction course.

—*MacQuigan Report* (1977), para 265

During my time as a team leader, I identified many gaps in our training and knowledge that would have left us open to liability, criticism, and risk our safety. I began to amass a library of informative and instructional books on our tradecraft. Some books were books published for "Police Use Only" on topics that we should have had knowledge of as Peace Officers and Team Members such as:

- Officer Survival
- Riot Tactics
- Use of Force Techniques for Tactical Teams
- Comprehensive Instruction on the use of Chemical Agents
- Distraction Devices
- Public Safety
- Street Gangs
- Supervisor Survival

I bought these books myself and had them installed in the Team's Ready Room in a bookcase for the members to sign out as required for their own study. The *Criminal Code* of Canada was one of the publications I placed in our Team library as there wasn't a single copy of it within the institution.

It was disappointing to see that after several years of having access to them, only two team members signed any books out. Most of the team members relied upon their leaders to acquire and have the knowledge and tactical skills required to deal with an emergency and didn't feel that they had to bother themselves with learning these skills on their own, without being paid to do so.

None of the books in our Team Room were available in the library at the Correctional Staff College because the Service felt that they were unnecessary and would not purchase them or any instructional or educational books concerning the Use of Force or Emergency Management.

The CSC Investigators did not have this knowledge, including, in many cases, even a rudimentary knowledge of the *Criminal Code* that they should have in order to conduct thorough and fair investigations. Madam Justice Louise Arbour proved that it was strikingly apparent that officers and managers usually did not know the law or how to apply it in an institutional environment. This was the primary underlying cause of liability within the CSC at that time.

I directed my team with integrity, honesty and strict adherence to policy and the *Criminal Code*.

I led by my example.

I didn't fear the inmates, I didn't fear the guards and I didn't fear the corrupt managers.

Integrity, Courage and Honour Inside the Chaos.

# PART 34

## The Canadian Police and Peace Officers' Memorial March

"A formal, national Memorial Day gives Canadians an opportunity each year to formally express appreciation for the dedication of police and peace officers, who make the ultimate, tragic sacrifice to keep communities safe."

—Solicitor General of Canada, September 27, 1998

### A Legacy of Indifference

In the 1980s, you trained in your issued uniform and graduated in it just like police and military. The dress uniform was for special ceremonial occasions like parades and funerals. The Canadian Police and Peace Officers' Memorial March held in Ottawa each year is one of those ceremonies.

I remember going to that memorial one year in our "Service Industry" style uniforms – the blue and white striped shirts and grey pants. You had a blue blazer with the CSC crest on it along with a baseball cap.

That was not a dress uniform, it was our day to day.

We left our baseball caps in the van as we thought it was disrespectful to wear them on parade. We stood with most of the Canadian law enforcement contingents mustered in front of the Superior Court in Ottawa and then marched over to the parade square on Parliament Hill for the ceremony. While waiting for the command to march past, we witnessed the Commissioner of the Ontario Provincial Police inspecting their Honour Guard. The Commissioner of the RCMP was doing the same for his officers.

We stood there looking up and down the line for a senior representative from CSC to inspect us or even acknowledge our attendance. No one turned up either before the parade or after. This same scene was repeated every year I attended.

We were on our own.

We had no value to the executives of the CSC who continued to demonstrate that fact year after year by their conspicuous absence and disrespect of the frontline officers and their families who attended the Police and Peace Officers' Memorial March on their own time.

If any senior managers did attend the Police and Peace Officers' Memorial March, they would never be seen with the officers on parade. They would stand where they had the best opportunity for the CSC senior executives to see them. They were not there for the fallen officers; they were there to benefit themselves.

The commissioners of the CSC of that time left a very profound legacy of indifference to all Correctional officers across the country by their failure to acknowledge our attendance at the annual Police and Peace Officers' Memorial March. This may sound truly outrageous to law enforcement officers across Canada, but this was the kind of systemic disrespect we experienced day after day while working for the CSC.

## Systemic Disrespect

If you wanted to attend the Police and Peace Officers' Memorial March you were not permitted to do so if it cost the CSC any overtime to replace you. You had to go on your days off or take annual leave. All my institution would contribute was a van to drive up to Ottawa and you were not permitted to stay overnight as that would cost money for a hotel and meals.

Many officers wanted to attend but were not issued with one of the recycled uniforms, so I told them to wear a suit and tie and march with us anyway.

I remember seeing one of our pitiful CSC baseball caps lying on a scarlet pillow alongside the peaked forage hats of police officers killed in the line of duty. The hats represented a fallen officer of that service. Our

**"Our symbolic baseball cap looked like it represented the fallen member of a company baseball team."**

symbolic baseball cap looked like it represented the fallen member of a company baseball team.

There were enough complaints and enough public embarrassment suffered by officers nationwide that the CSC finally gave in and got a limited number of dress uniforms. Only a small number were sent to the institutions as the managers thought that outfitting every officer was just too expensive. These "new" uniforms were not really new at all, they were not designed and produced specifically for the CSC. They were the same uniforms that were issued to Canada Border Services, now with the CSC insignia sewn onto them. At least they came with a peaked hat.

At that time, there were no official policies on how to wear the uniform or under what circumstances it would be worn. The last formal dress policy went out the door when the service industry uniform came into being. No rank insignia, no years of service badges, no direction as to the display of CD honours.

There was no officially sanctioned protocol with respect to conducting funerals for staff members or attending formal organized CSC functions. This was left up to the individual institutions and to those members who were issued the new uniform.

Each prison had their own idea as to how things should be done, and this created many areas of conflict. Even when I approached the CSC in writing requesting some guidance in this matter, the written requests were ignored. We were left on our own. I decided to design new "years of service" badges, paid for them with my money to be embroidered and sent them to National Headquarters to have them approved.

NHQ did what NHQ always did with respect to submissions from a frontline officer... they ignored me and my 'years of service' badge presentation.

Had the idea come from a manager, things would have been much different, and the manager would have been awarded with a citation for their initiative. The CSC managers did not wear uniforms then, so there was no reason to develop a ceremonial protocol, rank insignia, or years of service badges.

The 1980s-issue uniform had firearms badges that represented a score achieved in CSC issue weapons. The Commissioner at the time thought these looked too militaristic and threatening to the offenders and so removed them from the scale of issue. This is the same Commissioner who removed the old dress and duty uniforms for that same reason and went with the Service Industry employee look, ball cap and all.

# PART 35

## Regional Correctional Staff College

"If you have the Methods of Instruction training, you can teach any topic."

—Manager, Regional Correctional Staff College

### Still A Prisoner of the System

My first encounter with what was to come while working as an instructor at the Regional Correctional Staff College occurred the very day I started. There was no orientation training for me at all. I was shown the office that I was to occupy for the next two years and the storage room where the student module handouts were kept. I was given a schedule and got to work teaching that very day.

That afternoon, I witnessed two instructors teaching new recruits a skill that they were both totally unqualified to instruct: how to don and operate a self-contained breathing apparatus. This is the kind of equipment you will see firefighters wear when entering a smoke-filled building or an area where they are exposed to fire and toxic gases. SCBA is a topic that only certified and experienced instructors are to be teaching. But in this instance, you had two inexperienced staff members, who have never even had the equipment on their backs in their lives yet are showing the new Officer Recruits how to use it by reading the instructions directly from the manual.

There was no requirement for foundational experience for many of the modules taught at the RCSC, but in the opinion of the principal, "If you have the Methods of Instruction Course, you can teach any topic."

The Correctional Service suffered a long reputation of employing some staff members who had no practical foundational or frontline experience teaching some the topics assigned to them as had been demonstrated on my very first day. There was much reading from the instructional handbook and or watching videos employed as the method of teaching topics that the instructor had no experience in.

So, you may have someone teaching you how to use a body belt, handcuffs and leg irons that never once put them on an inmate. You may have someone teaching you how to deploy chemical agents like mace or pepper spray and yet had no experience deploying them in a dynamic situation in a real prison. Someone teaching you Use of Force and never having used force in a correctional service environment.

I remember the phrase "experience is the best teacher." This phrase clearly was not practiced in the CSC at that time.

As you begin your career and are exposed to situations that require you to rely on your training, and then find out that this training is somewhat inadequate. You are now at risk having your personal safety challenged because what you were taught to do is not working for you as I had experienced many times.

For example, riot team members being trained on the 10-day basic were being instructed in riot team tactics and formations that were, in some cases, totally impractical to the institutional environment. Riot Team formations were used to move the team down range, through hallways or in the exercise yard and gym. We were taught this by people who had no experience being tasked with suppressing a prison riot. We were told that the Team could enter the prison yard full of convicts and extract an injured staff member or inmate using these formations. I knew better through my extensive experience leading prison riot teams and never even suggested this tactic to a crisis manager.

Most of these riot team formations were completely useless is a large open area like a prison exercise yard. We would require massive numbers of IERT members to attempt any of these suggested formations. The cons would simply surround us with their superior numbers and slaughter us.

Yet we were told that this would work.

Placed in a situation just like this the Millhaven response team refused the order from the crisis manager to enter the yard and remove an injured inmate. The Team refused because it was unsafe for them to do so and filed a complaint of unsafe working conditions that was investigated by Occupational Health and Safety.

*Occupational Health and Safety Tribunal Canada concluded on appeal that: *"Correctional officers have not received the training necessary and recourses to enter the recreational yard at Millhaven Institution under an emergency situation to clear this area and extract an inmate in need of medical assistance."*

Constructing policy and creating lesson plans in the area of use of force options for the prison environment takes years of frontline practical experience to determine what works within a law and policy framework and what does not. It takes first-hand knowledge of your correctional clients and just what they are capable of doing in given circumstances like a riot or a hostage-taking.

You would spend days drilling on these riot formations so the team could execute them on the order of the Team Leader. The trouble with that was the Team Members could not hear the Team Leader giving these orders. The riot helmets impaired your hearing, and the gas mask muffled the Team Leader's commands. The cons are screaming, smashing glass, and playing their music at its highest volume and that would completely mask the orders of the Team Leader. You could see the Team Members standing stock still, confused, and afraid to move as they could not hear the orders from the Team leader due to the noise and the bulky helmets covering their ears.

---

* Occupational Health and Safety Tribunal Canada, "Correctional Services of Canada and Union of Canadian Correctional Officers – CSN, 2013 OHSTC 11

This kind of hesitation, lack of communication and indecisive action was a giveaway to the cons that we were unorganized, and they could take tactical advantage of that. You could never keep a tight formation because in a prison riot there is debris scattered all over the ranges, plus fires, and barricades made from beds, mattresses, washers and dryers, fridges, and freezers.

The cons have broken into the fire hose cabinets and are spraying you with high-pressure hoses. They are tossing down firebombs from the second tier and condoms filled with the gasoline and motor oil they stole from the institutional garage to light you up with.

I remember as a Riot Team Member for the Toronto Police seeing Tactical Paramedics with small fire extinguishers strapped to their lower legs to put out the fires started from the rioters throwing Molotov cocktails onto the Riot Team officers.

It's just not the same as marching in formation along the polished gym floor at the Correctional Staff College pretending that you are in a riot.

## Correctional Officer Physical Abilities Test (COPAT)

This program was introduced in the mid- to late-1990s, more or less because the RCMP and other Police Services were using the same system to test physical and aerobic abilities of their recruits. It was certified by the CSC as a "Bona Fide Occupational Requirement" for the job. All new recruits had to be successful in challenging this test before being hired.

The CSC went ahead a purchased many of these COPAT Push/Pull machines and trained staff members to administer the tests. One of these machines was installed in the gym at the Correctional Staff College so that staff members could practice with it.

Some other Staff Instructors and I, after observing many people having a go at the machine and doing so ourselves, concluded that the initial weight load was simply too much for many people. It was set at a standard weight for everyone.

Since the recruit had to use their own body weight to move the weight and keep it suspended while performing a back-and-forth shuffle, the test weight should be proportionate to the body weight of the recruit.

Of course, because we wore a uniform, our evaluation wasn't worth much at that time in the Correctional Service of Canada and no one was "rattling their zipper" to hear our opinion on this matter anyway.

We brought our concerns to the manager of the college, and they of course interpreted our observations to mean that "women" were not capable of successfully challenging the COPAT.

So, after making a successful COPAT test a Bona Fide Occupational Requirement in order to be hired by the CSC, the next class of recruits were entirely male. Shortly after that, the weight on the COPAT machine was adjusted to be more proportionate to the body weight of the person challenging it.

## A Midnight Search

When I taught at the Regional Correctional Staff College, I brought a class of new officer recruits into Collins Bay Institution on a midnight shift to give them some experience on the Inside searching the Prison.

One of the recruits brought me a device that he found hidden in one of the institutional shops. He wasn't able to immediately recognize it, but it looked out of place to him, so he seized it. What he found was a homemade flame thrower. The maker had brilliantly cobbled together this weapon using a variety of different pieces of metal and parts welded together to form a fully functional flame thrower. A propane regulator hose with a tank attachment and a flow control knob was fixed to a metre-long pipe, insulated, with hand grips welded to it. A spark plug was inserted into the barrel of the tube and a copper gas line ran to the muzzle of the weapon.

Prison-made flame thrower

When the shop instructor was questioned about this weapon found in his shop, he told the management team it wasn't a flame thrower at all, only a wand for a pressure washer. Not many pressure washer wands have a BBQ regulator hose and connector valve on them, nor do they have a spark plug welded onto the barrel of the wand. It was further discovered that there was a full propane BBQ tank and a BBQ in his shop. He told the management that he cooked his meals on it at lunch time.

These items were all prohibited. There was no excuse for them being Inside the prison in the first place.

## Hazing – With a Difference!

In the nineties, there was a national concern about the hazing of military recruits. The Staff College principal gathered the staff and insisted that there be no hazing of the Correctional Officer students.

As an instructor, at the graduation party of one of the classes, I was standing behind the bar with one of my co-instructors. We had a bottle of something called Shark Attack. This was a clear blue vodka the colour of Windex window cleaning fluid.

We poured this into a clear plastic bottle with a spray head attached so that it looked like the window cleaner that the cleaners used. We gathered the graduates up to the bar and poured each of them a shot into a glass. We announced that we were toasting them the way the cons do – with window cleaner. Reassuring them that the cons drank it all the time and that it would not hurt them, we had even poured some actual window cleaner into the bar sink prior to the prank so they could smell it.

There were some tentative looks going around as the peer pressure kicked in. They timidly took their glass in their hands and smelled the liquid. They knew then it was just a prank. But the principal and her major domo did not. They came screaming across the room yelling, "They're hazing the students! They're hazing the students!"

Shortly after, the principal had the bar removed from the College. This was not done as a result of the prank; it was done to save money. She also removed the longstanding tradition of the Graduation Dinner for the new Officers that had been held at the College for many years. This dinner was replaced with a lunch, which did not cost her anything as the students got their lunch meals at the College anyway. Yet another way that the lowest-ranking staff members were marginalized in favour of making your budget look good and getting your annual performance pay.

## Urine Testing

The Urine Testing Module was a dry subject to say the least. I didn't know much about it because it was specialized work, and the line officers did not do it. So, I attempted to make it more interesting, I improvised on the teaching model that required the instructor to stand before the class for two hours and deliver this subject straight out of the book.

I began by going to one of the local institutions and getting a supply of urine testing equipment: empty plastic sample containers and blank forms, rubber gloves, goggles, and testing agents. I had all the equipment required to do the actual testing of convict urine. I even had false positive chemicals for every drug tested.

I first made a batch of urine using water and food colouring. I even varied the shade of urine to make it more believable. I labeled the plastic containers with fake inmate names and FPS numbers and added a positive reaction chemical and I even left some of them agent free for more realism.

The students were given the theory and cautionary instructions about handling biohazards and universal precautions. Then they had to "test convict urine" using the proper equipment and safety clothing. They filled in the paperwork according to the results they got from their con's pee test. When it was all over, one of my co-instructors leaned back in his chair, when he had everyone's attention he picked up a plastic container of urine and took the lid off saying "This is how we test con piss at Millhaven" and tipped the whole container into his mouth and swallowed. Amid the gasps and screams of the students he then pronounced that the urine was "Clean!". It was always a good time teaching with this guy. He knew his stuff and had the experience to back it up. He also had a good sense of humour that was required to work Inside the Chaos.

The cons always have a way of beating the urine test. If they were dirty through drug use, they would buy clean urine from another con and put it into a clean toothpaste tube. They would hide this in their pants and fill the bottle from the toothpaste tube rather than fail the test. This financial investment was a good deal and paid off for them because some of the Correctional Treatment Programs required a series of clean piss tests in order to secure a temporary absence pass or recommendation for parole.

It's playing the game.

## Hold My Beer

Another test that was being used in the institutions was the buccal swab to detect the recent use of alcohol. This was always a favourite with me as it raised many eyebrows at the college. I would ask the recruits if any of them had any beer in their rooms. Alcohol is not permitted in the recruits' rooms while in residence at the college so no one would admit to it. I would tell them that I was going to close my eyes for five minutes and when I opened them, I expected to see a beer in my open hand. There was much scrambling and the patter of feet to be heard. Often, when I opened my eyes there would be several cans of beer lined up on the desk. I had to answer for this because some of the recruits were caught rushing through the hallways with a can of beer in their hands. When queried by a manager as to why they were running with beer they would reply "Because Dave Woodhouse wanted one". I would ask for a volunteer to drink one of the beers and there was always no hesitation in complying with this request. After downing the alcohol, we would use the swabs to wipe the inside of the volunteers' mouth and check the colour of the swab.

## Patricia the Stripper

There was a module taught in the Correctional Officers Training Program called Searching and Frisking. Inmates get very good at hiding things both within their physical environment, on their person and in their person.

As an inmate you have get good at this because if you are holding for someone and you have the goods confiscated you still have to pay it back. In many cases, if you can't pay you have to run for the hole to preserve your health.

The searching and frisking module would instruct on how to properly perform a "Pat Down" search checking the inmate for items hidden in his or her clothing. This was a common day to day procedure within every institution coast to coast. The recruits would hide weapons and items of contraband on themselves and have their fellow recruits frisk them to try to find the items.

Then there was the "Strip Search". No one liked to do these. It was not a glamorous part of the job, yet it had to be done. Most strip searches were performed when you had to escort an inmate into the community or to another correctional facility. Sometimes it was performed when there were grounds to believe that they had hidden contraband.

Body cavity searches were not performed by staff members. A medical doctor performed these when the inmate was suspected of concealing contraband within their body that would be hazardous to their health. This evidence was usually confirmed by an X-ray.

Everyone in the classed enjoyed performing the pat down searches as it was fun to try to put one over on your fellow class members when they missed an item that you had hidden.

Then when it came to the instruction portion about "strip searches" the cheerful atmosphere in the classroom disappeared. The instructors would ask for a volunteer to be strip searched in front of the class. (This never took place and was used as a set up to prank the students) There was much avoidance of eye contact, much awkwardness, much tension. The instructor would then advise the students that because we expected no one to volunteer we arranged to have one of the cleaning staff place an X in masking tape on the underside of one of their chairs at random. The person in the marked chair would be our volunteer.

It was actually the instructor who placed the X under the chair before the class started. The student chosen was usually the one of the most timid in the class.

Then everyone would stand up with a look of dread on their faces and peer under their chairs. The reactions were predictable. Those who did not find an X under their seats were the most relieved they have ever been in their lives. The one poor person with the X had one of two common reactions. The first was denial, they just pretended that it wasn't there. The second was outright refusal to participate. When it was revealed that this was a joke on the entire class there was much relief, especially from the poor selected student. I still have former students who remember these hoaxes fondly as one of the highlights of their training.

# PART 36

## The True Nature of the Beast

Overall, I have to say my time at the College was a refreshing break from the violence and stress of the prison. I was working with some very experienced and knowledgeable officers who made the College a

**"Trying to find some way to present without being hypocritical was the challenge."**

great place to be. These were staff members who, like me did the job and had been IERT Team Leaders and Firearm and Gas Instructors at their respective prisons and they brought a wealth of frontline knowledge and experience to their lessons. The only downside of working at the College was that the systemic corruption that was in the jails was also here. It was just something that was unavoidable in the CSC at that time.

One of the greatest challenges we faced as experienced instructors was trying to present the CSC in a positive light after each of us having faced the true nature of this beast and been wounded by it. We discussed this topic often among ourselves because we could not tell the students what really went on down Inside because they would run screaming from the building. Trying to find some way to present without being hypocritical was also a great challenge. We all experienced the deceit and spin doctoring that went on when we were on our initial training, and that fact that we were not prepared properly for this kind of working environment in the least back then. Do we just throw them into the water to become chum for the sharks in the cell blocks, the predator guards and the corrupt staff wearing suits?

We sold the product with a great degree of caution without forcing them into situations of great anxiety and outright fear that would most certainly be brought on if we told them about our many bad experiences and the subsequent lifelong nightmares that they produced for us.

Just the thought of visiting a prison is fodder enough to produce nightmares for most people. Very soon, they were all going to be in the thick of it and it was no different from what we experienced in our

> **"We knew that what awaited them on the Inside would destroy most of them."**

time as new recruits. We had to maintain a professional demeanour while having to suppress the constant urge to scream "RUN!" during our lessons.

On the day of their graduation, the experienced instructors would gather the recruits into a classroom for the final time, just an hour or so before their formal graduation ceremony and swearing-in to be full-fledged Correctional Officers and Primary Workers. We wanted to give them something that we didn't get when we graduated. It was a highly charged emotional experience for us because we all had our physical and emotional scars from being down Inside for so long. We would look at these young, fresh-faced mostly naive people, hoping that we prepared them as best we could for the evil that they were soon going to face. But also knowing that even if we had them under our charge for a full year of instruction, we could never have adequately prepared them for what they were going to face – no one could.

We knew that what awaited them on the Inside would destroy most of them. What could we possibly do for them in these final few minutes before they entered our world of bad dreams?

All we could offer them was ourselves as a coping resource when things inevitably got tough on them. We had already been there and suffered through what would be the impending and unavoidable machinations of the unrealistic world that is the CSC. We told them we would be here for them when the time came that they required a trusted friend and advisor to give them honest counsel and advice when the system lets them down. That's all we had to offer. That's more than what we had when we started.

Even when I left the CSC and went to work for the Toronto Police Service, sitting at my desk in the Detective office, I would still get calls from former students who had been traumatized, lied to, cheated, thrown under the bus and let down by their managers. They turned to me for advice they could trust.

# PART 37

## "The Duty to Act Fairly"

Justice must not only be done but must be seen to be done.

—Lord Howard, Lord Chief Justice of England (1924)

After running a competition for the position of Staff Instructor at the Correctional Staff College in 1995, the principal of the College forced her new staff, through coercion, to sign a bogus employment contract that she and her second in command fabricated. I was one of these staff members. Their fraudulent contract required the new Staff Instructors to work at their substantive level of pay for performing work designated at a supervisor's level, at the time this was a CX-3 rank, two levels above my pay grade.

This ruse was used by the principal in her attempt to deceive by simply changing the classification of the position and designating the job as a "Developmental Assignment" rather than an Acting Position. The thinking was that if it were called a "Developmental Assignment" she would not have to pay her new instructors at the appropriate level designated for that position as per the Master Agreement Employment Contract. This was yet another example of how CSC Managers redefined a term to deflect, deceive, and defraud.

This was the same kind of spin we witnessed when the CSC attempted to use new terminology such as, "Crisis Negotiator" rather than "Hostage Negotiator" or "Isolated Disturbance" rather than "Riot", "Structured Intervention Unit" rather than "Segregation". If you call it something else then that makes it something else to suit your immediate needs it would seem, regardless of what the contractual, legal, and ethical designations make it.

Thie senior managers deliberately and with foreknowledge through article M-27.07 of the Master Agreement knew that what they were doing to their staff was dishonest and so cheated many of these dedicated staff members. Some of these instructors worked from six in the morning to eleven at night without any compensation for their overtime. This was during a period when, up to that time, the highest volume of recruits ever trained in the history of the College was being undertaken. There was so many that some had to be put up in the local hotels as the in-house accommodation was at capacity.

Prior to the posting of the Competition for Staff Training Instructor being released, the principal received a letter dated July 8, 1993, from one of the indeterminate staff members at the College. The memo copied below was written and given to the principal prior to the pending competition. It addressed her intent to have the new instructors paid at their substantive level rather than at the appropriate, contract-negotiated level of a Staff Training Instructor.

> *"If the positions are not to be acting positions, the following actions are required (according to the Chief of Staffing, Ontario Region):*
>
> - *have you checked with the DC (Deputy Commissioner), is he in favour of this action?*
> - *we will likely have grievances filed from current staff, they will likely be upheld, and we will have to pay $ (possibly retroactively) then at STI-02 level*
> - *do we have the $ to pay instructors at this level?"*

There was no job description provided to us other *than "will carry out the function as Staff Instructor, reporting to the Manager Training Programs and carry out all of the operational tasks and responsibilities of that position plus such other duties as may be assigned by management from time to time."*

We were not provided with an Organizational Chart or statement of duties. The org-chart would have provided us with the position titles, classification, and salary of each employee. From a brief examination of this chart, you could see the glaring difference in the pay scales from the indeterminate College instructors and those on "Developmental Assignment" who actually had a higher workload than the much higher paid staff instructors.

The acting instructors did the majority teaching of the practical and knowledge components of the training provided to the new Officer Recruits and to experienced staff members. Of the fifty CTP Modules required, I taught forty-eight of them. This unquestionably does not sound like someone who is on a "Developmental Assignment".

Three of the new instructors already had the knowledge, experience, and ability to teach the majority of the CTP modules before they even started at the College so this could not possibly be construed in any manner as a "Developmental Assignment" as they already had what it took to hit the ground running by teaching on the very first day without any orientation training at all.

As for the assignment being a "Rotational Developmental Assignment" there was no developmental training offered or granted to us over the entire two years that we were there. I received one-half day of Franklin Time Management over my two years.

Written requests for training were rejected and eventually ignored by the employer. The reason given by the manager was, "We will not waste the College's money training someone who is only here temporarily." Further proof that the "developmental assignment" wording was just more of their guile.

After discussing this issue with the management of the College, they were adamant that my co-instructors and I had signed a "legally-binding document" and advised that we could give thirty days' notice, terminate our secondment, and return to our institutions and they would take on the person who was "next on the list".

They were then questioned about CSC Policy of "the Duty to Act Fairly" and "managing the service with openness and integrity."

They were advised that we would then be pursuing a grievance against the College on the issue of pay. But they strongly advised against taking such action as, "No one in the history of the College had ever filed a grievance against them before."

We told them that the Master Collective Agreement is clear that when acting in a position one is entitled to be paid at that level. In the bogus "Memorandum of Agreement" that we were coerced into signing, it clearly stated that we would "retain all inherent entitlements as calculated to the applicable agreement." The Collective Agreement took precedent over their deceptive "Memorandum of Agreement".

After conferring with legal counsel, we were advised that the Memorandum of Agreement was indeed not legally binding, particularly because it dealt with the issue of pay. It was just a fabrication constructed with the intent to deceive and confuse the new staff members. We were further informed that we had a strong and valid claim, with several pay equity and Human Rights issues.

Knowingly breaking the established rules certainly serves as an indication of a guilty mind and the line into criminality is not crossed until there is a willful act of deception as we experienced. That fact had already been established in that the management of the College knowingly and deceitfully placed our financial interest at risk.

The Deputy Commissioner and the Assistant Commissioner Personnel and Training at National Headquarters were also made aware of this act and did nothing to rectify it. This neglect just reinforced the corrupt corporate culture from the top down that permeated the Service at that time.

The side issues were how negatively this process affected us. Privately, some of the other staff told us that we would be perceived as whiners, not team players, and that we could no longer be trusted by the CSC Management. Others said we should've just accepted it. Some said we would never be able to work at the College again, that we have been blacklisted because no one had ever filed a grievance against the Regional Correctional Staff College before this.

In the end, many of these predictions came true.

## Play It Safe or Commit Career Suicide

The principal's corrupt practice was challenged by two of the staff members through the grievance process. We two who initially wrote the grievance brought it to the attention of the other staff members who had also been duped and asked them if they would like to file a grievance along with us. The others declined. They did not want to jeopardize their relationship with a Senior Manager by challenging their corrupt acts formally and publicly. They well knew the consequences to their careers if they were to do that.

After the grievance was upheld at the adjudication level, it was only then that abstaining staff members, who originally declined to grieve, came forward and filed their own claim to recover the money that they were duped out of. These abstainers wanted to play it safe and let the others stick their necks out and risk the wrath of management. Only when it was safe for them to do so, and posed no risk to their career, did these staff file to recover their pay. This 'play it safe' manoeuvre was indicative of most CSC staff members who knew full well that to challenge their manager at any level was to commit career suicide and be labeled with a terminal rank designation. They often declined to stand up for themselves out of the fear of that very real fact. If someone else wanted to stick their neck out it was fine with them. If they were successful, then all can benefit from the courage of the risk-takers, if they were not successful, well, their position with their manager was safe. Although cowardly, it was a means for them to survive the beast.

Integrity, Courage and Honour Inside the Chaos.

## Win Grievance – Lose Back Pay

The formal grievance hearing was held in Kingston on April 27, 1998, where the evidence was heard by a member of the Public Service Staff Relations Board. I was called to give my testimony concerning Article M-27, Pay Administration of the Master Agreement.

There wasn't much deliberation required by the Public Service Staff Relations Board member after hearing the evidence and examining the deceptive Memorandum of Agreement. It was a cut and dried matter of deceit and breach of contract on the part of the management of the Correctional Staff College.

Our grievance was upheld, so that in future any staff members assigned to the College would be paid at the appropriate, contract negotiated level.

As for our financial remedy, we were once again out of luck. We received a limited amount of acting pay, as it was not calculated over the full two years we worked there.

In the Management Decision, File #2359-0 from the Deputy Commissioner of Ontario Region and File #ON-96-0002(402) from the Assistant Commissioner Personnel and Training, they upheld the grievance but only permitted us six months of acting pay out of the full two years we were entitled to. The Master Agreement article 27.07 clearly states: *"The employee shall be paid acting pay calculated from the date on which he or she commenced to act."*

Even at the higher rank of a Deputy Commissioner in the CSC, the opportunity and rationale used to commit an act of betrayal like this was strongly influenced by the lack of values and ethics adopted by those in authority at the highest levels of the Correctional Service of Canada at the time.

In addition to being cheated out of our acting pay, I was required to assist the Kingston Fire and Rescue Training Officer with the practical training and testing of SCBA. As an experienced and qualified SCBA instructor, I was the only option to help out in this training. It was held at one of the local smoke house facilities located at Collins Bay or Joyceville Institutions. The training took place in the evenings and sometimes went to eleven o'clock at night.

I had worked over 140 hours of overtime for the College doing this training without any compensation. When I questioned my direct supervisor about this corrupt practice she simply stated, "the College does not pay overtime." She went on to suggest, "Keep track of your hours and cash them in as time off when you return to your Institution." The collective agreement does not permit officers to get time off instead of cash for hours worked in overtime. I knew what my Warden would say if I approached him for time off earned at another correctional facility. And to even suggest such a thing said a lot about the quality of the management in place at the Staff College at that time.

This was the kind of unethical working environment we had to endure under these two managers while we worked at the Regional Correctional Staff College in Kingston.

I was one of the two Instructors who dared to challenge the dishonest practices of the managers. I didn't really expect the Mission Statement or Core Values to have much value in this workplace as they never have. The time I spent at the College was proof enough that the poisoned and corrupt work environment that was the CSC in my time with them, was not limited to the institutions alone, it was systemic.

One of the hardest experiences in the CSC is seeing corrupt staff promoted and then having to work under them. It eats you up inside and leaves you with a frustrated outlook on the system. How long can you go on and on experiencing this kind of corruption day after day before it wears you down? This was the greatest contributor to the enormous amount of stress related illness suffered by the front-line staff members in the CSC at that time.

The managers were never spoken to by the Regional Deputy Commissioner or by the Chief of Staffing RHQ about their actions, even though they knew full well that this had taken place after being advised in letters dated February 28, 1997, and March 21, 1997. These letters were simply ignored by the Senior Managers of the Ontario Region. The Deputy Commissioner Personnel and Training was the final decision-maker with respect to fair restitution for our loss, but he too failed to do the right thing by his low-level employees.

The Principal and her Training Manager never expressed regret for what she had done to her staff. Both were in complete denial that they had done anything wrong.

Both her and the Regional Deputy Commissioner and the Deputy Commissioner Personnel and Training never sought to apply a fair and adequate remedy this situation, as was their duty.

So, the injured staff members were further victimized by the Service through Senior Management's total failure to act with even a modicum of ethics and professionalism.

I remember the incumbent Regional Deputy Commissioner at that time quoting the classic statement: "Justice must not only be done but must be seen to be done" while addressing one of the new Correctional Officer graduation ceremonies.

Had the shoe been on the other foot and a low-level employee cheated a manager in such a deceitful way, the internal and the criminal investigations would have been convened in full force against them.

As a result of the ongoing corruption and betrayal by those in positions of trust, power, and authority, a highly dedicated and professional staff member so injured by this violation of trust and lack of support by his senior managers, left the Service a few years after.

\* \* \*

Throughout all of this, the college management staff were hiring their relatives on personal services contracts over the summer and did this using the same "Memorandum of Agreement".

In the not-so-distant past, the hiring of relatives was used as a conflict of interest that got a former Prison for Women Warden fired. I often wondered if that was the real reason for her dismissal because that corrupt practice of hiring relatives has continued even beyond that very public example of her being fired from the CSC for it.

What good is having a Collective Agreement that has been certified by the Public Service Staff Relations Board when its' contents can be displaced by this "Memorandum of Agreement" that appears to have omnipotent power over a certified, government sanctioned framework that provides orderly and efficient labour relations between the employer, the union and the employees?

This form was still being used to avoid transparency and manipulate staff members long after I had left the service.

In 2016 a female officer from Fraser Valley Institute for Women was attending and IERT 10-day basic training course. This woman was brutally harassed by her male cohorts throughout the training. In the aftermath of the incident, she was issued an apology from the Commissioner and handed a Memorandum of Agreement that would place her into the position of a community parole officer in exchange for agreeing not to file a grievance or take legal action and only if the terms of the agreement were kept confidential. The officer, Nubia Vanegas refused to sign. In a quote from lawyer Elizabeth Grace over this incident "public institutions such as federal prisons have to be held to a higher standard of transparency and should not be forcing employees to "keep their mouths shut" in exchange for justice.

*(CBC Radio Canada posted 06 Nov 2017 Erica Johnson)*

## More Grievances

This was not the end of the questionable staffing practices carried out by the Regional Correctional Staff College. After returning to Collins Bay Institution, I was elected their Union President and investigated grievances filed by the staff members. One of two such grievances were over the selection process for the position of Staff Instructor at the Regional Correctional Staff College.

I looked into the marking, scoring, and the assessment of my grieving members' competition test scores for the position of Staff Instructor. I compared them with the other candidates' scores and assessments along with their personal suitability ratings. The testing and scoring was conducted by a panel of three managers from the Staff College.

After examining the Master Assessment Sheet that recorded the candidates' scores, it was determined that the officer I was representing actually scored higher than the successful candidate due to mistakes in adding up the marks.

While attending the disclosure hearing on June 8, 1997, and investigating deeper into this matter, it was revealed that only one of the four candidates submitted the required Performance Evaluation before the closing date, as required. As well, the preferred candidate did not meet the current appraisal requirements as defined by the very people running the competition.

The preferred candidate did not have a personal stability mark recorded on the test sheet. The preferred candidate did not even submit their application to the competition until after the closing date yet was allowed to compete. The same took place for some of the supporting documentation with respect to demonstrating previous teaching experience and letters of reference by their supervisors. None of them submitted this documentation within the designated time period with the exception of the grieving officer.

Any one of these omissions was an automatic disqualification to compete for the position. Yet, the preferred candidate and the others who were all lacking the required documents were permitted to do so against all selection process policy.

A great many of the competition posters within the CSC contained the following Screening Qualifications statement:

> The onus is on you, the candidate, to fully demonstrate in writing *at the time of the application* that you possess the above screening qualifications. Failure to do so may result in your application being screened out without further consideration.

Had the officer not challenged the competition through the grievance process, the preferred candidate would have gotten the position through acts of guile.

The grievance examination clearly exposed the deceit of the competition process held by the management team in order to place their preferred candidate into the position.

With their chicanery now exposed, the manager of the staff college revoked the competition rather than take the successful candidate who was deliberately placed last on the list but was the only one who competed fairly.

After a short period of time, their preferred candidate got the job they wanted at the staff college and eventually their preferred candidate became an executive within the CSC. This was one of two grievance presentations I investigated that demonstrated that the Regional Correctional Staff College was once again neglecting their "Duty to Act fairly" and doing so with impunity.

## A Bogus Screening Requirement

In the screening qualifications for a teaching position at the College it stated that the candidate must have: *"Fully satisfactory and extensive experience working in a correctional environment in security, programs, or case management."*

Yet, in an appeal hearing decision rendered in 1997 by R. J. Ojalammi, Chairman, Appeals Board, he clearly stated that: "For the foregoing reasons, the experience requirement established by the department (selection board) (that of 'Fully satisfactory and extensive experience working in a correctional environment in security, programs, or case management') was held *not to afford a basis for selection* according to merit."

It was clearly established through evidence, that the screening qualification in use was *"not a bona fide requirement in selecting candidates according to merit."* Further:

> *"If the intent of the experience requirement is to screen candidates for certain expertise rather than to simply ensure that the temporary instructors do not stay for more than one posting, then it should be written and assessed more explicitly."*

Even after the decision was rendered, the college and other sites in the CSC continued to use this bogus screening qualification statement in future competitions, completely disrespecting the Chairman of the Appeal Board's ruling.

## A Full-on Catch-22

While working at the College, I had applied to six competitions within the Ontario Region. I was screened from everyone of them because I was working at the College and did not have "Current and extensive experience working in a correctional environment." Even when I applied to teach at the College for another term, I was screened out because I worked at the College.

Truly a Catch-22 situation.

After gathering the evidence and facts in this matter, I addressed the issue to my Warden, Chief Human Resource Manager, Staffing Officer of Ontario, and the Principal of the College in the form of a four-page letter. It was ignored by all. I was a low-level officer of terminal rank.

## Defining Merit in Hiring and Promotion

The Government of Canada has a *Public Service Act* that oversees the integrity of the hiring and promotion system and makes sure that the hiring process is not compromised. The Public Service Commission performs audits across the staffing system, examining hiring and promotion files, to ensure that employees are hired and promoted based on merit.

Merit refers to the use of essential qualifications during the hiring and promotion process. This means that people who are hired and promoted in the public service *must* possess certain competencies, skills, and experience, rather than being based on political connections or partisan affiliations.

The merit principle requires that every person who is appointed to the public service has met the essential qualifications and requirements established for the position. Yet even though this system is in place, the CSC routinely did not adhere to it, and continued to promote and manipulate the careers of their staff members as they saw fit, whether they merited it or not.

\*    \*    \*

# PART 38

## In Too Deep

> "The suicide deaths of husband and wife prison guards were linked to a major corruption investigation at Kingston Penitentiary, according to testimony by police and prison officials."
>
> —*CBC News*, February 27, 2002

In the very first class I was in charge of there was a student who had failed the training program. She was unable to complete the firearms portion of the course and several other aspects of the training modules as well. Had she been successful, she was designated to work at one of the male prisons within the Region. She was to be dismissed as per CSC policy because she failed the training.

However, a manager at the College decided that she would be better off at Prison for Women as the officers there did not require firearms training. The manager overturned the decision to release her and off she went to P4W without successfully completing all the required and essential training to become a Peace Officer.

Some years later, she was working at a male maximum security prison within the Ontario Region. She was also living with another guard who worked at the same prison and the two of them bought a home together.

The finances for the home they purchased was arranged by one of the inmates.

One thing led to another as they got in over their heads in debt to the inmate. The con wanted them to bring drugs and other contraband into the prison for him and was using the loan as blackmail to compel them to lug in the goods. So, being caught between a rock and a hard place they decided the only way out for them was suicide. They killed themselves and left a note identifying their co-workers who were involved in the same corrupt activities.

# PART 39

## Launching a New Ship

### A New Philosophy for Treating Women Offenders

Grand Valley Institution (GVI) located in the Ontario Region was the brand-new Prison for Women. This was going to be the flagship for Corrections' new philosophy for the treatment of women offenders. After the scathing reports that came out of the *Arbour Commission of Inquiry into Certain Events at the Prison for Women in Kingston* (1996), the CSC had to put on a new face and Grand Valley was it.

The new Staff Members being hired for Grand Valley were to be designated as Primary Workers, at the CX-2 level. The women and some men selected for this position by the CSC were handpicked by the newly appointed Warden of GVI and her staff.

In 1996, they arrived at the Regional Correctional Staff College ready for their training. Each CTP (Correctional Training Program) had a Staff Instructor assigned to their class throughout their training. The responsibility of class leader for the instructors was rotational and changed with each new class. According to the rotation schedule, I was to be their assigned Instructor. But I was removed from this position because "I was a man" according to the managers of the College.

I protested this as a clear example of discrimination based upon my gender. But "You are a man, and the new recruits are women" was the answer given by the all-female management team like it was the obvious and righteous decision.

The issue was finally settled by appointing a second Instructor, a woman, alongside me as liaison. This was the first time in the history of the College that two instructors were in charge of one class.

## Same Aliens … Different Planet

A mockup model of the new Grand Valley Institute for Women was brought to the Staff College. This, along with photos of the construction phases for the build gave us and the Primary Workers an idea of what the new facility would look like. One of the experienced instructors took note of the picket-like fence surrounding the prison with its motion detection sensor and asked when the chain link fences were being installed. The reply from the newly appointed Warden, as she looked down her nose at him was, "This is a new facility for women, and security fences are a thing of the past."

"But" the experienced instructor replied metaphorically, "aren't you just taking the same aliens and placing them on a different planet, and by virtue of that expecting them to behave differently?"

She didn't like this comment either.

Very soon after the inmates boarded this new flagship of the CSC, the escapes and contraband smuggling ran completely out of control. The residents in the surrounding community were outraged and complained. The CSC was forced to enhance the perimeter security level to rival that of maximum-security institutions.

Very few of the original members of that first training course of Primary Workers at Grand Valley Institute remained there. Many soon left after finding out that what they were sold by the management team that hired them wasn't a true reflection of content of the Mission document that was used as a brochure to sell the product to them. Some just quit, others transferred to male institutions, some took positions outside of uniform. The "aliens" were not how they were depicted to be in the recruitment sales pitch. The meaningful interaction between staff and offender took on a very different meaning than what was described to them in the job offer. Some staff said that the women offenders were worse than the men.

Just because you would like an inmate to behave differently in their new accommodations doesn't mean they will, regardless of how hard you try to sell your new product to them and to the public. A prison is a prison, and a con is a con. It's up to them to make the changes in their lives using the tools and encouragement you provide for them. This is not something you can wish upon them or force upon them. It's their choice.

Once again, and not for the final time, the Monday morning quarterbacks and knee-jerk reaction policy makers did not understand the behaviour and the potential for violence that their correctional clients possess.

The Author Teaching at the Gas Range

# PART 40

## The Old College Try

### Loaded Shooters

I remember my Firearms Instructor Course in the 1980s. The training was held at the CSC shooting range located on the local army base. You had the good ol' boys going to the bar during their lunch break and coming back 'loaded' to continue their training. The instructor trainer never acted on this because he was having his drinks bought for him at the bar by his students. This was a sure way to pass the course even if you were unable to stand, let alone handle a firearm safely on the range. This was the way it was done back in the day of buying whisky in the old boys' club.

This same instructor trainer had an ongoing scam running at the Correctional Staff College. Twice a year or more, he would take the spent brass cartridges from the firing range to the local metal recycling plant. There would be cases upon cases of brass casings that would fill the rear bed of a pickup truck up to the rails. The brass would be weighed, and a cash payment would be made to him for the metal. The money was supposed to be returned to the Correctional Staff College.

When I took over those duties, I handed the College two cheques, one for $353.50 and the second for $258.30 worth in total $611.80[32] for just one trip to the recycling yard. They were shocked because this had never happened before and wanted to know where the money came from. They were unaware that the expended brass from the ammo was worth so much.

## The Key to Many Doors

I remember one occasion when a stone mason worker found the barrel of a 38-calibre revolver hidden in the wall of the building he was working on at the Correctional Staff College. He turned it in and there

**"The inmate had a key to more ammunition and gas than the local police force possessed."**

was an internal investigation into how it came to be there. One of the recommendations from the completed investigation was that all the locks on the buildings be changed.

Shortly after the locks were changed, I went into the library at the College early one morning to get some videotapes for my class and had to wait for the female offender who worked there to get in and open the library door with her key. I figured that while I was waiting, I would try my key. To my surprise, it fit, and the door opened. I became curious after that and when the offender got to work, I took her key and tried it in several locks at the College. It fit many, including the safe that contained all the keys to the ammunition room and the room where we stored all the tear gas agents. The inmate had a key to more ammunition and tear gas than the local police force possessed.

## About Those 45 New Rifles Outside

Stranger still was the time that the College received a shipment of semi-automatic 9mm carbine rifles. Whenever firearms are delivered, they have to be signed for and accounted for by someone who has access to the secure storage vault located within the College. A delivery truck arrived, and the driver was looking for someone to take the firearms off his hands. I told

---

[32] Receipt numbers 004357 and 004401.

him that he would have to return another day, as I did not have access to secure storage for the weapons. The driver wandered around until he found someone that would accept delivery and sign for it.

A convicted offender, who is employed at the College as a groundskeeper signed for the firearms. The driver left 45 semi-automatic 9mm carbine rifles on the front step of the College all night.

This was where I found them the next morning when I arrived for work.

# PART 41

## Weapons Training

The Author instructing on the firearms range

Custodial personnel must have full opportunity for continuing professional educational development and should be required to spend a minimum of one week a year in refresher courses or upgrading.

—*MacGuigan Report* (1977), Recommendation 7

Part of the induction training program was the safe use and deployment of Service firearms. In the area of weapons, the CSC had a profound degree of inexperience that even a layperson with limited knowledge of firearms can plainly see. At that time, the firearms Correctional staff were trained and issued with:

- Smith and Wesson Model 10 .38 Special revolver
- Colt AR-15 .223 Cal Rifle
- Colt 9MM carbine
- Remington 870 12-gauge shotgun

I remember *The Andy Griffith Show* and the revolver that Barney Fife always carried. The CSC used the exact same firearm along with the same holster as seen on that classic TV sitcom of the 1960s; our equipment was just that old and outdated. I remember Barney carried his bullet in his shirt pocket, his *one* bullet. Well, life imitates art in that the CSC was not too far off the mark from that classic comedic concept.

The old leather holsters that were issued by the CSC were constantly in a state of disrepair. The leather strap that covers the hammer and secures the firearm in the holster was always stretched out of shape so that it never secured the revolver inside the holster. The weapon was always falling out when you got in and out of the mobile patrol vehicle. Most officers never even wore the weapon when deployed to their control posts, towers and mobile patrol vehicle because of this. Often you had to look for the revolver when you relieved the mobile patrol as it had often fallen off the seat onto the floor or between the passenger door and seat of the vehicle.

There were usually three varieties of holster for the .38, two strap holsters and one flap holster that were manufactured in the 60s and 70s and were issued by the CSC right into the 1990s' and all of them out of date, impractical and in sad shape for active use.

The Firearms Act is very specific with respect to the use of a well designed, constructed and maintained firearms retention system for caring a gun while on duty as a Peace Officer. But this simply went ignored for years and years by the CSC even after being brought to the attention of the Security Branch at National Headquarters in the 1990s.

The old holsters were finally replaced by a surplus of RCMP holsters. The RCMP were issued with semi-automatic pistols and no longer required their stock of used wheel gun holsters, so they were going to be destroyed. The CSC stepped up to take them off of the RCMPs' hands and issued them across the country.

Yet, at the time the Security Manual Part III Firearms page FA33 still stated that the "Operational" holster is the RCMP Full Flap Holster DSS NATO #1095-21-898-778. The Security manual was never updated to include these newly issued Firearms Retention Systems.

The new holsters were a secure system designed to retain the firearm if someone to attempted to disarm the officer. They were classified as a firearm retention system, threat level two.

The CSC issued these new holsters Nation-wide without any training on how to draw the revolver from them and without the proper gun belt to secure the holster in place.

As a result of this negligence, you had officers wearing the new holsters who could not even draw the revolver from this retention system if they had to. You had officers wearing a right-handed holster on their left side and visa- versa. There is no way of getting that firearm out of these holsters using the cross-draw method. The holster itself has to be firmly secured to a proper web belt, not just slid into place on the standard male or female issue belt, which was being done across the country.

This information comes directly for the supplier of the holster with the warning that it is negligent to deploy it in any other manner.

This logic was totally lost on the Security Branch at National Headquarters, as they have no experience or extensive knowledge of Service Firearms, ammunition or retention systems in the field. The memo sent to Personal and Training dated 27 November 2000 expressing concerns about this issue was ignored and all written complaints and concerns were ignored as well. It does not take a firearm expert to see that this is a very serious safety issue. When enough pressure was applied in the form of a formal complaint to Labour Canada as well as bringing this issue to the attention of the Health and Safety Committee, the excuses began rolling in from RHQ and NHQ. We at the Institutional level attempted to have this serious safety issue resolved by going through the usual channels but these methods are routinely ignored. Yet you still have to demonstrate that you attempted to resolve it at the lowest level before advancing to the next.

The finger pointing began and it was directed at the Firearms Instructors at the Institutions. NHQ didn't understand that these holsters needed to be secured to a proper compatible web belt in order for them to work safely. The holsters were free, but web belts were not. Money would have to be spent on the nation-wide purchase and distribution of compatible belts. Proper instruction on how to use this equipment was not free either. We offered to incorporate it into the annual firearms refresher training. But on till that time we recommended that the staff members who did not have this instruction were not to use the holsters. The recommendation was ignored. We never made a formal complaint without offering up a variety of solutions otherwise, it's just complaining. As the IERT Team leader I supplied several proper duty belts that we had in our Team Ready Room. I fastened the holsters onto the belts myself and placed them at the main gate control center so that the officers working the mobile patrol would have them. This issue was still ongoing when I left the Service.

National Headquarters don't seem to get that fact that we, as Firearm Instructors are trying to protect the CSC in bringing this information to their attention. They are reluctant to act on this when they have no knowledge or experience in the field with any of these firearms to make an informed decision. They don't want to appear uninformed, and so are unwilling to take the advice from or act on the recommendations of their own experienced staff, even from the very person who wrote the National Training Manuel for Firearms for the Service.

It's they themselves who have to be brought up to speed on the reality of the way it is on the front lines as they are so far removed from it they have no idea about what goes on behind the walls.

You cannot be expected to deal with an issue when you have absolutely no knowledge or experience on the ground dealing with the day-to-day reality of working in a Prison. Many people in positions of authority and policy making did not consult the Officers at the front line before the implementation of a new security equipment or policy. It has been my experience that if a consultation is made it is only to say that they "have consulted with experienced Officers". Often the policy, decision or equipment has already been decided upon beforehand and the consult is just to add weight to the final draft. Your years of experience, knowledge and trade-craft mean absolutely nothing to the managers at National Headquarters. And when their final product blows up in their faces the policy makers have now so distanced themselves from it that they cannot be held responsible.

When I left the Service for the Toronto Police and then retired from there, I had returned to Kingston to live. Early one morning I was at the Kingston General Hospital with my father-in -law who was ill. I remember sitting in the waiting room and noticed a couple of guards escorting an offender sitting in a small office by the main door to the emergency department. The guard was sitting in a chair with his legs stretched out across the open door to the office, sleeping. The other guard was not there in the office with them at the time. The con was handcuffed to the front and was sitting there smiling at me and anyone who passed the open door. When he caught your attention, he would nod his head in the direction of the guard who was sound asleep. On his hip was a revolver in one of the old leather (Barney Fife) holsters. The firearm had slipped partially out of the old holster because the retaining strap no longer fit. I was shocked by this but more so alarmed that the CSC was permitting armed escorts outside of the prison carrying this shoddy equipment under the control of inferior guards. This was never done in my time. The inmate could have easily taken the revolver from the neglectful sleeping guard and the inmate knew it.

So nothing had changed in the CSC since the time I left.

In the future, on another hospital escort, an inmate did take advantage of an armed escort by attempting to disarm the guard. The inmate had his handcuffs removed for him by the guard so he could use the washroom. When he exited, he went for the officer's gun and during the struggle over the firearm one round went into the wall and the other struck a civilian in the foot. The offender was charged with aggravated assault, criminal negligence cause bodily harm, illegally discharging a firearm and take firearm from a Peace Officer. He was convicted and seven years was added to his sentence. The con was the brother of another high-profile offender who died in custody years earlier.

*Dave Woodhouse*

## The Emergency Reload

During the course of fire for the revolver, you were required to perform a tactical skill called an "emergency reload". In the event that you ran out of ammunition you were to perform this task by emptying the revolver and reloading the weapon with one bullet.

To accomplish this, you would first have to eject the six empty casings, insert one bullet into the cylinder and turn the cylinder so that this round will be in a position to fire right away. "This skill could save your life," we were told by an instructor. We were taught this without the history and theory behind this required skill being explained to us. I had no doubt that the instructor in that period had no idea what the reasoning for teaching this tactical skill was all about.

The reason for training in the emergency reload stemmed from a tragic event referred to as "The Newhall Incident" of 1970 in Valencia California. A shootout occurred between two heavily armed criminals and four California Highway Patrol Officers. In less than five minutes, all four officers were shot dead. The officers' training required them to reload their revolver with all six rounds of ammunition at once rather than just a few at a time as required.

**"This skill could save your life."**

Because they relied on their training, some of the dead officers were found with their spent brass castings in their pockets in order to "keep the range clean" as they were trained to do, rather than dumping them on the ground. They were found dead with four out of six rounds loaded in their revolver. In the middle of a heated gun battle for their lives, some were caught with their heads down concentrating on reloading their revolver with all six rounds and shot dead, when loading just a few could have saved their lives. The Newhall Incident was taught to me as an Auxiliary OPP Officer in my firearm training and taught once again in my training as a Toronto Police Officer.

This was the reasoning behind the "Emergency Reload" training but the firearms instructors at the College did not know this or they just didn't explain it. They did what the training manual said without explanation or

302

theory behind the tactic and without having the foundational experience to back up what they taught.

The only trouble with applying this skill in the CSC is that there is no way that it could ever be accomplished in the field: you were only issued with six bullets.

That's it.

On all the posts where a .38 revolver was located at Collins Bay institution the only ammunition you had is what was already in the revolver.

*You didn't have any extra to reload.*

The CSC was teaching emergency reloading when you were not issued with any additional ammunition to reload. I wondered how this training was supposed to "save your life".

This appeared to be a typical issue with most of the firearm training in the CSC at that time. Thoe who determined what the lesson plans would contain had no frontline practical, foundational experience in the area of firearms.

**"If you knew what's good for you, you'd do what you were told to do even when you knew it was wrong."**

Some of the people instructing these skills at that time and even up to the time that I left Corrections had no experience in the field, so they did what National Headquarters told them to do even when they knew it was impractical, dangerous, and a waste of training time. But, if you wanted to stay in your position, you allowed yourself to be an instrument of those in authority over you.

This kind of complacency appeared to be systemic in the CSC during the '80s and '90s. If you knew what's good for you, you'd do what you were told to do even when you knew it was wrong. This was the jackpot that got many CSC staff members into serious trouble, e.g., the Ashley Smith murder.

## No Sniper Team in the CSC

In my time with the service there was no official "gun team" or "sniper team". The firearm training was not specialized for the IERT. They get the same training in firearms as the rest of the guard staff, that of timed fire from a measured distance at stationary B27 targets.

The officers who teach firearms training do not have specialized knowledge, experience, or training in anything other than firing at static paper targets. None of the firearms in the CSC are specifically sighted in for an individual staff member. Whatever is on the security post or comes out of the armoury is what you got and you are expected to deploy that weapon responsibly and with accuracy in an emergency.

## "Shotgun Training Injuries" – February 2000

The report on Shotgun Training Injuries written by Chris Van Duyse, author of the *National Firearms Training Manual* for the Correctional Service of Canada.

Shotgun Training Injuries was a well-written and comprehensive report authored by an experienced instructor that explained in detail how and why our staff members were constantly injured by the use of duty issue ammunition being used for initial qualification and refresher training in the 12-guage shotgun.

The injuries sustained by experienced staff and new recruits were always viewed as something beneath the notice of CSC management. Many, many attempts to resolve this were brought to their attention, but they simply did what they always did and pointed their fingers at the complainants. "The instructors must be doing something wrong"; "There is nothing wrong with the ammunition or the methods that we are using now"; "You must have an agenda because none of the other institutions are reporting these injuries."

In fact, all the institutions doing shotgun refresher training had many staff members sporting bruised faces, shoulders, and arms. These injuries were not reported or tracked because you were perceived as being weak if you complained about it and you were put upon by your peers. This was the prison culture… you can't take it because you are not tough enough to do the job.

One of the Deputy Wardens at Collins Bay Institution who was on board with us about this issue had mentioned to me a conversation that he had with a neighbour who worked at Millhaven Institution. When the DW saw the neighbour and his friend, who also worked at Millhaven, with their arms severely bruised, he asked them how they got injured. The Millhaven guard told him that it was from the re-qualification training with the shotgun. The DW asked them if they reported the injuries, and the guards told him that they didn't do that at Millhaven, as they would appear weak in the eyes of their peers.

As an instructor at the staff college, I remember taking a female recruit to the hospital early one morning with large bruises on her jawline and cheek as well as her shoulder and arm, all caused by firing the shotgun during her induction training. The staff at the hospital thought she had been beaten by her spouse and questioned her repeatedly about the nature of her injuries while looking suspiciously at me.

To complicate the matter, after returning to the school with the recruit, I was called into the principal's office and dressed down for "fraternizing" with a female student and threatened with termination of my teaching assignment. One of the female instructors saw me arriving at the school early in the morning with the student in my vehicle, drew her own conclusions from that and reported me to management. This happened twice to me while I was teaching at the staff college. In the second incident I had driven a female recruit to the hospital in the early morning because she was having an asthma attack. Once again, upon arriving back at the College with the student I was paraded and grilled about my "fraternization" with the women recruits.

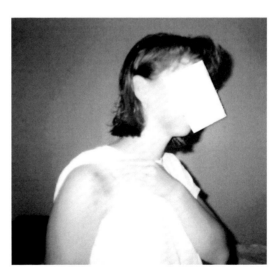

Injuries from the Shotgun

The author of the shotgun injuries report and I offered several solutions based upon our research and our many years of firearm training and teaching experience in the field to the matter of the injuries experienced from using the shotgun. The solution that would eliminate the injuries almost entirely was to use the lighter #8 "birdshot" for training purposes. It would reduce most of the injuries and be less expensive than the heavier buckshot. Buckshot is used to kill large mammals like deer. It's the same man killing ammunition used in Police shotguns.

Birdshot is used in the hunting of upland game such as partridge or in skeet shooting where you may fire many rounds in a day without the adverse effect of recoil injuring you.

Train with the lightest loads possible for this gun. For the same price of ten rounds of buckshot you can train properly with twenty-five rounds of inexpensive birdshot without the injuries.

When I taught firearms at the college, live fire drills were conducted with light birdshot loads as we were trying to install a positive training experience with this weapon. There is no better way to discourage a new shooter than to have them fire many rounds of buckshot through this gun over a short period of time.

But the reply we received from headquarters was that the firearm training in the Service had to be as realistic as possible, so the more powerful duty ammunition would stay and be used for initial training and requalification requalification. In a quote from a regional manager concerning this issue dated February 1, 2000:

> *"Furthermore, the Service adopted many years ago the practice to use "operational" rounds during training. This is to train and qualify our members on the ammunition that would be used in a real-life situation, etc. It makes little sense to train persons on something otherwise."*

Our counter and experienced reply to this dismissive and uninformed answer was that the much lighter, less expensive 38-calibre revolver 115gr wadcutter ammunition is being used for induction training and re-qualification rather than the duty issued 158gr +p hollow point ammunition. So, their argument for realism in training was completely shattered in that one sentence. The 38-calibre 115gr wadcutter is not an "operational" round and never has been an operational round, it is a "training round of ammunition" and this is what we were asking for in our shotguns, a lighter training round.

Another argument from RHQ that they were trying to sell us was from the same memo...

*"Approximately ten years ago (1990/91 I believe) EXCOM approved the use of number 4 Buckshot for IERT use when responding to emergency situations. To change to 7 1/2 would require EXCOM review and approval."* (We were not asking them to change to 7 1/2 shot to use in an emergency situation. Clearly, they did not know what we were talking about.)

*"Secondly, using this lighter shot that does not equate our operational #4 buckshot, could result in a situation during an emergency where the wrong ammunition is used and would be ineffective resulting in injuries or death etc. We must remember that it is under these conditions when the shotgun is to be used. Whether the 7 1/2 is to be used for training, there are no guarantees that there would not be any possible mix-ups of this ammunition as the #4 and the 7 1/2 would be kept in the armory."*

They were referring to an incident where there was a mix-up of shotgun ammunition and the wrong one was deployed. This was not the first time that firearm ammunition had been mixed up in the CSC. Staff members are trained to identify the proper caliber of duty-approved ammunition as part of their induction and refresher training. This same training is given to Police, Military and even to the general public when they attend classes to get their firearms license. All are required to identify the proper ammunition for the firearm and are tested on this.

The 38 cal+p revolver ammunition is kept in all the Institutional armouries along with the 38 cal wadcutter training ammunition. Yet another argument from an inexperienced manager shot down by the staff with extensive operational experience.

At that time, the Ontario Province Police and the RCMP did not subject their officers to this kind of punishment by using operational loads to train with. (The RCMP was using #8 Birdshot, the same shot size that we were recommending.)

The CSC issued recoil pads for the shotgun, which extend the length of the firearm so that small statured people find it difficult to mount, fire and control the gun.

The many photos of staff with their faces and arms bruised from shoulder to elbow with blackened eyes and jaw lines still don't seem to convince them.

The decision makers at NHQ and RHQ were invited to attend and experience a demonstration of the two types of ammunition and their effects on the human body. But they chose not to attend and "lead by example" as they would have you believe they do by the contents of their Mission Document and its Core Values.

All of this information was sent to NHQ Security Branch.

The final decision, answered in half a paragraph, from the Director General NHQ Security Branch dated September 20, 2000, left us completely dumbfounded:

> *"My department in co-operation with…(the company that they bought the ammunition from) have conducted a joint review of the #4 Buck and #00 Buck Shotgun Ammunition as a result of field inquiries regarding the Remington Model 870 shotguns recoil when fired. The Current CTP training and recertification program was also reviewed.*
>
> *The outcome of our review does not provide a strong preference of one ammunition over the other, however, there is some indication that the #00 Buck, reduced load, would be more user friendly. Both rounds have been found to be effective for our purpose.*
>
> *Therefore, I do not recommend we change from the current 12-gauge ammunition (#4 Buck) at this time. However, that is not to say when the current stock is depleted, we couldn't reassess and opt to change to a round we find more suitable at that time."*
>
> *Original Signed by*
> *Director General, Security Branch*
> *NHQ*

This was the reply we received after all of the research we performed on our own time to produce a well written investigative report into an issue that was consistently causing injury to our staff members.

The Director General, Security Branch at National Headquarters clearly had no idea what we were talking about, and he himself, through this ridiculous memorandum, demonstrated the fact that he had absolutely no experience with the Firearms and Ammunition purchased by, issued by and controlled by the very department he was in charge of. There was never any "open and honest two-way communication" between Security Branch and the institutional firearms instructors in an attempt to resolve this.

The Director General, Security Branch consulted with an outside agency (the company that they purchase the ammunition from) rather than with their own experienced staff members on this serious matter of health and safety.

Nothing was mentioned or suggested in any of the many, many pages of correspondence or mentioned in the Van Duyse report on Shotgun Training Injuries about the substitution of #4 Buckshot with #00Buckshot as our operational loads. Where National Headquarters got the idea that we were suggesting the use of #00 Buckshot we didn't know. It was made very clear in all of the facts and evidence presented that we were asking for #7 1/2 or #8 Bird Shot for *Training Purposes Only*, to reduce the ongoing injuries to staff members.

Also, Security Branch NHQ would not provide us with results of their "joint review" with their ammunition supplier.

Clearly, no one at the National Headquarters level gave our reports any serious thought and certainly the Core Value Statement, "Our strength and major resource in achieving our objectives is our staff" is meaningless to those in positions of power at that time.

The decision makers at NHQ simply lacked any knowledge and experience in this area and refused to listen to those who did as this was a non-issue for them. They were not the ones being injured.

They have never heard about tunnel vision, or auditory exclusion experienced while under stress and the impact on a human body subjected to the firing of 20+ rounds of #4 Buckshot.

The primary issue that prompted our report was centred on the adverse effects of recoil on the staff members during initial training and re-qualification. Clearly, the premise that recruits and staff have been, and continue to be injured by the shotgun have been proven and this fact was completely lost on the decision makers. You simply can't argue with the physics of recoil on the human body.

What remained was for the CSC was to select from among the options presented in the detailed report provided and contribute to the effective reduction in the potential for injuries to their employees.

But once again, the CSC at National Headquarters were trying to argue methods against mathematics, unable to separate the two.

If you are firing this shotgun and it is hurting you, you will learn to fear it and you will never be confident using it in any situation let alone in an emergency where your stress levels are off the scale. After years of experience on the Inside and the Outside witnessing the deployment of this firearm and using it myself, I cannot say that I would have any confidence in it being used by the majority of staff. They just didn't have the experience and the skill required to use this weapon properly.

Being in the middle of a full-on Prison Riot, armed with a shotgun and having to assess the threats that are all around you changing by the second, dim or no lighting, very high levels of noise, smoke and fire, people running and screaming, your radio blaring in your ears and tear gas in your eyes is very different from standing on a clean outdoor firearms range shooting at stationary paper targets on a sunny day.

As an IERT Team Leader, I would only designate this gun to hand-picked Team Members who I knew had the confidence, knowledge, and experience to use it safely, accurately, and according to law and policy.

At the time of this writing, #4 Buckshot was still being used for induction training and requalification purposes within the CSC.

## The Unpredictable Bounce Shot

Another round in the CSC course of firearms pertains to the use of the 12-gauge shot gun and the "bounce shot". What is being referred to here is a ricochet shot. The idea of the bounce shot is to slow down the speed of the entire shot pattern, by striking the ground first and then deflecting the pellets into the intended target.

The thinking behind this deployment is that a bounce shot is a lesser degree of force because you are instructed to fire at the ground in front of the rioting cons causing the pellets to bounce up and strike no "higher than the shins". This method of fire is totally unpredictable.

The policy makers did not take into account the kind surface that the pellets would strike before bouncing. During your training to perform this shot, you fired at the grass just in front of your intended target. Different surfaces other than grass were not used to examine the results of the rounds fired. Most of

**"You don't bounce bullets or shotgun pellets off the ground and expect them to act in a predicted fashion."**

a prison where this weapon is deployed is made of concrete and metal. These materials do not absorb a great deal of energy, so the deflection is generally increased, causing more penetration and damage than intended from deflecting the round off of a grass surface.

During a prison riot, the floor is covered in debris like water, concrete pieces, and all sorts of glass and metal fragments that will hinder and affect the result of the shot spread.

It sounds good in theory, but in reality, the pellets will often strike in the chest and face area depending upon the surface the shot is ricocheting off and the angle at which the pellets strike the surface. You cannot predict the outcome of a bounce shot.

The use of a bounce shot is a very dangerous and negligent way to deploy a shotgun in any situation. Take a moment to ask the training department of any police service what they think of a bounce shot.

Police do not train their officers how to bounce around the lead discharge from their shotguns. If you are ever in a position to have to use a firearm to defend your life or that of another person, you don't bounce bullets or shotgun pellets off of the ground and expect them to act in a predicted fashion.

When you have to apply lethal force from a firearm, there are no 'lesser measures' once the lead leaves the barrel of the firearm. It's a last resort to defend your life or the life of someone else where other means have proven insufficient.

For the most part, it's been my extensive experience that the average officer handed a shotgun or any of the CSC-issued firearms, is not capable or experienced to use it confidently, faced with the overwhelmingly stressful conditions that they would face within a prison. You cannot recreate the conditions of a prison riot for the purpose of a training exercise. Police services do try to ramp up their training to make it as practical as they can by using modern technology in the form of paint ball style firearms, FATS (Firearms Training Simulator) and intense role playing.

The College instructors, at that time, did not have any experience in the use of a shotgun or any CSC-issued weapon in an actual prison setting or during a prison riot and so followed the lesson plan without question and without having the answers to the difficult questions.

## No NHQ Response on "Flash Bangs"

Persons unknown decided that the IERT needed a 'distraction device' as part of their scale of issue. So, the Def Tec No. 25 was brought in. This is also called, in police vernacular, a "Flash Bang". It is a pyrotechnic device that when deployed creates a 100db+ retort along with a million-candlepower flash of light.

Okay, we have these devices, we are trained in their use, but what are the guidelines and policies behind their deployment?

When and where do you use them?

Should we not have an approved carrying pouch for them rather than just having them in your shirt pockets? This proved disastrous for a police service when the device detonated inside an officer's shirt pocket.

A written request submitted to NHQ containing these questions received, as usual, no reply. With no guidelines in place as to their deployment in the field it was now open to unrestricted and dangerous misuse of these explosive devices.

When I left the CSC there was still no policy in place for the controlled deployment of these explosive devices. This was an example of deliberate indifference on behalf of NHQ in failing to provide us with guidelines and policy for the use of this dangerous equipment.

\*　\*　\*

The frontline staff are the ones who require up- to-date training. They need to be well-equipped, supported, and encouraged just as the decades old *MacGuigan Report* strongly recommended. Instead, we suffered the most from the systemic neglect and indifference by our managers from National Headquarters down to frontline supervisors.

# PART 42

## IERT Team Leader Suspension

Another example of the complete lack of "open and honest communication" between those that make the decisions and those who have to act upon those decisions took place after an involuntary transfer of an inmate from Collins Bay Institution to Millhaven.

> **"who enabled this person to suspend a Team Leader without due-process or having any investigation into the facts in issue"**

The con that we had to transfer to higher security was involved in a serious assault on another inmate while in the yard. All the cons that were outside at the time of the assault were brought back inside the prison and searched. We were looking for weapons and looking for evidential defensive marks and injuries related to the assault. The one con suspected of being involved in the stabbing was non-compliant in the search and that escalated into him assaulting one of the Officers. The con was taken to the hole and continued to act out while there. The Emergency Response Team came in and prepared him for a transfer to Millhaven Institution. While getting him ready for transfer he kicked a Team Member in the groin. He continued to try to assault the Team Members by kicking, spitting and uttering death threats. He kept up this behaviour throughout the drive to Millhaven Institution.

He spat at the officers and at the video camera that was recording the transfer. The camera lens required frequent cleaning enroute.*

Once at Millhaven, I as the Emergency Response Team Leader in charge of the transfer ordered that the con be walked backwards into the prison, so that he would not have the opportunity to spit on any Millhaven staff members while being taken to the segregation unit.

Once this was all over the reports were written up and the video tapes copied and sent to Regional and National Headquarters. The video recording was reviewed by someone, somewhere who somehow determined that walking the con backwards was an excessive use of force ordered by me.

So as the Team Leader who gave the order, I was suspended from active duty with the Emergency Response Team. I tried to find out who made this decision and upon what evidence it was based. But all my requests for disclosure were completely ignored by the Institution, Regional Headquarters and National Headquarters. And there was no criminal charges of assault peace officer brought against the inmate.

This suspension went on for several months without any "open and honest two-way communication" as to the reason behind the decision, what evidence it was based upon and who made that decision. The word got out to the other Institutional Response Teams within the Region, and they threatened to withdraw their voluntary services in protest.

Very soon after that the Regional Deputy Commissioner had to step in to resolve this issue. He attended a meeting with the Collins Bay Response Team and reinstated me.

When queried as to who made the decision to suspend the me and upon what evidence they had to make that decision the DC had no answer. When asked what happened to "open and honest two-way communication and due process" he had no answer.

What experience did this mysterious person or people have with the Criminal Code of Canada, IERT tactics, training and the Use of Force and who enabled this person to suspend a Team Leader without due-process or having any investigation into the facts in issue. He would not even name the decision maker. Possibly he didn't even know who it was himself.

---

\* Although there was a device called a "spit hood" to prevent this, the CSC had not purchased them in that time.

All of this clearly flies in the face of their Mission Document and Core Values.

No answer.

At that point he just hung head clearly embarrassed.

He had to take the bullet for someone at National or Regional Headquarters or somewhere over this.

So there you have that enigma rearing its' head once again about these mysterious people at NHQ or somewhere who make their decisions without accountability, shrouded in anonymity and layered in secrecy and mystery, who have no clear understanding or experience of what it's like to work on the front line in a Federal Prison. What kind of conclusion can be drawn from this kind of management?

In a gesture of contrition, the DC offered to pay for our newly minted IERT Badges, Wallets and business cards. These badges were an idea conceived by, designed by and paid for by me as a reward to my Team Members. This was given in recognition of the volunteer officers on my Team who consistently performed in a professional manner with Integrity, Courage and Honour Inside the Chaos. This was in a time when the CSC senior managers would not award these same officers with a piece of paper that cost them nothing to produce in recognition of these values.

I handed the DC my reciept for the Badges in the parking after retrieving it from my car. His eyes went wide when he looked at it as he didn't expect the cost to be so high. I told him that his gesture was all that mattered to me and to forget about reimbursing me the cost. He insisted and a few weeks later I received a check for the full amount. This, or a Memorandum of Agreement, was how the CSC eliminated their duty to act fairly or be held accountable for their decisions and actions in my time.

There were many other purchases for the Team that came out of my own pocket in the form of Team clothing and accessories. Most in the service would have thought me out of my mind for spending my own money in this manner, but I believed in leading with Integrity, Courage and Honour to offset the Chaos on the Inside.

# PART 43

## From My Two Decades of CSC Experience

"Success is not final, failure is not fatal:
it is the courage to continue that counts."

—Winston Churchill

### A Bankrupt Justice System

Our federal prisons offer yet another chance to provide and enable someone to achieve what they may not have had the opportunity to do while on the Outside. Treatment programs, education, health care, psychological care – endless programs to address every criminogenic factor that you have on your road to a federal sentence. Here it is. Free. You now have all the time you require to take advantage of everything offered. But it's your choice. Just like on the Outside, these opportunities cannot be forced upon someone. You have truly want to make those changes in your life.

After a couple of times around, you get to know the ins and outs of the court system and you know how to manipulate it to your advantage. It's no secret that this is a game to be played and many rounders know how to play it well and to their maximum benefit at every turn. Just because someone is given Federal time does not mean that they are going to complete the years doled out to them by the judge who formulates their sentence.

Today, Canadian prisons are not the deterrent they were meant to be. They are not a place of penance and rehabilitation as they were meant to be. Canada's permissive justice process has excused and removed the onus of guilt and responsibility from the accused and turned those compelled to appear before the courts into victims. The guilt is often placed on the different branches of our social systems, claiming it is their failure, they dropped the ball, they as a whole are now the cause for all of the evil done in our communities. The individual is no longer responsible for their own actions according to our new society, which is now based entirely upon deflecting guilt away from the accused and putting it straight on some perceived societal wrong either in the past or the present.

In the US as well as here in Canada, we are seeing more and more violent crimes committed against innocent people: bystanders, the elderly, and children. We have now become a society that avoids responsibility for our actions at every turn.

We have created a truly bankrupt system of justice without breaking the cycle of crime and the only ones who do a life sentence as a result of this are the victims.

> **"The only thing that is on trial in the courts of Canada today is procedure."**

The Canadian public had lost faith in our system of justice as being too soft and make no mistake, the freedom of the individual accused and the convicted is more important in the eyes of today's judicial system than the safety of those who protect and contribute to our communities as law abiding citizens.

A criminal trial in Canada today is no longer about the crime.

A criminal trial in Canada today is not about the guilt or innocence of the person before the courts accused of committing that crime.

The only thing that is on trial in the courts of Canada today is procedure.

The main objective of our prison system in my time seemed to be to get them out as soon as possible. If, as a victim, you are of the mind that the person responsible for the damage they have inflicted upon you and your family is being punished via incarceration in prison you are very wrong in that thinking. Once on the Inside you may think that the convicted are settled in for a long stay of years. But in reality, the minute they enter through the prison gates, the CSC is working to get them out. Their needs are assessed and their programs and treatment plans are devised in order for them to work on their exit strategy. With respect to a federal sentence 50/50 was, in my time the goal of the CSC: 50% on the Inside and 50% out the door as soon as possible into a community facility, healing lodge, or halfway house.

I often saw the convicted transferred to a lower security institution or healing lodge after only a short evaluation stay in a Medium Security Institution or sometimes a Max, in order for them to avail themselves of a program offered there that is on their treatment plan.

Cons placed in Native Healing lodges who are not even Indigenous is a common occurrence in Canada now. Sometimes, there is public outrage against this practice and the offender is sent back to an institution. But that only occurs if a victim on the Outside has knowledge of the transfer and has their voice publicly heard, otherwise it's done behind closed doors.

Transgender cons being transferred to female institutions where vulnerable women and their children live is happening now – even when the trans has a lengthy conviction record of sexual assaults against women and children.

## A Wasted Life

Ultimately, the decision to go straight is entirely up to the con.

I have had many discussions with my correctional clients and the majority have no interest in going straight and see prison life, in Canadian prisons, as just a brief time-out for them. They can spend their time comfortably in their cell or on their ranges sharpening their close-quarter battle skills by playing first person shooter games on their PlayStation and their computer and making connections with their fellow criminal counterparts while watching TV.

## There are Many Opportunities to Go Straight

In the current system, which we have maintained for decades, every opportunity imaginable has been on the table for our correctional clients to take advantage of. At their very first conflict with the law, the accused is offered a chance at redemption and given the tools and the time required to build themselves up.

But these opportunities are often refused, ignored, laughed at, and spat upon in favour of an easy way off the hook. It takes effort and determination to live the straight life, and many believe that going straight is for suckers and have no desire to enter into a crime-free lifestyle.

Most think they're tough guys and work very hard at trying to keep up that reputation. The only tough guy, in my extensive experience in our federal prisons and on the streets of Toronto, is the man or woman trying to juggle two jobs and keep their family together and do so without committing harmful criminal acts.

It's easier to sell dope or stick a gun in someone's face to get fast money and no amount of programming is going to change that thinking in the mind of a young criminal. Being labeled a gangster and a bad guy is a badge that many young people and rounders strive to earn on the Inside and on the streets today.

Canada puts rehabilitative policy and action into our prison system at many levels and offers it freely to all those incarcerated within it. But rehabilitation cannot be forced upon someone, it can only be offered. It is a choice and choosing to do the right thing for their own betterment is often ignored by those who live their lives by the sword.

## The Final Score is No Big Score

I have found that it's only when cons get older that they start to examine their life and come to the conclusion that it has been a wasted one. That "Big Score" that the rounders are always talking about, and forever in pursuit of, never comes in their lifetime. And even if they do score big money off a job, it is squandered foolishly, and they are right back in the thick of it again.

I have heard it said from more than one con that it's too late for them, they are too old now to change and there is nothing out there for them anyway.

Wrongs committed by you against another con are never forgotten and they always catch up with you because there is no place to run when you are behind the fences and walls. Even when you get out, the beef is still waiting for you on the other side of the razor-wire fence, and it will find you eventually.

I always felt sad for these guys who, after a lifetime of Playing the Game, finally admitted their defeat and the complete waste of their life. Sometimes, some of them finally gain some insight into the harm they have caused others throughout their lives and experience sincere remorse. This kind of inmate is now a very different person from who he was when he was younger. And within the circles and lifestyle of the violent criminal or drug addict it's a rare outcome to live to a pensionable age.

I once boxed up all the cell contents for an inmate who had died. Either through murder or overdose, suicide or natural causes I don't remember now. But when an inmate dies, you have to move fast and padlock his cell right away otherwise the other cons on his range will steal everything he has, even while he's lying there getting cold.

I remember thinking, *this is all that this guy had to show for his entire life – one cardboard box. How sad is that?*

You lived your whole life and all you had to your name is what was in your prison cell at the time of your death. Very often, there is no one – no family member and no friends or relatives to send his property to. The majority of the time they are buried by the state because there is no one willing to front the money for a funeral.

This is without exception the end result of a wasted life.

## The Great Enabler

These observations come from extensive frontline experience working within our judicial system on the Outside and on the Inside. Our entire justice system has turned into the great enabler for those in conflict with the law at every level. From traffic court to the Supreme Court of Canada, it's all about the accused and the convicted getting every advantage no matter how unjust, outlandish, and insulting it may be to their many victims.

As we now enter the third decade of the twenty-first century, all the CSC can do is offer an opportunity for incarcerated people to better their lives through programs and education. But the majority of prisoners in Canada do not take advantage of these opportunities. Their lifestyle is crime, and it is reinforced by their peers and even family members. It is what they do for a living to augment their social benefits. In most cases, it is the environment many were raised in. This is what the CSC has to battle against with its arsenal of programs and its attempts at meaningful interaction between staff and inmates.

Canadian criminals are given an opportunity through incarceration to become law-abiding citizens. They have the opportunity to obtain an education that they may never have had the chance to get while on the street. This new and often alien lifestyle cannot be forced upon them. It's a choice to be made by the individual just as much as it was their choice to murder, rape, or rob.

But can a government-run system pitted against a lifetime of poverty, ignorance, peer pressure, and substance abuse be expected to convert criminals into law-abiding citizens?

It's an idealistic crusade that has been crammed down the throat of the Canadian public for years. The Service is trying to impose our social morality upon a criminal population that is, for the most part, totally foreign to those who have lived a life of crime as the baseline nature of their existence. The United States has tried all these methods to give their incarcerated the chance to break free of their lifestyle and live the straight life starting from the very first time they offend right up until some land themselves on death row.

We in Canada have often copied their methods of Unit Management and prison reform. But now the US uses its three -trike rule, knowing that to have some people free on the streets is just too much of a risk for innocent and vulnerable citizens. So, they build more prisons and put more and more people behind their walls and fences for life, where life means life.

Canada is now a society of permissiveness when it comes to criminal behaviour. In our current system, great amounts of our resources are being used up by criminals without seeing much in the direction of positive outcomes from that investment.

Canada is giving a free pass to criminals to do whatever they please, time and time again. Just look at the increase in the murder rates in Toronto now that pro-active policing and street checks have been removed because someone might be offended by this strategy. The current system of justice has been of the mindset to remove responsibility from the criminal act by painting all offenders as victims of our society.

There have been decades of avoiding the fact that most criminals are primarily responsible for their own actions and yet the blame and cause has been the failure of society, the educational system, social programs, the police, the school system, and so forth. The finger of guilt has been diverted from the accused and pointed to anything other than the individual responsible for the crimes that they commit. This style of blame management continues to escalate and has been nothing but destructive to our society and a great enabling tool for criminals to avoid responsibility.

For the most part, many convicts I have dealt with believe they are entitled to do whatever they want because it's not their fault they are told, you had a hard life they are told, it's no wonder you hurt others because you yourself were hurt.

You are not responsible.

Defence lawyers always attempt to diminish violent crime by explaining it away. Deflect the intent and responsibility away from the accused and the convicted and put it straight on societal issues. It appears that the matter of guilt or innocence in a criminal case is not what a trial is about anymore. It's seems to be all about how the police conducted the arrest, gathered the evidence, and presented it without being in violation of someone's rights, actual or perceived:

- Was the accused offered free legal counsel in a timely matter upon their arrest?
- Did they have the charges and their rights under the Charter explained to them in their language of choice?
- Was the search conducted properly?

The biggest get out of jail free card has been the right to a timely trial. When the first line of defence of the accused is to stall:

- postpone
- fire your lawyer and search for a new one
- extend and request still more time for documents to be produced
- have them translated if required

- produce and depose expert witnesses
- arrange medical and psychological exams performed by hand-picked experts
- schedule independent coroner's examinations and private forensic and DNA lab analysis

All of the above is done in a deliberate attempt to argue that the accused had their right to a speedy trial violated and thus having the charge against them dropped. Playing the Game.

Some judges and Parole Board members appear to make their decisions based upon the convenience of the accused and the convicted rather than restoring a sense of justice to the victims.

My view is, let the criminal act speak for itself and let the punishment reflect the severity of the crime because, from my extensive experience, we are truly at the limits of our failed attempt at progressive prison reform.

A life sentence in Canada does not mean life. It means that after the convict is released, they are still under the conditions set by their parole for the remainder of their lives, but they are in all other respects free.

Many callous, cowardly criminals have proven to us that they will commit violence again and again. The risks they pose are so great that extended and even permanent incarceration is the only appropriate measure to protect Canadians.

**"You cannot induce a criminal not to commit crime by absolving them of the crimes committed by them."**

In the streets today, there are not enough police to serve and protect our society and the police themselves are not permitted to do their jobs because of the profound lack of courage and common sense demonstrated by politicians more concerned about their critics and the security of their own positions of power than in the protection of the people they are elected to serve.

Under the current microscope of the uninformed and inexperienced anything bad that happens to a criminal is either the fault of the police, social services, or the prison system. The onus of responsibility has been almost completely removed from the accused and the convicted in favour of unlimited excuses for the crimes they commit.

You cannot induce a criminal not to commit crime by absolving them of the crimes committed by them. Yet this appears to be the truly absurd recent past and current trend in our system of Justice.

My career path has enabled me to observe this system through the eyes of incarcerator, law enforcer, and victim. It's a unique combination of frontline experience that gave me a broad perspective of Canada's permissive laws, our unaccountable prison system, and the truly dismissive treatment of victims.

Taken together, these are a strong indication that our current system – on the Inside and the Outside – is strained and broken.

## INITIAL SUMMARY

**"There was no cultural change strategy in place in those days because CSC didn't think that there was a need for it."**

An entire book can be written on the corruption of the selection process alone. "Appointments to the Correctional Service are based upon merit" is a major deception that has demoralized staff for years in the CSC. I have seen staff members promoted that have longer criminal records than the offenders. These are the people who are held out to us to be leaders. Those staff that have integrity and perform the job to the best of their ability are most often left back in favour of the squeaky wheels, liquor buyers and ass grabbers that have to be shuffled around from jail to jail because of the damage they do and the danger they pose to other staff members.

The staff members who face the constant day-to-day struggle to perform their duties with integrity and professionalism must deal with the enormous psychological and moral conflict between selling themselves out for advancement and maintaining their values. It is so much easier to throw up your hands in surrender to the dark and corrupt side of the Service. They see so many dishonest staff get ahead by doing what they are told even though they know that it's legally, morally, and ethically wrong.

The successive legacy of managers and other staff members perpetuated this over decades, from Institutional to Regional to National levels, are the ones who are directly responsible for the systemic harassment and appalling environment that we worked within in my time.

It takes its toll on the honest individual and their family. In speaking with the majority of frontline staff you will hear the following quote, 'It's not the cons I worry about … it's the staff." For the most part, the offenders are not the major contributors to the stress that CSC staff experience. It has been the people they work with and work for.

I have always had difficulty with the Mission Statement Value "We lead by example" and the contents of this book, in my opinion, is what leadership meant in the CSC back then. There were many good supervisors and senior leaders. But the balance between the good and the bad was greatly skewed.

Many of the bad ones were promoted, awarded medals and given free reign. Many of the good ones walked away from the CSC when faced with the corruption. They became highly successful in other fields and never looked back. Others like me, who got out, are compelled to look back by the impact of intrusive thoughts, nightmares and flashbacks. The specter of intense violence is constantly looking over your shoulder.

This was the culture we worked within in my time and there was no cultural change strategy in place in those days because the CSC didn't thingk there was a need for one.

The Author beginning a new career with the Toronto Police Service.

# FINAL SUMMARY

The strong wording contained within the *MacGuigan Report* describing the poor prison management, morale, and the reports of the corrupt working dynamic of the CSC may well have been written on the very day that I started with the CSC and were still just as accurate on the day I left.

The extensive stress related harm and the betrayal perpetrated on the line staff in my time cannot truly be measured because the wary remnants of the guard culture still prevent the victims from seeking help. Ever the "tough guy" they still do not want to appear as being weak or in need of help, just like the inmates. Even today I see people that I worked with in the prison from decades ago who are but a shell of their former selves.

The final and greatest parallel that I can draw between the inmates and the Correctional Service of Canada is that throughout the years, the CSC and the people that it incarcerates have had many opportunities to correct themselves but continue to fail to do so to the detriment of their many victims and to the safety of all Canadians.

# APPENDIX A

## Key Excerpts from the MacGuigan Report

In 1977, under the chairmanship of then Member of Parliament Mark MacGuigan, the House of Commons Standing Committee on Justice and Legal Affairs, Sub-Committee on the Penitentiary System in Canada presented its Report to Parliament.[33] Based on "intensive and extensive" research, the Report spoke to a framework for change, large scale reforms, immediate implementation, utmost urgency, immediate action for reform and renewal in the field of Corrections.

The report identified a great many shortcomings within the Service at that time and made many recommendations for change. Some of those recommendations were implemented by the Service to the benefit of the offenders, but just as many were ignored to the detriment of the frontline staff members.

Issues that I have already identified in this writing were reported with great accuracy by the *MacGuigan Report* and in previous studies and committees. Yet these same issues of systemic neglect, the guard culture, racism, and sexism still very much dominated the workplace and continued to cause great harm when I started in the Service in the 1980s and throughout my time on the Inside.

---

[33] Canada, Parliament, House of Commons Standing Committee on Justice and Legal Affairs, Sub-Committee on the Penitentiary System in Canada, *Report of the Sub-committee*, 30th Parl, 2nd Sess, 1976–1977 (Chair: Mark MacGuigan). Accessed October 3, 2020, https://johnhoward.ca/wp-content/uploads/2016/12/1977-HV-9507-C33-1977-MacGuigan.pdf.

The CSC failed to establish trust in its position of authority and most certainly created no incentive for the line staff to aid them in the succeeding in their Mission. The line staff were the only ones who had direct daily contact with the inmates and by virtue of that had the greatest opportunity and impact to encourage rehabilitation. No one else in the entire CSC had that degree of access to the cons. So, to have those frontline positions composed of guards instead of Officers the CSC was not providing the best role models for the inmates.

Some of these issues are quoted below from the 1977 *MacGuigan Report:*

233. Morale is generally low among custodial staff. We attribute this primarily to a lack of discipline. By "discipline" we do not mean polished buttons and military creases in the trousers. Rather we refer to the interlocking trust that every correctional officer must be able to repose in each of the others, reflecting a confidence that each person, whether peer or superior, will do his duty. True discipline is a result of professionalism."

234. The "guards' code" appears to be just as strong, and just as destructive, as the "inmates' code". Every custodial officer realizes that his safety, his satisfaction with his work and his success in the conditions in which he finds himself all depend not only on his own behavior but also on that of each of his associates. Yet officers in more than one of our institutions are genuinely apprehensive about misconduct, troublemaking, or ordinary stupidity by their fellow officers—which, in a prison setting, can be potentially disastrous. Despite this they are under intolerable pressure not to break the rule of silence that the custodial staff, in their insecure and embattled insolation have imposed on and tolerate among themselves. If they report such breaches of discipline, they are likely to find little support from their colleagues.

We do not suggest that the custodial staff is the only aspect of the system that must change. The problem is in fact three-sided, involving staff, management, and prisoners, each of which is separated from the others by entrenched attitudes of confrontation, mistrust, and deep suspicion. These mutual antagonisms stem from factual causes that can and must be corrected by a significant reform effort involving all levels of the penitentiary system. Penitentiaries have been subjected to a great deal of tinkering, which has done more to unsettle matters than to improve them. At this point, success will only be achieved through a determined, far-reaching and courageous commitment to fundamental reform."

237. All this can be summarized by saying that a correctional officer, in the argot of the prison sub-culture, is under extraordinary peer-group pressure to demonstrate that he is not a "con lover". In terms of the psychological reality of the penitentiary, as opposed to the official picture presented by the Penitentiary Service for public consumption, a correctional officer can only maintain his personal integrity, self-respect and the respect of his associates by conforming to the group attitude of militant and belligerent solidarity."

238. Given that this is almost on the fundamental level of a personal survival need, the perceived threats to the custodial officers come not only from the inmates but also from the administrative staff responsible for directing and managing the penitentiary system and the institution. There are many directives issued from above that attempt to implement modern penological techniques and approaches aimed at fostering rehabilitation of inmates. From the point of view of the staff officer in contact with prisoners, these often are inconsistent with his experience, and are seen as requiring him to behave in a way that contradicts his own perception of what he must do in order to function successfully in the bizarre and twisted world in which he works. Management is therefore no less of an enemy to the correctional staff than the inmates.

274. A major factor bearing not only on staff efficiency but also on morale, discipline, and attitude, is the lack of continuing training for persons who have made a long-term commitment to the Penitentiary Service. Such training is necessary to enable career officers to upgrade skills in order to qualify for advancement. In the absence of adequate educational programs, we find a widespread conviction among correctional staff that promotion standards are unfair, arbitrary, and sometimes based on favouritism rather than established abilities.

275. Proper advanced staff training could add much needed elements of intellectual discipline and professional purpose to the way in which Penitentiary Service personnel perform their duties, in the same way that advanced training for intermediate and senior officers enhances the efficiency and accomplishment mission of the armed forces. We also point out that such training could provide an appropriate avenue for

the introduction into the intellectual horizons of the custodial staff of new concepts of penology, as well as a testing-ground for all aspects of correctional theory and practice.

284. We observe that not all aspects of what happens to a correctional officer working in contact with inmates are negative. Although bad habits tend to be perpetuated by transmission from the old to the new staff, work on the range or even on the perimeter is a learning experience about problems that do not exist in a vacuum or without cause. Without having gained first-hand personal knowledge of the actual dynamics of staff-prisoner relationships—something that is far removed from the ordinary experience of people —much of the contribution made by supervisory personnel and program and classification officials to prison management and problem-solving fails to address itself to reality as it exists on the inmate ranges. We are of the view that it would ultimately enhance the team effort required in a penal institution if all persons who eventually will work in supervisory or collateral staff positions were first exposed to what it is like to work in daily contact with inmates, and to the problems experienced in practice by the custodial staff in carrying out the directives and policies by which penitentiaries are run.

Staff appointments above the initial level should either be made by promotion within the system, or appointees (other than professional persons or those who already have equivalent experience) should be required to spend a period of six months gaining experience in security before assuming their positions. It is vital that the service hold out the probability of promotion for the deserving officer.

All staff and inmates should be accountable for their behavior and actions. Neither should be allowed to use anonymity as a shield for any misdeeds. Anonymity has been employed by the worst guards in the worst institutions. They do not wear identification and typically refuse to tell inmates who they are. Because of the general breakdown in leadership, discipline, purpose, and morale in Canadian penitentiaries, it is not uncommon for "accounts to be settled" behind the protection of anonymity. This sort of behavior by the staff, so long as it is kept out of sight, can be officially disclaimed, and is in fact often tolerated.

298. Irregular enforcement procedures by the staff may even be seen as useful to the system to keep things "looking good on paper". The smaller

the number of formal disciplinary actions required to be taken against staff, the more effective the management of an institution seems to be. In a penitentiary system without goals that rise much above warehousing human beings, the importance of maintaining good appearances and unblemished management "track records" becomes proportionately much greater than the importance of the eventual success in society of men unfortunate enough to have been "rehabilitated" through such expedients."

## Selected MacGuigan Report Recommendations

### Re: Correctional Staff

The subcommittee made sixty-five specific recommendations as a result of the findings described in its report. The most pertinent of these for the purposes of this book are presented below with their original report numbering:

7.  Custodial personnel must have full opportunity for continuing professional educational development and should be required to spend a minimum of one week a year in refresher courses or upgrading.
8.  A sufficient number of training positions must be established to allow for the full and adequate training and continuing professional education of custodial personnel without depriving institutions of necessary staff. This number should be established annually.
9.  Staff appointments above the initial level should either be made by promotion within the system, or appointees (other than professional persons or those who already have equivalent experience) should be required to spend a period of six months gaining experience in security before assuming their positions. It is vital that the service hold out the probability of promotion for the deserving officer.
10. The period of probation for new employees must be one year after the completion of the initial training course.
11. Staff must be paid in keeping with their training and status and we find the R.C.M. Police to be the appropriate model.
12. In order to increase staff experience and, to enhance the quality of Canadian penology, there must be regular programs of exchange

of manpower for periods up to a year or two with penitentiary systems in other countries.

13. As far as possible, all staff members should have dual responsibility for security and program.

14. All staff members and all inmates in penitentiaries must wear name identification.

15. A "no deals" rule should establish that no agreements of any kind will be negotiated in hostage-takings while hostages are being held.

16. Each maximum and medium security penitentiary must have a tactical unit of staff trained to deal with hostage-taking and other crises. When necessary, a director should also call on the assistance of police tactical forces. The decision as to the role of Inmate Committees, if any, should also be left to the director.

17. Women should be employed on the same basis as men in the penitentiary service. Selection must be according to the same criteria used for men to ensure that recruits have the aptitude, maturity, stability and self-discipline required for penitentiary work.

18. When the new system of qualifications, pay, promotion and pensions is being instituted, all present penitentiary staff should be re-examined with a view to determine their continuing suitability for penitentiary service. Those who are not deemed suitable should be transferred to other government departments, retired from the Service with appropriate pensions, or dismissed.